Doing Work Based Research

Education at SAGE

SAGE is a leading international publisher of journals, books, and electronic media for academic, educational, and professional markets.

Our education publishing includes:

- accessible and comprehensive texts for aspiring education professionals and practitioners looking to further their careers through continuing professional development

- inspirational advice and guidance for the classroom

- authoritative state of the art reference from the leading authors in the field

Find out more at: **www.sagepub.co.uk/education**

Doing Work Based Research

Approaches to Enquiry for Insider-Researchers

Carol Costley, Geoffrey Elliott and
Paul Gibbs

Los Angeles | London | New Delhi
Singapore | Washington DC

SAGE Publications Ltd
1 Oliver's Yard
55 City Road
London EC1Y 1SP

SAGE Publications Inc.
2455 Teller Road
Thousand Oaks, California 91320

SAGE Publications India Pvt Ltd
B 1/I 1 Mohan Cooperative Industrial Area
Mathura Road
New Delhi 110 044

SAGE Publications Asia-Pacific Pte Ltd
33 Pekin Street #02-01
Far East Square
Singapore 048763

Library of Congress Control Number: 2009934594

.

British Library Cataloguing in Publication data

A catalogue record for this book is available from the British Library

ISBN 978-1-84860-677-7
ISBN 978-1-84860-678-4 (pbk)

Typeset by C&M Digitals (P) Ltd, Chennai, India
Printed in Great Britain by TJ International Ltd, Padstow, Cornwall
Printed on paper from sustainable resources

Mixed Sources
Product group from well-managed
forests and other controlled sources
www.fsc.org Cert no. SGS-COC-2482
© 1996 Forest Stewardship Council
FSC

From Carol, love to my parents, Ron and Mary.

From Geoffrey, love to Trudi.

From Paul, love to Jane.

Contents

List of tables and figures

Figures

Tables

Acknowledgements

The authors would like to acknowledge and thank the following for their contributions to this book:

Monira Begum, Editorial Assistant at Sage Publications, for helpful advice and support throughout.

Professor Michael Crossley, Professor of Comparative and International Education, Joint Co-ordinator, Research Centre for International and Comparative Studies, and Director, Education in Small States Research Group, University of Bristol, for permission to make use of his research guidelines in Chapter 11.

Dr Helen Fairlie, formerly Commissioning Editor, Sage Publications, for her confidence in the project.

Annette Fillery-Travis, Principal Lecturer, Middlesex University, for identifying and collating much of the student work based learning project extracts used in Chapter 10.

Stan Lester of Stan Lester Developments for invaluable advice on developing a methodology in Chapter 7.

Dr Margaret Volante, Head of Practice Learning and Education, Centre for Research in Nursing and Midwifery Education, European Institute of Health and Medical Sciences, University of Surrey, for reading and thoughtful comments on draft chapters.

Alison Williamson of Burgess Pre-Publishing for her expertise and excellence in text preparation and indexing.

Elda Nicolou-Walker, Senior Teaching Fellow and Head of Work Based Learning, Queen's University Belfast for her invaluable advice and insight. For permission to use extracts from their work based research projects, participants past and present carrying out work based research towards postgraduate and undergraduate awards of the following universities: University of Worcester, Queen's University Belfast and Middlesex University, namely:

Brian Ash
Tom Best
Carey Bongard
Catherine Brady
Loraine Burke
Alison Cambray
Jane Campion
Adrian Casha
Eileen Cassidy

Mary Colvill
Katrina Cremona
Annette Fillery-Travis
Simon Godsall
Ailbhe Harrington
George Hutchinson
Kitty Lloyd-Lawrence
Kelly Mangold
Nick Papadopoulos
Kathryn Pritchard
Ashley Anastasius Rego
Valerio Rossic
Carla Solvason
Catherine Steele
Des Thompson

The authors are grateful to all those who granted permission for material
to be reproduced in this book including:

Table 4.2 – Kvale, S. (2006) Dominance through Interviews and Dialogues,
Qualitative Inquiry. London: Sage.

Table 5.1 – Robson, C. (2002) *Real World Research*. Oxford: Blackwell.

Figure 7.1 – Burrell and Morgan (1985) *Sociological Paradigms and Organisational
Analysis*. Farnham: Ashgate.

Table 12.2 – Brodie and Irving (2007) Assessment in work based learning:
Investigating a pedagogical approach to enhance student learning,
Assessment & Evaluation in Higher Education, Taylor and Francis.

About the authors

Professor Carol Costley is Head of the Work Based Learning Research Centre at Middlesex University. She works with individuals and organizations in the private, public, community and voluntary sectors internationally in the teaching and learning of work based programmes, particularly in Cyprus where she has developed the Work Based Learning Doctorate in Professional Studies programmes since 1996.

Her research interests are in examining methodologies and epistemologies in work based learning, looking particularly at work based learning as a field of study, especially issues relating to trans-disciplinarity, equity, ethics and the insider as researcher.

Carol has been the convenor of the Universities Association for Lifelong Learning, Work Based Learning Network, since 1998 until the present, and executive member of UALL.

Professor Geoffrey Elliott is Director of Regional Engagement at the University of Worcester. He has worked in school, further and adult education, and has previously held posts in the School of Independent Study at the University of East London and the Open University teaching on the professional doctorate programme in education. His research interests are in post-compulsory education and public policy, and he has authored many books and articles on these and related topics. Geoffrey is Chair of the UK Further Education Research Association (FERA), the sponsor of the international peer-refereed journal *Research in Post-Compulsory Education* which he has edited since its launch in 1996. Geoffrey's most recent book (with Chahid Fourali and Sally Issler) is *Education and Social Change* (Continuum, 2010). Geoffrey is married with two sons, and lives in Bewdley, Worcestershire.

Professor Paul Gibbs works in the Institute for Work Based Learning at Middlesex University and is interested in the nature of being revealed through work, marketing and education. He has published widely and has developed an interest in Heidegger and Wittgenstein in the context of education and business ethics, reflected in his book which addresses a Heideggerian perspective for the university entitled *Trusting in the University: The Contribution of Temporality and Trust to a Praxis of Higher Learning* (Kluwer Academic, 2004). His most recent book is *Marketing Higher Education: Theory and practice* (Open University Press, 2009).

Introduction: the context of work based research in higher education

With the advent of a global, knowledge-driven economy, conditions for higher education have changed. Universities now face a proliferation of expectations and demands. Higher education's contribution to the socio-economic success of both developed and developing nations and of individuals has been widely recognized, marked by its inclusion in the General Agreement on Trade in Services (GATS). Moreover, the World Bank (2000) sees development of the knowledge economy being led by tertiary education, encouraging the European Union to develop both European higher education and research areas. These trends in massification, accountability, privatization, marketization and an unprecedented level of participation[1] have caused a shift in the boundary between the public and the private sectors (Altbach, 2002). This shift has seen the university, according to Bleiklie and Kogan (2007), move from a republic of scholars to a stakeholder organization.

In higher education during the 1980s, the emphasis on human and social capital grew, as did the emphasis on related concepts of entrepreneurship and enterprise. For individuals, the financial benefits of higher education may be measured in terms of anticipated lifetime income and access to interesting jobs. These changes have brought a need for educational institutions to adapt to a competitive world through embracing that in which they operate. This has led to an increased desire for academia to be relevant to our everyday lives, explicitly to be relevant to work (Elliott, 1999).

As well as government-funded work based learning initiatives, work based learning is seen as a way to widen participation in higher education and, in particular, to focus learning in the projects of individuals and groups doing work, paid or unpaid. Work based learning can offer project research and learning that reflect the interests of a wide range of people and is not instrumental in serving the economy, but is socially significant.

Higher education is changing in response to new work practices and social, economic and cultural changes within societies (see Schmidt and Gibbs, 2009, for a discussion of these changes in the UK). Arising from this are new ways of making meaning, and new ways of framing questions and making enquiries into meanings. Multi-disciplinary approaches to knowledge are now necessary to answer the questions of complex societies. It is with this background in mind that work based learning as a field and mode of study in higher education took up in the UK in the early 1990s a unique approach to programmes of study or individual work based modules. Many programmes or modules were developed from a perspective other than subject discipline, used generic assessment criteria and focused on practice that had a particular work context. Work based and professional studies, which developed most rapidly in the former polytechnics, usually have a multi-disciplinary and inter-professional approach to their learning programmes, reflecting an increased responsiveness and accountability of new universities to the wider market.

In the context of knowledge economies, the role of knowledge based on a binary distinction between creator and users has become blurred. This is the central premise in Gibbons et al.'s (1994) notion of a distinctive 'mode 2' knowledge which is produced and valued outside the university and is not discipline based. The significance of mode 2 knowledge is taken up in a growth of interest in knowledge management and intellectual capital in the business literature. Gibbs and Garnett (2007) have argued that the university in the past has concentrated on human capital which has the potential to be transformed through employment to structural capital of the organization and that the changing missions and business models of universities mean that they share a responsibility to enhance the practicality of institutional learning.

The recent turn to work based research and experiential knowledge in higher education indicates the significance of these debates and how they have impacted upon its curriculum, hence the need for a book on work based research.

The emergence of work based learning

The background of work based projects is that it has partly emerged from independent study, which in the 1970s and 1980s drew upon a humanistic educational tradition that emphasized participants on university courses taking responsibility for their own learning, choosing and initiating their study.

Project activities often include those undertaken through work experience, work shadowing, mentoring schemes or the conventional placement period. While there are many varieties of work-related, workplace or work based learning in higher education, this book focuses more on existing workers who wish to undertake higher education study drawing on their own working environment. These modules and programmes take research projects firmly outside the university, and acknowledge existing expertise and self-directed learning.

Despite the differences in the implementation of work based learning across the UK and internationally, programmes that include elements of work based learning as a mode of study still have much in common with those that treat it as a field of study (Costley and Armsby, 2006; Gibbs and

Garnett, 2007; Helyer, 2010). There are shared or similar approaches to knowledge and understanding as generated outside of the university in a context of practice. There are similar pedagogical approaches, where students are 'experts' in the sense that they are or have been in a particular work situation and have understanding of its nuances, micro-politics and so on. Students researching their own practice are common in work based learning programmes of study.

Practitioner-led research and development has become a principal means of developing organizational learning and enhancing the effectiveness of individuals at work (Costley and Stephenson, 2008; Rhodes and Shiel, 2007). Change in organizational practices has meant flatter management hierarchies and individual practitioners taking greater responsibility. A higher education response is to construct programmes of learning that enable practitioners to take a critical, reflective and evidenced-based approach to change and development at work. Practitioner-led research and development is now an essential capability for people at work.

The curriculum in work based learning is a new and emerging field of study in higher education (Boud and Solomon, 2001; Gibbs and Costley, 2006). Universities are now beginning to establish a research infrastructure that promotes and develops excellence in practitioner-led research and development and to apply quality assurance to the delivery mechanisms of research and development at work. To this end, there has been a steady growth of undergraduate awards, Master's degrees and Professional Doctorates (Scott et al., 2004) that focus on professional areas of learning. This book has been devised to meet the needs of people undertaking professional courses in higher education that have a professional orientation– that is, the course is related to work. As part of a work-related programme of study, there is usually a focus upon work based enquiry. The enquiry, or piece of research, is focused on real-time work practices.

About the book

The main focus of the book concerns the nature of the work based project and a particular approach to work based research and development that has a wide relevance to many other programmes in the higher education sector (Boud and Costley, 2007). The book emanates directly from the higher education curriculum, principally in the field of work based learning and professional studies, and focuses on the continuous learning of people already at work. This is because experienced practitioners provide a rich source of data that informs the 'real time', 'real world' projects that form the subject of this book. Superficially, it relates to the growing interest in practitioner-led research and also builds on the body of work that has been undertaken on reflective practice. Recent research across the university curriculum (Costley and Armsby, 2007) has shown that many subject areas are involved in practitioner-led research. Participants on courses with placements use work experience for reflective practice and practitioners who are in work use their unique knowledge to drive their work based projects. Professional practice can be enhanced by practitioner-led research (Bourner et al., 2000) and by the ability of practitioners to evaluate research and to take an ethical stance (Costley and Gibbs, 2006; Gibbs et al., 2007).

The authors have a particular interest in work based research. They are all higher education practitioners who work in this area and have research interests in the field.

The book is in the multi- and often trans-disciplinary field of work based learning. It identifies not just research methods and methodologies used by practitioners doing research and development projects undertaken at work, but the contexts that surround the research site and the nature of academic engagement in the workplace.

The book has 13 chapters which offer a comprehensive approach to work based research within an academic context. Chapter 1 introduces key concepts for the insider-researcher and provides a general orientation and induction into work based research, focusing on the characteristics that make it both distinctive and powerful. Chapter 2 deals with issues of knowledge and information, how to find what you need and how to use it in an appropriate manner for work based research. It deals with the often problematic issue of a literature review where the relevant literature is not always, or often, in the standard form of academic authority, and it explores how a whole range of literature that is relevant to the nature of the enquiry can be used to contextualize your work based study.

Chapters 3, 4 and 5 deal with ethical issues central to undertaking a work based research project. The first of these deals generally with the ethical issue of being an insider-researcher, and the next deals specifically with privilege, power and the politics of the workplace. The third in this trilogy considers access to the research site. Within all three is an overriding ethos of care and gratitude for the workplace participants in the research. These themes are a thread linking all the chapters of the book. We then move on to Chapter 6 which looks at one of the mechanisms that enable workplace research to be effective: the learning agreement and what this entails and contains.

The next three chapters are the core of this work. They present research approaches which address how people with expertise and contextual knowledge can best develop and research a project in their own site of work. In Chapter 7, we use the intellectual capital in universities and organizations outside of higher education to introduce practice-based methodologies, develop a useful resource and build a theoretical framework for the teaching and learning of practice-based research and development projects. Chapter 8 illustrates how many research projects at work seek to find the potential of a system and collaboration and in so doing enable the researcher to take immediate reflective, practitioner-led action. Chapter 9 seeks to demystify reflective practice and shows how work based research can lead to useful theory building, and the steps involved in this.

Chapter 10 then offers practical examples drawn from live, work based research projects. These illustrate many of the issues and dilemmas facing the insider-researcher. It helps to bring everything together by presenting a window on key aspects of real workplace studies with a commentary and advice on the approaches employed.

The next three chapters build on the understanding you have developed and show how you can use this to write a research proposal (Chapter 11), understand and develop outcomes for the research (Chapter 12) and, finally, make recommendations to others based on the research (Chapter 13). The making of recommendations that will lead to action and impact is distinctive of work based research.

Although the book is structured linearly, each chapter is designed both to fit the pattern of the book and to be read separately. The order of reading each chapter could be approached in many different ways, depending on what you are looking for and the preconceptions you have when you come to the book. For example, if you want to know outcomes to help understand the beginning, it may be better to start with Chapter 11. Alternatively, you may wish to start with Chapters 10 and 12.

Each chapter contains discussion questions to help you reflect on what is being presented and to locate it in your own research practice.

The readership

This is a book that is for people doing research at their own sites of work. It is therefore aimed at the 'insider-researcher' and the kind of research that includes a substantial amount of development along with the research process. Specifically, the target readership is the postgraduate level learner undertaking a research project based on their work practice as part of their award. The learner is likely to already have some expertise in the work area in which they are doing their research and have insider knowledge and understanding of that particular context. They may be studying for a professional Doctorate or a Master's degree. The book is also highly appropriate for those in the final year of a Bachelor's degree who are undertaking project work through investigative methods. The book is also relevant to people doing research whilst on placement and those researching whilst reflecting on work with which they have had first-hand experience.

Note

1 The Higher Education Policy Institute (HEPI) estimates that UK growth in participation in higher education between 2007–8 and 2029–30 will be between 8 and 25 per cent (HEPI 2009).

References

Altbach, P. (ed) (2002) *The Decline of the Guru: The Academic Profession in Developing and Middle-Income Countries.* New York: Palgrave.

Bleiklie, I. and Kogan., M. (2007) 'Organization and governance of universities', *Higher Education Policy* 20(4): 477–93.

Boud, D. and Costley, C. (2007) 'From project supervision to advising: new conceptions of the practice', *Innovations in Education and Teaching International* 44(2): 119–30.

Boud, D. and Solomon, N. (eds.) (2001) *Work-based Learning: A New Higher Education.* Buckingham: Society for Research in Higher Education/Open University Press.

Bourner, T., Bowden, R. and Laing, S. (2000) 'Professional doctorates: the development of researching professionals', in T. Bourner, T. Katz and D. Watson (eds) *New Directions in Professional Education*, pp. 226–37. Buckingham: Society for Research in Higher Education/Open University Press.

Costley, C. and Armsby, P. (2006) 'Work based learning assessed as a field or a mode of study', *Assessment and Evaluation in Higher Education* 31(4): 21–33.

Costley, C. and Armsby, P. (2007) 'Methodologies for undergraduates doing practitioner investigations at work', *Journal of Workplace Learning* 19(3): 131–45.

Costley, C. and Gibbs, P. (2006) 'Researching others: care as an ethic for practitioner researchers', *Studies in Higher Education* 31(1): 89–98.

Costley, C. and Stephenson, J. (2008) 'Building doctorates around individual candidates' professional experience,' D. Boud and A. Lee (eds.) *Changing Practices of Doctoral Education*, pp. 261–85. London: Routledge.

Elliott, G. (1999) *Lifelong Learning: The Politics of the New Learning Environment.* London: Jessica Kingsley.

Gibbons, M., Limoges, C., Nowotny, H., Schwartzman, S., Scott, P. and Trow, M. (1994) *The New Production of Knowledge: The Dynamics of Science and Research in Contemporary Societies.* London: Sage.

Gibbs, P. and Costley, C. (2006) 'Work based learning: discipline, field or discursive space or what?', *Research in Post-Compulsory Education* 11(3): 341–50.

Gibbs, P. and Garnett, J. (2007) 'Work based learning as a field of study', *Research in Post-Compulsory Education* 12(3): 409–21.

Gibbs, P., Costley, C. Armsby, P. and Trakakis, A. (2007) 'Developing the ethics of worker-researchers through phronesis', *Teaching in Higher Education* 12(3): 365–75.

Helyer, R. (ed) (2010) *The Work-based Student Handbook.* New York: Palgrave Macmillan.

HEPI (2009) *Demand for Higher Education to 2029.* Bailey, N. and Bekhradnia, B. Available at www.hepi.ac.uk/466-1366/Demand-for-Higher-Education-to 2029 [accessed 2 October 2009].

Rhodes, G. and Shiel, G. (2007) 'Meeting the needs of the workplace and the learner through work-based learning', *Journal of Workplace Learning* 19(3): 173–87.

Schmidt, R. and Gibbs, P. (2009) 'The challenges of work-based learning in the changing context of the European Higher Education Area', *European Journal of Education* 44(3), Part I.

Scott, D., Brown, A., Lunt, I. and Thorne, L. (2004). *Professional Doctorates: Integrating Professional and Academic Knowledge.* Milton Keynes: Open University Press.

World Bank (2000) *Higher Education in Developing Countries: Peril and Promise.* Washington, DC: The World Bank.

1

Key concepts for the insider-researcher

Key points

A most important aspect of work based research is the researcher's situatedness and context. Within this, the unique perspective of the researcher inevitably makes a difference to the research. An understanding of the critique of insider research, along with the specific issues that often arise for insiders, such as the need for sensitivity towards colleagues when undertaking research, appears in this chapter. The development of the self and the potential impact that insider research can have in a particular organization or professional sphere are emphasized.

An important aspect of work based research is that it is within the researcher's own work practice. The concept of 'social situatedness' originally put forward by Vygotsky (1962), and situatedness in terms of learning developed by Lave and Wenger (1991), is that the development of individual intelligence requires both social and cultural influences, and the multiple perspectives needed for understanding are provided by context. Situatedness arises from the interplay between agent (you, the researcher), situation (the particular set of circumstances and your position within it), and context (where, when and background). Organizational, professional and personal contexts will affect the way a piece of research and development is undertaken. In the organizational context, the culture and structure of your work situation and the actions and thinking of colleagues are likely to shape your work. When researchers are insiders, they draw upon the shared understandings and trust of their immediate and more removed colleagues with whom normal social interactions of working communities have been developed.

Some people take learning very seriously, not only as a phenomenon to be studied, but as a way of living. Antonacopoulou et al. (2005) expanded on this to show that learning may become a part of working life and that working and learning are both integral parts of life's journey. The term 'lifewide' is also a concept that recognizes the 'non-formal' and implicit learning that occurs within work based contexts as social action environments and the continual development of oneself (Alheit and Dausien, 2002). Lifeplace learning is another term that has been introduced and linked to work based learning (Glasgow Caledonian University, 2009) and which situates self, work and learning within a whole life setting.

From your professional life, professional bodies, partner organizations and colleagues will have an influence and from your personal life, family, career goals, values, principles, financial security and so on will all be relevant to how you choose your interests, your research topic and the way you undertake your research. All of these influences, from the individual level to the organizational and professional background, must also be placed in the wider context which will have a bearing on your project through international networking and other influences, market forces and cultural background. As a work based learner undertaking the project as part of a programme of study, another layer needs to be added to these individual and contextual issues. This comprises the influences of the educational institution requiring an academic underpinning to your work based research project. Figure 1.1 illustrates the influences and contexts impacting on work based projects.

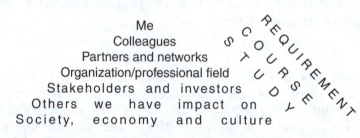

Me
Colleagues
Partners and networks
Organization/professional field
Stakeholders and investors
Others we have impact on
Society, economy and culture

REQUIREMENTS COURSE STUDY

Figure 1.1 The influences and contexts impacting on work based projects

The context and purpose of work have consequences for the value and use of knowledge. The way universities have constructed paradigms concerning knowledge (see Chapter 7) and the systematic (research) process by which new knowledge is created and judged are shifting to better reflect the nature and complexity of the information society in which we now live (Barnett, 2000). Crucially, contemporary societies involve work roles that are subject to change; jobs for life are a thing of the past and lifelong learning implies continually developing oneself into new and varying positions (Antonacopolou et al., 2005).

What makes an insider-led work based project?

As an insider, you are in a unique position to study a particular issue in depth and with special knowledge about that issue. Not only do you have your own insider knowledge, but you have easy access to people and information that can further enhance that knowledge. You are in a prime position to investigate and make changes to a practice situation. You can make challenges to the status quo from an informed perspective. You have an advantage when dealing with the complexity of work situations because you have in-depth knowledge of many of the complex issues. This is vital when exploring a problem or issue in a detailed and thorough way. Amongst the complex issues that insiders can often go some way to understand are the tensions between the specific and the general. Some work issues are beset with paradox and ambiguity, but an insider is often able to unravel and comprehend such intricacies and complications.

Reed and Proctor (1995: 195) identified 'idealised' criteria for practitioner research in health care that has relevance for insider-researchers in a range of settings:

- a social process undertaken with colleagues
- educative for all participants in the projects
- imbued with an integral development dimension
- focused upon aspects of practice in which the researcher has some control and can initiate change
- able to identify and explore socio-political and historical factors affecting practice
- able to open up value issues for critical enquiry and discussion
- designed to give a say to all participants
- able to exercise the professional imagination and enhance the capacity of participants to interpret everyday action in the work setting
- able to integrate personal and professional learning
- likely to yield insights which can be conveyed in a form which make them worthy of interest to a wider audience.

When reading about research in general, it is important to remember that the scale of a work based project is likely to be relatively small. The nature of your project is likely to be something quite specific that is making an improvement, suggesting something new and creative or perhaps evaluating a particular practice. Work based research concerned with specialized practice may not bring about results that transfer exactly to another similar situation. In university research practice, this has been an issue of debate. In work based research, we cannot assume that one work situation will be the same as another, but we can make what Bassey (1999: 12) has called 'fuzzy generalizations'. These are generalizations that arise from the particular research project and may have some general application in a similar context. Predicting easy solutions to diverse and complex issues involving a range of people is not realistic. Work based research may not transfer exactly to another situation, but it involves the application of research which has usefulness and application to a particular situation. It has usefulness to the community of practice and to the individual researcher, and it has the potential to generate theory. It embraces complexity and can be empowering and innovative, saving time and money by making improvements.

A compelling rationale for insider-researchers is to make a difference in a work based situation in which they have a range of investments. To have this impact at national, regional and local level or in your own organization, you may need evidence. Work based research can provide this evidence to influence policy and decision making, and can also make a difference to individual practice.

Work based research undertaken by an insider can be constrained by funding, resources and opportunities because of location, internal politics and so on. These constraints are a feature of real time, real world projects that may sometimes be overcome by, for example, changing the focus of the project. Other challenges of insider research can be the conflicts of interest between workers and between worker and organization. The guidance given in Chapters 3, 4 and 5 should be helpful in making these considerations. Do not forget that, as an insider who is immersed in work, it is possible to fail to see the obvious and you need external feedback on what you are doing.

As an insider-researcher, you are going through a learning process. Reflection upon current practice, evaluation of your research work against university criteria and the adoption of a reflexive approach to your work are crucial aspects of the learning of work based projects. Self-development in this area requires you to understand your professional self in relation to your personal self. Having to build effective relationships between your professional occupation and the university and justify your work, achievements and intentions to critical audiences in work and academe can promote greater self-belief, wider acceptance amongst peers, intellectual skills and a commitment to continuing self-development in the context of your work. The self-management of the insider-led work based project is a prime means of inducing self-managed learning. Debates about the learning process itself are of particular importance, because of the growing awareness of the role of high-level personal or 'soft' skills and qualities in professional work (Eraut, 2004).

If you are party to a learning agreement or contract as part of your university course (see Chapter 6), your work based project is usually endorsed by someone in the professional field who knows about your area of work. They can confirm that the project you are undertaking is likely to have worth to the organization or professional field. Your goal when deciding on a research project is to find a project that adds value to your work situation, that you feel a commitment to undertake and that also has academic value.

It is worthwhile considering the literature on change in organizations, and the growing field of literature on reflection, particularly professional reflection at work. We do not discuss the literature on organizational change and change management in this book, but it may be an important source of information, depending on the kind of project undertaken. Chapter 9 provides a discussion of reflection that is vital to a practitioner contemplating a work based project.

Engagement with your community of practice

There is clearly a need for insiders to have a particular sensitivity to colleagues; for example, consulting colleagues about your research and informing people what you are doing is a matter of courtesy, especially if it is likely to affect their roles. After all, people usually work in teams so the success of your project is likely to depend on others, their input and their willingness to act upon your project's recommendations or changes. Where you undertake your work based project may also be your critical community, that is, the place where you get and give feedback about your ideas and your work. Your professionalism and respect for colleagues will sustain you in your practice community.

Sensitivity to colleagues extends to the organization or professional field to which you are contributing. You should show by your actions an acknowledgement of the culture of your community of practice. You will need to show that you have respect for the values of the organization, its purposes and ways of doing things and to show the relevance of your project, what has been termed its 'fitness for purpose'. It is advisable to pay attention to effective communication which is likely to include consensual techniques for enlisting others' support and opinions, empathetic understanding of the colleagues who are your participants and their needs, demonstrating care for others, and being approachable and good humoured.

Due to the familiarity of these relationships, addressing the ethical issues of insider research discussed in Chapters 3, 4 and 5 is not straightforward. Examples of challenges include:

- negotiating access to your own work situation as an area being researched and securing consent for the research to take place
- promising anonymity and confidentiality to your own colleagues
- possibly challenging the value system of your organization or professional field in some way
- interviewing your own colleagues
- managing the power implications of your work and your positioning as a researcher and as a practitioner within your research project.

Making an impact from the inside

Raelin (2008) recognizes the growing body of evidence suggesting that work based projects may prove immensely beneficial to the long-term success of companies. Nixon (2008) demonstrates that engaging in reflection at work and undertaking insider-led research can make significant contributions to work practices.

You will need to give due consideration to the positive impact the project can make and, of course, any possible negative impact. Making an impact on practice can involve your practical action at work as well as your research abilities. Encouraging the results of your work based project to be taken seriously by colleagues and putting them into practice is part of the project's implementation strategy which needs to be thought through at the outset.

Your insights as an insider are valuable because of your depth of knowledge, but you should also demonstrate that you are critical of your own work and understand a range of perspectives. It is usually the case that every perspective has its weaknesses, but one may be preferable to another and you should give reasons that are compelling (including research evidence) to substantiate your views. It is important to monitor your research processes and also the reaction to your work from those whose opinion you value. Action to implement the findings of research may be taken during or at the end of the project. If you want to put the results of your research into practice in your own community, it will be important to take a balanced view and recognize the opinion of others. See Chapter 13 for further discussion on implementation.

Rights and responsibilities of an insider as a researcher

As an insider in your professional field, you have expertise and experience that gives you an advanced level of knowledge of issues in your area of practice. As such, you have the right to be acknowledged as a practitioner of good standing. To some extent, as a researcher, you have to take on the tradition of what is accepted as good research practice in your professional area of research. If you are able to combine these two roles well, you will be a successful insider-researcher.

You should be aware that several research traditions can put forward a criticism of work based projects in relation to their use of insider-led research. This is because of the issue of the subjective nature of researching your own practice, where there may be a lack of impartiality, a vested interest in certain results being achieved and problems concerning a fresh and objective view of data. Do not forget that all research is subject to criticism, as both criticism and critique are considered good practice in discussions about research. The criticism has some validity, and because of this it is vital that gathering data as an insider is given careful attention, especially concerning questions about insider bias and validity (Murray and Lawrence, 2000: 18). It is important to state and give due consideration to these aspects of insider research. There are many steps an insider can take to guard against bias in the work, for example careful attention to feedback from participants, initial evaluation of data, triangulation in the methods of gathering data and an awareness of the issues represented in the project.

The criticisms and general critique of insider research is balanced against the value of work based projects. Insider-led, work based projects are approached from the perspective of bringing about contributions to practice that are informed by underpinning knowledge. The purpose of the project is to bring about actual change, either during or at the end of the research project, and constitutes a particular constraint to researchers as they are working within systems where there are limits to research practice and change. You need to access particular insider information, inform and bring about significant changes to practice. There is usually a right time and place for innovation to be introduced. The success of projects may be in some part due to insider-researchers' ability to negotiate around systems and practices with creativity and ingenuity. You are the primary agent of control and the exercise of this agency within critical academic and professional environments is the basis of the impact that the project can have upon you and your workplace or professional area.

Your challenges are, to some extent, set in the demanding context of having to justify achievement and progress to critical partners in the wider profession and the less familiar world of academe.

References

Alheit P. and Dausien, B. (2002) 'The double face of lifelong learning: two analytical perspectives on a silent revolution', *Studies in the Education of Adults* 34(1): 705–13.

Antonacopoulou, E., Jarvis, P., Andersen, V., Elkjaer, B. and Høyrup, S. (2005) *Learning, Working and Living: Mapping the Terrain of Working Life Learning.* London: Palgrave.

Barnett, R. (2000) *Realizing the University in an Age of Supercomplexity.* Buckingham: SRHE and Open University Press.

Bassey, M. (1999) *Case Study Research in Educational Settings.* Oxford: Oxford University Press.

Eraut, M. (2004) 'Informal learning in the workplace', *Studies in Continuing Education* 26(2): 247–73.

Glasgow Caledonian University (2009) *LIFELEARN Project.* Available at: www.icll.gcal.ac.uk/lifelearn/index.html [accessed 8 July 2009].

Lave, J. and Wenger, E. (1991) *Situated Learning: Legitimate Peripheral Participation.* Cambridge: Cambridge University Press.

Murray, L. and Lawrence, B. (2000) 'The basis of critique of practitioner-based enquiry', in L. Murray and B. Lawrence (eds) *Practitioner-based Enquiry: Principles for Postgraduate Research.* pp. 16–34. London: Falmer Press.

Nixon, I. (ed.) (2008) *Work-Based Learning Impact Study.* Available at: www.heacademy.ac.uk/assets/York/documents/impact_work_based_learning.pdf#search="Nixon+impact+work-based+learning" [accessed 25 June 2009]. York: Higher Education Academy.

Raelin, J. (2008) *Work-based Learning: Bridging Knowledge and Action in the Workplace.* San Francisco, CA: Jossey-Bass.

Reed, J. and Procter, S. (eds) (1995) *Practitioner Research in Health Care: The Inside Story,* London: Chapman and Hall.

Vygotsky, L.S. (1962) *Thought and Language.* Cambridge, MA: MIT Press. [Original work published in 1934.]

2

Search and review of relevant knowledge and information

> **Key points**
>
> This chapter explains issues encountered in the search and review of knowledge and information for a work based project. Conventionally, a dissertation might identify a 'knowledge gap' in the academic literature, but a work based project is more likely to look for knowledge and information to create new practices or solve a practical problem. The issues include insiders as researchers, the practice-based project, widening thinking around a particular context and reviewing professional sources. The chapter includes information about important academic conventions, for example referencing and avoiding plagiarism.

There are two activities covered in this chapter; one is the search for relevant knowledge and information (commonly called a 'literature search') and the other is the selection and review of this knowledge and information (commonly called a 'literature review'). Searching through the great quantities of information available in our present-day information society may require complex activity in finding and referencing the items. Reviewing involves more analytical and evaluative abilities, using critical skills. In terms of extending your knowledge, as well as developing critical skills and reflexivity of writing, you should develop an ability to synthesize academic knowledge and theory with your own professional practice.

A search and review of relevant knowledge and information may constitute an essential chapter of a project or dissertation, or it may be integrated into the project or dissertation during the course of the research study, dispensing with the traditional discrete chapter. Another possibility is that it may be a self-contained review of writings on a subject that may or may not be later used to inform further research on that subject.

Usually, a search and review is a demonstration of existing knowledge and information in the area of the project that is being researched and developed. Although this may be an essential area, it is likely to involve more than just academic, peer-reviewed literature on the topic and include more professionally based knowledge and information found in work-related sources. This is because a work based project is likely to seek to communicate research and scholarly ideas found in academic literature and also to apply information and provide professional knowledge and understanding from professional sources.

The search for knowledge and information depends on the kind of work based project being undertaken, the purpose of the project and the purpose of those undertaking the project. The process of research itself often acts to clarify the research issue, changing the focus of the project and thus the relevance of different sources, knowledge and information. The main findings of a research project often highlight unforeseen themes that may require extending the search and review.

When planning, organizing and writing critically about the knowledge and information that you have located, you will need to establish which knowledge and information is most pertinent to your review and be able to synthesize, evaluate and critique the relevant materials. Do not underestimate the planning stage; having a sense of the overall organization of your literature review may expedite the process.

A search and review for a work based project is undertaken to:

- establish a familiarity and awareness of practitioners' current thinking on the subject area by means of collected knowledge and information so that your expertise in the project area is evident; you have an insider's awareness
- demonstrate understanding of not only the immediate context, but the wider field in which the project takes place. Whilst the focus of the project is to change or inform an immediate practice, you need to think about and search for related and widespread issues that may creatively inform the project, hence the saying 'to think globally and act locally'. It is possible that these considerations may involve a national or international search and networking with different groups of colleagues
- show a working knowledge of current practice and conceptual professional understanding that demonstrates practice-based knowledge and information. Presenting your project relative to prior work shows that you are engaging with a conversation and stepping into a debate that, in some ways, has already started
- develop a theoretical understanding of the topic through a search and review of relevant academic literature that will help to show how theory relates to practice
- uncover relevant areas with which you are not familiar and include these in the review
- cite and discuss approaches and ideas that are contrary to your own perspective
- provide the reader with an informed and up-to-date discussion on issues relevant to the project, so that a complex and sometimes specialized area can be related in a concise and accessible manner. Reviewing knowledge and

information provides you with a guide that keeps the reader up to date in the field. It should be relevant, appropriate, useful to the reader and at the forefront of current thinking

• explain why areas have not been included, or alluded to only briefly.

Ideas come from many different sources

Knowledge and information are likely to come from a range of sources: from standard academic literature, the professional sphere and elsewhere. Professional knowledge is likely to be emphasized in a work based review. The literature cited is likely to include the review and critique of relevant professional documents such as policy documents. The work based project requires this eclectic search because the projects are real world developments that take place in specific contexts, so the approach to literature is likely to be both multi-/trans-disciplinary and inter-professional. For example, the following extract shows that sources of knowledge and information can be very specific:

> there may be practice 'on the ground', particularly with specific groups, that is considered effective but that doesn't necessarily get written up into the type of review level publications considered in the review. There are however numerous publications containing information about, and evaluations of what is considered to be good/effective practice published by e.g. service providers, service funders and the like which are rarely viewed beyond the confines of small interested groups. (Coomber et al., 2004: 3)

Academic literature comprises publications that report original empirical and theoretical work in the natural and social sciences and within a scientific field, often abbreviated to 'the literature'. Academic conventions of citation and reference can be found in numerous published books on the subject, for example Rumsey (2008), Neville (2007) and Hart (1998). Not all academic literature is peer-reviewed. For example, in a peer-reviewed journal, the papers are, but the book reviews are usually not. Literature that is not peer-reviewed can be sometimes regarded as having a different status. Irrespective of its peer review status, all literature should be subjected to the same evaluation processes for the purposes of a review and referenced properly.

Depending upon the design of the particular research and development project, sources of knowledge are likely to include those used on a day-to-day basis within the workplace. Work based researchers may refer to a range of professionally generated materials. The types of knowledge and information might be internal policy documents, professional journals, books, government documents, popular media, Web-based materials, reports, informational brochures, teaching materials, newsletters, posters and minutes of meetings, and may also draw upon conversations and contacts with colleagues, as well as many other kinds of written items and artefacts.

Sources and their characteristics	Characteristics of use
Reference works: • provide a good starting point for research in an unfamiliar topic • may provide quick information • are good for new vocabulary, synonyms and so on • may provide bibliographies, lists and so on.	• may be available in paper form, where topics are usually listed alphabetically • are often available on the Web and accessed by keyword search.
Broadcast and World Wide Web material: • is usually current and updated regularly • can disappear as quickly as it appears • can be a good source of primary information – interviews, video footage, and so on. • may be biased or sensational.	• material on the Web can be searched easily • broadcast material may not always be known about in advance – constant vigil is required in searching listings, and so on • material may not be archived and can be lost for all time. It is important to take references when the material is found and make copies.
Books: • generally provide a broader view of topics • explore ideas in some depth • often contain bibliographies • are not generally current because of the time taken to publish • are quite dense and time-consuming to read • may contain essays expressing a variety of views.	• use library catalogues to discover local collections • use catalogues of deposit libraries and publishers' sites to find the latest material.
Academic journals: • are written by and for scholars (peer-assessed) and are, therefore, authoritative • contain bibliographies • are up to date in their content • provide in-depth analysis of narrowly defined topics • may be available in both paper and online format.	• use the library catalogue to find which journals the university holds or can provide access to • use electronic databases to search journal contents.

(Continued)

(Continued)

Newspapers: • contain information on current issues and debates • are easily available • may be biased or sensational.	• all British newspapers are available to research at the British Library Newspaper Library, Colindale • full-text British broadsheets are available online through UKProquest, which is listed amongst the electronic databases.

Policy and law:
 	
 • may be applicable at international, national and local level
 • may be available on the Web
 • are often discussed in broadcast media and newspapers
 • are often implemented through procedure and local policy documents.
	• commentary on policy and law may often be found in newspapers
	 • several specialist sites may provide access to full-text resources and catalogues. Examples include:
	    – www.Barnet.gov.uk
	    – www.opsi.gov.uk/
	    – www.europa.eu/index_en.htm
	    – www.un.org/

Conference papers: • contain a text version of papers presented at conferences • usually contain the latest ideas in a field of interest.	• these may be available online or through higher education or specialist libraries – for example, see the British Library catalogue at: http://catalogue.bl.uk
Documents in use (sometimes called 'grey literature'): • include any printed material which is not available through the normal publishing channels, for example pamphlets, brochures and guides. You may have relevant material available locally.	• ask relevant organizations if they have the material required. Try searching: http://bubl.ac.uk/link/subject browse.cfm • the British Library catalogues are a starting point.
Invisible college: • includes any communication shared by people with a common interest • can be acknowledged as a source of information, for example email, conversations, telephone calls, minutes of meetings.	• these are not catalogued or generally available. They may come from your personal collection, but must be properly referenced.

Selecting sources

The scope of the knowledge and information review will depend on the size and focus of your work based project. Higher level projects would take account of a broader context and are likely to have a wider brief for knowledge and information.

Example 1: A Master's project with the title 'Towards the creation of a professional IT association'

The candidate reviewed knowledge and information within the following areas: professional societies and ethics, development of systems thinking and systems practice, the IT profession, future directions and development, professions and their organization, professionalization, certification and professional development.

Knowledge and information was mainly located within books, professional journals and other professional publications and newspaper articles.

Example 2: A Bachelor's project with the title 'Involving parents in classroom activities'

The candidate used mainly course material, lesson plans, activity sheets, and so on, communications and testimonial.

Example 3: A Master's project that assesses the practice of adult education and catechesis (deepening and maturing of faith throughout life) within the Catholic Church in order to determine a new paradigm of mature faith education

The literature review encompassed the literature of research, selected adult learning theories, ecclesiastical documents specific to adult education, Christian interpretations of adult formation and literature relating to the role of the educator in such a setting.

Example 4: A Bachelor's project that critically evaluates the introduction of a specific learning method as a whole-school approach

There was investigation of policy documents (specifically relating to *Every Child Matters* and the National Curriculum), the original research articles on the learning method as well as the later professional articles by the same author on how the National Strategy team had been advised on its implementation.

An important critical ability is that of determining which knowledge and information makes a significant contribution to the understanding of the topic. You need to develop the capacity to filter knowledge and information, deciding to include some and exclude others. Remember also that it is usually important to include relevant and recent developments in the area and show that you have kept informed about current initiatives. You also need to apply principles of analysis to determine the reliability and validity of the sources, demonstrating that you know where to access material that has credibility in your field.

An ongoing search

The focal point or issue upon which the project centres has often come out of your pre-understanding of the particular area of your practice, and you are searching for material towards enhancing a particular aspect of this practice. The project may have been identified in consultation with an employer and/or other stakeholders in the project area. Within the work based learning context, relevant knowledge and information is less concerned with constructing a picture of theoretical knowledge. It is concerned with using knowledge and information to achieve the needs of a 'real life' work based project at the point where new knowledge adds another element.

The search is therefore likely to be ongoing, and in this sense you may find that you do not perform a comprehensive search and review before starting the primary data-gathering stage of the project. You are more likely to continuously refer back into literature of various kinds as the project progresses. The ongoing needs of the project are better served in this way than treating the search and review primarily as something at the outset to scope and focus the project. In terms of the work based purposes of the project, it may be irrelevant whether the proposed project corresponds with a gap in the academic literature on the project's topic.

Understanding the project's context

You are at the stage of searching for and reviewing the knowledge and information that already exists about the area or subject of your research. As a work based researcher and practitioner, you already have a level of knowledge about your area of work. You are also likely to already have extensive understanding of the work based project context. To a large extent, the authority for the content and style of the search and review therefore rests with you, as the expert in your work area. You may also be advised by a tutor to search in more academically focused areas.

It is important that, as a worker-researcher, you use your own experience when selecting what to review. As a worker, you know where to look and who to ask. You have a detailed understanding of the context in which the project is to take place. It is important that you are also able to place the project in the context of the national and international sphere. It is the particular context of the project and your individual propensity to undertake it that make your project unique. You have a standpoint within a particular context on the kinds and sources of knowledge and information important for your project.

As a worker, you are likely be in a role related to the research project and your position may determine the readily available sources of knowledge and information, because it is often the case that senior workers have wider access to sources. Insiders have access to information and may or may not also have power and control over its use. This is an element of your search that you should take into account.

Insiders usually belong to several networks and know who will tell them what. Your understanding of the area is likely to be affected by a whole range of different social interactions at different times. The knowledge and information you find is likely to reflect what is available in the context of the project's partners and stakeholders. There may not be much, especially if the project is particularly innovative. Some information is coded so only insiders can understand, and it may be that you are able to explain because you have a unique perspective and can bring together various pieces of codified knowledge, drawing on aspects to produce new knowledge.

Reading and critically evaluating the information that you locate

In order to write a cohesive review that offers an overview of significant knowledge and information published on a topic, you need to present a clear line of argument. This line of argument involves making your 'voice' clear; that is, your perspective, position or standpoint should be clearly identifiable in the review, as in the project as a whole. However, you are explicitly writing about other people's work and it can be easy for your own 'voice' to be lost. For this reason, you should be careful that the knowledge and information review does not read as a mixture of different tones and arguments, but has a consistent flow.

It is important that your position is clearly and strongly stated and that your critical evaluations form an integral part. Secondly, it is important that your language indicates whether you are relating your own or other people's attitudes to the question or issue. This can involve using critical comments from your reading notes to express an opinion.

In the initial stages, some people find that drawing diagrams of how the knowledge and information fits together is useful in providing a 'big picture' of the information to be incorporated.

You may need to follow guidelines provided by your course leaders and seek clarification from your tutor:

- Critically analyse the knowledge and information you use.
- Follow through a set of concepts and questions, comparing items to each other.

- Do not just list and summarize items, but assess them, discussing strengths and weaknesses.
- Avoid personal comments or language when talking about the arguments presented by authors. Use phrases like 'Denzin argues ... ', or 'According to Ying ... '.
- Avoid emotive and inaccurate language.

Read widely but selectively in your topic area. Pay attention to what you notice in passing; it may seem peripheral to your more focused search at the time, but might resonate with other material at a later stage. Examine its strengths and weaknesses in relation to your research project. Take notes, not only of the information that you read, but of your thoughts about this information. This will help you draw your ideas together when you start to write your review. Extracting or making summaries of each piece has some value, but does not constitute the building blocks of a good review; taking notes and making critical comments is likely to be more useful. Keep in mind that although taking notes is time-consuming, much of it will be directly usable later. For this reason, it may be useful to type notes instead of writing them in longhand, and not to think of the reading as being somehow separate from the writing. This can also contribute to a sense of the progress with your project.

Knowledge and information need to be read critically and impartially. There are many excellent resources and a great deal of knowledge and information where you need to keep a clear focus when selecting for review. This is the case whether or not the material has been peer-reviewed and is also true for information you find on the Web. Your evaluation should involve a critical awareness concerning the writing of others, for example whether it is based upon reliable practice or research and has a coherent rationale. When evaluating texts to incorporate into your review, the following questions could be considered:

- How does the text relate to the particular circumstance of your work based project?
- Are the authors familiar with working practice, and what do you know about them?
- What is the perspective of the writer? (Think about their context.)
- What would be the credibility of the text to the professionals who will receive and possibly use the results of your work?
- Why does the material exist and is it credible to a range of audiences, both professional and academic?
- Is the material up to date?
- Are the arguments logical and consistent with the norms of the context of your project?
- Is the evidence reliable and can it be related to the context of your project?
- Is the material correctly and fully referenced or linked to other information?

You should have some specific questions in mind as you read. These may be quite general or more specific and will help you concentrate and deal with the material in an active manner. If you are looking for specific information, you do not need to summarize the whole article or book.

- Keeping a list of questions in your mind will sharpen your analytical skills and help you keep an objective outlook on your material.
- When your findings conflict, you might find it useful to ask questions.

The questions will form the basis of your written review. Asking them as you read will tend to slow the process down, because you will be thinking as you read. However, doing this work early will make the process of writing a critical review much easier. If you take comprehensive notes in your own words as you read and think, you will have done the really hard work before you start to write.

Synthesize and evaluate the review according to the guiding concept of your research question. Good reviews are characterized by:

- a logical flow of ideas
- current and relevant references with consistent, appropriate referencing style
- proper use of terminology
- an unbiased and comprehensive view of the previous knowledge and information available on the topic.

The first step towards critical reading is to keep your purpose in mind as you read. Do not allow the arguments in the text to distract you from your reading agenda. Take a few moments to think about what you are expecting before beginning to read.

The way your notes are written and organized is not important, but you should ensure that:

- a difference is noted between your ideas and those of other authors
- there are clear references including page numbers, publishers and place of publication in case you want to look at the original material again, or cite it and reference it in your review.

Situation reviews may also be necessary

A situational analysis can be used as part of a case study approach, for example, it may be used as preliminary work for a case study. It originates from Popper's (cited in Oakley, 2002) philosophy of social sciences as a way of seeking explanations regarding choice and human conduct (Neves, 2004). It is a way of analysing a situation by a logical process of reconstruction of the component parts, as influenced by the people and context in which that situation occurs. An example is when an organization purchases a particular service from another company. There may be a problem with the provision of that service – perhaps it does not fulfil the first organization's requirements, or the expectation of what the service consists of differs between the two companies. Before such a problem can be rectified, the factors that influence that service have to be identified, described and explored in depth to see where the problem originated and what range of alternatives might be offered.

This analytical process therefore requires the researcher to explore the internal, external, social and institutional processes that combine to form a particular event, and to take a logical approach to see how these processes could be expected to contribute to the behaviour of those involved. This can be used to create a strategy to resolve the problem. Simplified, it can be presented thus:

- a description of the situation
- an analysis of the situation, considering, for example, internal, external, sociological, technological, political, financial and organizational factors
- an examination of the logical outcomes of these factors
- a rational explanation of the situation and consequent actions to be taken.

Conventions of referencing

In order to produce a rigorously researched work based project that has feasibility and validity, you need knowledge of the key academic conventions concerning referencing. This may entail how to reference information not usually found through libraries or publishers, such as workplace reports, working papers, leaflets and so on. In the academic world, these examples may be categorized as 'documents in use' (Hammersley and Atkinson, 1995) which usually comprise contemporary information not easily accessed by the public and unlikely to be controlled by publication, distribution or bibliographic systems. It may not be possible to distinguish the usual referencing information of author, publication date, place of publication and publisher. However, a wide range of knowledge and information may be necessary to inform a work based project, drawn from the professional sphere as well as the academic, and there are conventions by which it can be cited and referenced. Other examples are websites, although with the rise of online journals and repositories for academic work, such references are now more usual. There are also referencing conventions for works of art, dance, artefacts and so on.

When compiling the lists of relevant knowledge and information that you wish to use in your project, use an effective method that lets you retrieve information quickly and easily, for example, the use of a software programme such as EndNote (www.endnote.com) to help you organize and store your notes relating to the readings that you have undertaken. Remember that there is no single 'right' way to organize your materials. However, it is important to know where to find the knowledge and information that you have tracked down so that you can access it quickly and easily.

What is referencing?

A reference list is a detailed record of those items – books, articles, policy documents, conference reports, electronic resources and so on – that you have cited during the preparation of your work. It must include all the publications quoted, paraphrased or referred to in the text. These are identified within the text in a manner which directs the reader to their full details in the list at the end of your project. Serious problems can arise if you use sources and do not cite them within the text (see section on plagiarism, over).

A bibliography is usually meant as a list of all the material which you have found relevant while searching for knowledge and information but not necessarily cited or referenced. This lists in alphabetical order the sources referred to in the text, as well as other sources you have relied on in your project. This list should not contain page or chapter references. A bibliography comes at the end of the work, before the appendices. You do not need to have read all the items, only know that they further knowledge in your field and may be of use to others. Some subject disciplines use the term 'bibliography' in the same way as the term 'reference list' is used here.

Citation

Your completed work must acknowledge in the text itself the sources from which you have obtained your information and must also cross-refer to the reference list at the end. The following provides guidelines on how to cite (or *refer to*) those sources.

A *citation in the text itself* (see example below) is used as an acknowledgement of intellectual borrowing of ideas and facts and interpretations and so on, citing page references ('chapter and verse'!) and, in a minority of cases, a particular chapter in a book.

References in the text should be presented in this way:

'As Kolb (1984: 22–3) has observed … '

Or, in a more general reference, 'Kolb (1984) appears to be saying … '

For a work with three authors or more, give only the first name followed by 'et al.'

When citing the work of one author found in the work of another, you should acknowledge that you did not consult the original source, for example: 'Supporting evidence appears in a study by Black (cited in Smith et al., 2001: 64)'.

Plagiarism

In some cultures, it can be seen as correct, virtuous or even complimentary to reproduce the ideas or words of others without acknowledging their origin. Because a knowledge and information review is based on the work of other authors, you must be very careful to separate an author's evaluation of research from your own. Organization and scrupulous note-taking and referencing are the best ways to ensure that your work is correctly referenced. Make sure that you understand what needs to be referenced:

- Plagiarism of ideas occurs if you paraphrase facts or arguments without citation. Anything taken from a text, even if you write it in your own words, needs to have a citation or footnote.
- Plagiarism of words happens if you copy another author exactly without putting the words in quotation marks. This type may occur in conjunction with plagiarism of ideas or on its own. Even if you provide citation information, you also need to put the text in quote marks or you will be guilty of plagiarism. Citations of quotations should include page numbers.

Copyright and confidentiality issues

In the UK, copyright exists automatically in all original works under the Copyright, Design and Patents Act, 1988. Copyright does not have to be registered, but is automatically assigned the moment the material is created, published, recorded or, if the creator is unknown, released or publicly displayed.

One change in copyright law that may affect you is the fair dealing exception: 'Copying for private study or research' will now be restricted to 'Copying for private study or non-commercial research'. Any copying for commercial research will require permission and payment.

With regard to using personal data, you need to be aware of the Data Protection Act (1998). There are brief guidance notes issued jointly by the Publishers Association and the Joint Information Systems Committee (JISC) (1997) that may be useful.

Privacy or copyright issues may apply to the documents you gather, so it is important to inquire about these when you find or are given documents. If you are given permission to include what you learn from these documents in your project, the documents should be cited appropriately and included in the references section of your project. If you are not given permission, you should not use them in any way.

Where should knowledge and information be placed in a work based project?

A typical dissertation might include a chapter that is mainly a review of academic literature and another chapter on methodology that describes the research approach and methods. One of the methods might be a review of relevant documents and artefacts. In this way, documents and artefacts classified as 'documents in use', sometimes called 'grey literature', can be used as a way of including secondary data in an immediate analysis along-side primary data. A typical dissertation may include a later section that discusses the analysis of primary data in relation to works reviewed in a literature review chapter.

Relevant literature for a work based project is often an initial part of the project. Some salient literature is likely to be used at the beginning of a work based project report to argue and define the project, but further literature is more usually integrated into the whole. This literature may be used as a source of secondary data, often to make explicit what practitioners themselves may take for granted. So the review of knowledge and information in a work based project might consist of:

- a single chapter that reviews all the knowledge and information. The knowledge and information review itself, however, does not usually present new *primary* scholarship. It may critique sources and synthesize them in a new way, but data is usually drawn from the work of other authors;
- a single chapter that reviews published work whilst unpublished knowledge and information such as minutes of meetings, circulars and other professional documents are evaluated as part of ethnographically oriented approaches to data collection;
- a chapter that reviews the published work that appears immediately relevant; unpublished knowledge and information evaluated as part of the research methodology; and continuous search and review throughout the research that is factored into the study as the research takes place. Continuous review can thus take place whilst data are being collected, whilst being evaluated (as is common in the case of action research) and again when conclusions are being drawn.

Structuring a review chapter

A review may comprise the following elements:

- an overview of the subject, issue or theory under consideration, along with the objectives of the literature review
- a division of the works under review into categories (for example, those in support of a particular position, those against, and those offering entirely alternative ideas)

- an explanation of your agreement or otherwise with the material under consideration
- conclusions as to which pieces are best considered in the argument, are most convincing of their opinions, and make the greatest contribution to the understanding and development of your research project.

The following is a suggested structure for a work based literature review.

Introduce

Clearly identify and delineate the topic to be considered, and the function(s) of the intended work based audience. Define or identify the general topic, issue or area of concern, thus providing an appropriate context for the review. Establish your rationale for reviewing the particular knowledge and information, explain the criteria to be used in analysing and comparing knowledge and information and the organization of the review and, when necessary, explain the scope of the review by stating why certain knowledge and information is or is not included. How good was my information seeking? Has my search been wide enough to ensure I've found all the relevant material? Has it been narrow enough to exclude irrelevant material? Is the number of sources I've used appropriate for the length of my project?

Review

Depending on the function and range of the sources, this may be structured by type, theme or approach. Group research studies and other types of literature (reviews, theoretical articles, case studies and so on) may be grouped according to common characteristics, such as qualitative versus quantitative approaches, conclusions of authors, specific purpose or objective, chronology and so on.

Connect

Sum up individual studies or articles with as much or as little detail as each merits according to its comparative importance in the knowledge and information, remembering that space (length) denotes significance. You will not simply list your sources and go into detail about each one of them; consider instead what themes connect your sources together and their issues and arguments.

Provide

Give the reader strong 'umbrella' sentences at beginnings of paragraphs, 'signposts' throughout, and brief 'so what …' summary sentences at intermediate points in the review to aid the understanding of comparisons and analyses.

Summarize

Sum up any major contributions from significant knowledge and information to the project or topic area under review, maintaining the focus you established in the introduction.

Evaluate

Weigh up the current material you have reviewed and discuss whether or not you are in agreement with the points made and how useful the contents are in progressing your project.

Conclude

This should identify major themes which have emerged during the review and pick out the most important points for your work based audience and your own work based project. Provide some insight into the relationship between the central topic of the review and a larger area of study, such as a profession.

Discussion questions

1. In your own work area, identify possible sources of relevant knowledge and information.
2. Which sources are most difficult to acquire, and how would you deal with this?
3. Why is it important to ensure that your 'voice' is clearly identifiable in your review?
4. What benefits does software such as 'Endnote' bring to the researcher? Is there a downside?
5. Identify the source of guidance for the referencing system required for your university programme of study.

References

Coomber, R., Millward, L., Chambers, J. and Warm, D. (2004). *A Rapid Interim Review of the 'Grey' Literature on Risky Behaviour in Young People Aged 11–18 with a special emphasis on vulnerable groups.* Health Development Agency, Available at: www.nice.org.uk/nicemedia/pdf/rapid_review_risky_behaviour.pdf [accessed 1 May 2009].

Copyright, Design and Patents Act (1988) www.opsi.gov.uk/acts/acts1988/Ukpga_19880048_en_1.htm [accessed 1 May 2009].

Data Protection Act (1998) www.legislation.hmso.gov.uk/acts/acts1998/19980029.htm [accessed 1 May 2009].

End Note (2009) *Endnote: Bibliographies Made Easy.* Available at: www.endnote.com [accessed 1 May 2009].

Hammersley, M. and Atkinson, P. (1995) 'Documents,' in *Ethnography: Principles in Practice*, 2nd edn, pp. 157–74. New York: Routledge.

Hart, C. (1998) *Doing a Literature Review*. London: Sage.

Neves, V. (2004) 'Situational analysis beyond "single-exit" modelling', *Cambridge Journal of Economics* 28(6): 921–36.

Neville, C. (2007) *The Complete Guide to Referencing and Avoiding Plagiarism*. Milton Keynes: Open University Press.

Oakley, A. (2002) 'Popper's ontology of situated human action', *Philosophy of the Social Sciences* 32(4): 455–86.

Publishers Association and JISC (1997) www.ukoln.ac.uk/services/elib/papers/pa/licence/ [accessed 1 May 2009].

Rumsey, S. (2008) *How to Find Information: A Guide for Researchers*, 2nd edn. Maidenhead: Open University Press.

3

Research ethics and insider-researchers

Key points

By the nature of work based learning, the researcher is an insider, often working on organizational or wider professional issues. Learners are agents of their organization or professional area and also of their university, which is behind their work based academic award, additionally act for themselves alone. This chapter will set out the first part of a practitioner framework for research ethics for use by the work based researcher. Perspectives are adopted which relate to the nature of the research itself, the methodologies you are likely to use, the way the research is conducted, the analyses of the research, the range of stakeholders in this kind of research and the outcomes of the research. All of these issues need close scrutiny from an ethical perspective that often depends upon the values of differing work settings. Many of these would be familiar to all kinds of researchers, not just insider-researchers. However, the issues are often slightly different, with particular caveats or sometimes with an alternative point of view. From the outset, the way in which you conduct your research needs to be in the light of ethics from an insider perspective.

Insider-researchers such as yourself are usually experienced workers involved in research that may use colleagues as subjects in the research. Insider-researchers learn how to enquire using research techniques; you may draw upon literature, artefacts from the wider body of knowledge outside your context, your own experiential knowledge and your colleagues' knowledge. The subjects of the research and the organization in which the research takes place are therefore likely to have a vested interest in the process and outcomes of the research.

As a practitioner who is likely to be, at least to some extent, an insider in relation to the research, reflecting carefully on ethical issues that are particularly relevant to you is an important aspect of developing work based research projects undertaken as part of a university award. As an insider-researcher, you have to consider the ethical implications of your project from the point of view of the professional area in which you work. You must also ensure that you abide by the university's code of practice on research ethics, and you should be comfortable with your research from your own perspective, given that you may be asking colleagues for data and therefore using them as subjects of your research. The relationship the learner has with both organization and university is not new to higher education in the area of sponsored research, but it highlights role ambiguities for the researcher (and others), since it is likely that they have to work alongside colleagues they are researching in order to achieve a predetermined goal in a manner that satisfies academic criteria.

Most students who undertake research projects are advised to read about ethics in research by consulting research books and publications. In the case of researching within your own work context, it is important to understand the particular issues of being an insider-researcher and the pertinent ethical issues associated with your particular project and its unique context. In order to address the ethical issues that should always be considered in a practitioner-generated work based project, particular guidance and information should be sought through an extensive literature search and enquiry of research texts in both academic and professional spheres.

Your practitioner-led research presents unique challenges for engaging in ethical issues, because you are an insider in relation to your engagement with your research project(s).

The purpose of a work based project

When considering the overall moral and ethical implications of your projects, it is advisable to take account of a range of issues. Ethical issues or issues of value concerning the nature and aim of a work based, practitioner-led project are of particular significance. The project aim is likely to be research and development in an aspect of work that enhances working practice. The nature of the piece of research being proposed and whether or not it is morally and ethically appropriate (Robson, 1993: 30) will have to be considered by all the stakeholders in order to gain approval from a university and workplace perspective.

The aim is likely to be beneficial to a particular organization or community of practice. Not all 'work' can be considered ethically sound and it becomes the responsibility of the university to monitor the value of a work based project. For example, whilst it is clear that illegal and immoral work would not be acceptable, there are work areas that can engage researchers in high-level thinking, but which the university may not consider worthwhile – for example, work on astrology or feng shui.

You should give sound reasons for your aims and objectives, discussed in a justification and rationale for your project. It is suggested that an appropriate standpoint for work based projects would be to take account of the following three factors that combine social, economic and environmental benefits.

- To explore all the social implications of the project. For example, to whom is it beneficial and is there is any detriment to people (individuals, communities of practice, members of organizations) or other living creatures?
- To explore all the economic implications of the project. For example, is the research feasible, and will the research in some way bring about financial gain? If so, whose interests will it serve?
- To explore the sustainability of the research. For example, is it likely to cause any detriment to the environment?

Finally, the research might be justified in relation to all three factors working in harmony with each other:

> The role of the professional in a sustainable society is an increasingly dominating issue. Government, business and academia are generating interest and activity in sustainable development. Professional institutions and employers expect their members to be competent to undertake development projects that have solved any issues around sustainable development. (Harman, 2005: 110)

You need to rationalize the benefits and appropriateness of your project for your own development, for your organization or community of practice and for the university. Many researchers undertake modules or courses in research methods, and for these you will need to take a more in-depth view of these areas.

The methodological approach to the work based project

The point of view or ideology behind the project aim is a matter for your critical evaluation. Your chosen approach and methods also underpin your point of view or ideology and are often based upon a particular set of values that you may have taken for granted.

Not only are you working within your own point of view or ideology, but also within particular discourses, often associated with particular professions, work situations and cultures (see Chapter 7).

The rationalization for your research approach and methods requires you to justify why you intend to take that particular course of action. This justification entails asserting why the particular approach and methods are the best to use to discover what you need to know to get the best results for your research and development project. It also entails giving an account of your efforts to ensure that the methods of the research are appropriate and reasonable from the point of view of all the participants. As a worker as well as a researcher, you also do this within certain constraints, for instance, of time, context and position, and these constraints will also be factors in your justification. The ethical considerations are necessarily priority concerns when undertaking this justification. Here again, the three key parties who are concerned with your research and development project (yourself, your organization or professional area and the university) are likely to be the parties who are considered and consulted.

The investigative methods of particular organizations and work situations may tend towards a particular style or mode. For example, artists may tend towards ethnography and historical methods, while people in financial management might tend towards quantitative approaches. You may have to consider the appropriate approach and methods that fit in with both organizational/professional requirements and issues of ethics.

Organizational/professional context

There are significant ethical implications for your organization, professional groups or communities of practice. You may find yourself in various different contexts within particular professions and/or communities. It is your responsibility to recognize and understand the ethical codes of practice and principles that exist within the context in which your project is being researched (Messick et al., 2001). For example, if you are working for a health service, there are restrictions concerning the use of patients' records and ethical committees that consider the conduct of research within the areas of your jurisdiction. If you are working with minors (in the UK, children under 16), there are protocols regarding parental consent when interviewing and so on. You will need to consult specialist literature on ethics within your own field; this is part of your individual search of the literature.

Within your professionally oriented programme, you are well advised to seek feedback on ethical issues from your academic project advisor, but also, where appropriate, your employers/managers, and to consider regulations and protocols within your professional areas and the values, statements and codes of conduct in your organization or community of practice. You are undertaking a project within a particular situation where there are already policies and practices that you are probably familiar with or, at least, you will know how to familiarize yourself with them. Universities usually require research proposals to be approved by the university and benchmarked with ethical standards of organizational and professional codes of good practice where relevant, such as in the fields of social work, psychology, medicine and so on. This includes taking appropriate action such as gaining approval from ethics committees, where required. If your professional body or organization requires proposed research activity to go before an ethics committee, it is your responsibility to ensure that your research proposal has been endorsed by such a committee and to provide evidence. For example, ethical guidelines for conducting educational research can be obtained from the British Educational Research Association (www.bera.ac.uk) and, for conducting health-related research, the National Research Ethics Service which is part of the National Patient Safety Agency (www.nres.npsa.nhs.uk/).

However, you may be in a new and emerging professional area such as professional coaching, or in areas that are developing professional work at higher levels such as veterinary surgery and conservation.

Personal perception

There are ethical implications relating to your own ideological position in doing work based research projects. The project will take a great deal of your time and enhance your expertise in a particular area. The purpose of the project is likely to be a subject on which you feel it is worthwhile to focus your energies and you will rationalize this in terms of your own ideals, development and hopes for the future. Between this personal perspective and the considerations of the context of the work and the university lies a connection to the community and society in which you work and live. There is usually a process of reconciliation with these larger structures and/or conflict between your personal position and the ideological structures around you.

There may be organizational values to be considered from a personal and professional perspective and you may or may not feel a responsibility for your project work fulfilling the expectations of those who are stakeholders in your project's outcome (Murray, 1997). There is a sense in which your main responsibility is to yourself: to carry out research that you feel is right for you, for your organization and/or professional area, and also to adopt an appropriate approach to collecting data from colleagues that feels right for you and does not impose on others.

University context

Universities require all researchers to observe ethical codes, policies and practices. An example of a statement by one university is: 'All ... students of the University are responsible for ensuring that their actions are carried out in the terms of the general policy and codes of practice'. Students are usually required to sign a statement that acknowledges the importance of understanding and implementing all relevant ethical considerations. The statement is usually considered by a committee or panel that can refer problematic ethical issues to other ethics committees, if appropriate.

Ethical research codes and the responsibility of the researcher to have a framework in place are required for work based projects to consider ethical issues as they present at the initial proposal stage and throughout the conduct of the research. That is, ethical research practice is an ongoing process and does not stop when an external body gives the proposed research a favourable opinion. This 'ethical dependency' on others external to the project is to some extent counteracted by emphasizing the researcher's ethic of care (see Chapter 4).

There are also general principles and legal requirements to consider when undertaking research at work, such as the Data Protection Act and laws on copyright and equal opportunities.

Literature relating to research ethics and insider-researchers

Within work based, practitioner-led research, there is a growing body of literature that addresses research undertaken by practitioner-researchers. Robson (1993) describes the advantages and disadvantages of this role and Jarvis (1998) and Gray (2004) briefly examine its possibilities and limitations. Gray then goes on to relate in more detail how insider-researchers who use the methodological approach of action research can easily become concerned with ethical issues. For example, when insiders make observations of what is going on, people may not necessarily be aware that they are being researched.

This is even more so in work based, practitioner-led research where academic responsibility must take into account multiple communities of practice, each of which has its own epistemological and power agenda. Feminist participatory action research has often advocated reflexivity as a means by which power, position and perceived status can be interrogated and understood (Kemmis and McTaggart, 2000). Reflexivity has more recently been advocated as a way to be both reflective about one's own practice (Boud et al., 2006) – a common learning technique in the field of professional practice – and to understand one's own position and the position of others in the research.

From a feminist standpoint perspective, Harding (1987) found that women's situated experience was able to express knowledge that had hitherto been marginalized or ignored. Later, Haraway (1991) gave deep consideration to standpoint theory and found that knowledge claims can be treated differently according to the socio-economic positioning and location of the subjects of research and the researchers. Raised by feminist thinkers, these are salient issues for practitioner-researchers, especially in regard to their position at work. Sprague and Kobrynowicz (2004) note that to understand fully knowledge grounded in experience, account needs to be taken of understandings that are generated by people in their daily lives. Standpoint theory also notes that there should be recognition of the authority that comes from the experience of having studied, reflected and paid attention to the reflection of others. Insider-researchers fall into this category and Sprague and Kobrynowicz (2004: 92) further note that such a positioning means that they have to take responsibility for the authority of their experience.

In effect, the differing approaches to standpoint theory that have emerged over the last 20 years are a good source of literature for insider-researchers such as yourself, to help to inform you about your positioning as a researcher and as a practitioner within your research project (Hartsock, 1997; Hill Collins, 2000; Sprague and Kobrynowicz, 2004).

Ethical issues that relate directly to the methodology of insider research can also be found in the work of applied ethnography. For example, ethnographers might ask whether you should be involved in work that you yourself do not believe conforms to professional or personal standards of morality (Chambers, 2000: 864). The insider-researcher may have to ask similar questions of self in this regard. New qualitative approaches to methodology offer a range of approaches that insider-researchers could consider (Denzin and Lincoln, 2000; Guba and Lincoln, 1994). For example, the approach of 'bricolage' (Kincheloe and Berry, 2004) presents an opportunity to move away from traditional social science approaches and use rigour in research in a more adaptive and appropriate way.

Specific insider-researcher issues

There is the possibility that colleagues may feel obliged to cooperate with your research. This applies to your own organization, but may also apply to other organizations or communities in the professional area where you may be gathering data. Within your own organization or community of practice, you will normally have approached a line manager or other appropriate person regarding the research and development project(s) that you are hoping to undertake. You will need to consider the power dynamics involved in requesting colleagues or subordinates to be involved in your research and this is discussed in Chapter 4. Negotiating access is discussed in Chapter 5 and is an important part of the ethical issues you need to consider. As an insider-researcher, you will have to live with any mistakes and so should proceed carefully in negotiating with colleagues, following research protocols designed for insider-researchers rather than researchers coming new to a particular situation. There can be a kind of deception involved in being an 'insider but outsider' to the community being researched:

> to the extent that researchers are insiders, you are drawing on the normal ground rules of reciprocity and trust that pertain for social interactions in the community. To the extent that being a researcher means using these ground rules for research purposes, there is a risk of exploitation and betrayal. (Griffiths, 1998: pp. 40–1)

For example, in the case of your 'real world' and probably, to some extent, 'real time' project, some of your colleagues may be involved in the project anyway as part of your normal work, but you may ask them to spend extra time providing data. You may ask them to give interviews and/or complete questionnaires or you may ask them to take a more active part in your project. You need to be clear about what is expected of the participants in terms of both the project itself and the research element of the project.

You will need to be able to explain exactly what you mean by anonymity and confidentiality. In the case of insider research, it may be almost impossible to ensure real anonymity about the organization if it is known that the research is insider-led. There are several ramifications to this scenario and below are a few examples:

1. Any possible criticism that the researcher makes in evaluation of the research will be instantly perceived by the organization and could cause tension between the researcher/worker and the organization.
2. If the organization is known, then it is difficult to ensure anonymity of the subjects of the research, who can also be known.
3. Issues of confidentiality are also cast differently when confidentiality is offered not only to a subject of research, but also to a colleague. It is a more longstanding, confidential promise.
4. Insiders have more access to secondary data such as minutes of meetings, reports and so on and, even if you do not receive the permission which you establish you need to use these data, you still have knowledge that will inevitably affect your analysis and evaluation of the project as a whole.

This kind of insider-detailed knowledge is one of the reasons that insider projects can be so fully informed and, arguably, better placed to propose effective change strategies. In terms of ethical issues, it is also why insider research can highlight conflicts of interest between workers and between worker and organization. From the university's perspective, researchers are 'covered' if you ask for the organization's signature and make it clear to the signatory what data you wish to use. From the researcher's and the organization's perspective, the issues may be more complex and should be the subject of much reflection and consultation by the researcher.

Insiders have responsibilities regarding the rights of participants, who are also your colleagues and with whom you have a long-term relationship. From the university's perspective, you need to let all interested parties know what you are doing from the start and ensure that you are comfortable with procedures. You should always be in full command of your own involvement in the project and state that the purpose of the project is that it is part of your degree. Participants should be informed of the objectives of the study and what is to be done with the information that they provide. This is standard ethical practice when conducting research. However, for the insider-researcher, the added familiarity of the researcher to the researched adds a relationship dynamic that is not easily dealt with by protocols. For example, avoidance of being deceptive may become problematic because you have greater access to information, so you may take information from colleagues for your project and then allow them to believe that you need the information for another reason. Each small act and its possible impact on others may therefore need careful consideration as each part of the research project develops.

Clearly articulating an informed perspective

Issues associated with being an insider-researcher involve the close familiarity with the context of your research and the micro-politics of your particular organization or community of practice. The ethical issues that you anticipate arising in your project reflect your own thinking, which in turn will have been influenced by your situatedness within particular contexts. Like any other researcher, you determine which behaviours are observed, which are ignored and how the information is interpreted but, as an insider, you have detailed knowledge of the particular context. In research communities, this knowledge is sometimes represented as being 'subjective', which is deemed undesirable, since the goal of good research is seen in some research circles as objectivity. This has in turn been shown by some authors to be an epistemological impossibility. It is therefore important to articulate your own perspectives or premises clearly, that is to state your personal model of understanding of a situation. This process of articulating your own position will allow others to reflect on alternative constructions. Your insights as an insider are valuable because of your depth of knowledge, but you should also demonstrate that you understand alternative perspectives. Subjectivity, in this sense, is unavoidable because your particular interests in what and how the project is researched and developed will influence what is studied and emphasized, and the way it is evaluated. This is the case, of course, for all research, not just for the insider-researcher, but it is a particularly important consideration if you are 'in' the research.

As an insider-researcher, you may not be able, and may not wish, to distance yourself from the research, so there may be a subjectivity which you share with colleagues and other participants who are involved in the project – although it is also true that people in the same situations can construct reality in differing ways. You do have the final (and powerful) authority of interpreting and writing up your findings using your own constructions. You might try to minimize this power imbalance by calling on others to verify or contest your accounts.

Ownership of your research

In addition, it is necessary to reflect on whose interests will dominate the project work. You own the intellectual property rights of your own academic work, but you should consider who decides the nature of your project, the research and development process and output. If the project has been commissioned by your workplace or is necessarily part of your work role, the property rights are likely to be those of the organization. You may need to clarify the matter of ownership of your project with your organization and consider what constraints or opportunities your position as an insider-researcher in your workplace imposes upon or offers them, and who will benefit from the project's development. You will need to decide how you manage your position as a researcher/developer and your position as a worker in relation to colleagues. You should neither assume that colleagues will or should necessarily cooperate with your research, nor feel obliged to trust them. You have insider knowledge of the relevant people who can take part in the project and how best to approach them and should avoid putting people in a difficult position because you are a friend or colleague.

Interviewing colleagues

You need to consider the implications of working with colleagues and other participants who are your senior or junior, with all the difficulties that such situations may cause. You will want to undertake research about which you feel comfortable. For example, as an insider-researcher, you may have concerns about interviewing your own colleagues and should reflect on issues that may arise from doing so.

Colleagues often welcome the opportunity to discuss issues around their work and expound upon them. This is especially the case where the interviewer is someone familiar with their work problems and may in some cases be able to solve some of them, or at least discuss them with a common background of knowledge of the situation. It is possible that you may see the participant you are interviewing as a colleague who needs help or support of some kind. In this way, interviews with colleagues (participants) can act as a kind of 'therapy', whilst colleagues may also take the opportunity to air a grievance. You have to decide how you would deal with a situation if a participant tried to use an interview in this way.

Conforming to local laws and norms

In some cases, where there are international issues or if the research project takes place outside the country where your university is based, you may also need to consider laws and protocols with which the university is not familiar, such as laws of copyright. You are required to comply with local laws and practices as well as protocols of research practice in the university's own country, which may also affect the organization/community you are studying.

Discussion questions

1. Identify professional codes and research codes specific to your role as insider-researcher.
2. Identify relevant ethics/review committees and find out how they operate within their organization.
3. What ethical encounters do you anticipate in the conduct of your work based research and what framework would you develop to address them?

References

Boud, D., Cressey, P. and Docherty, P. (2006) *Productive Reflection at Work*. London: Routledge.

Chambers, E. (2000) 'Applied ethnography', in N.K. Denzin and Y.S. Lincoln (eds) *Handbook of Qualitative Research*, 2nd edn, pp. 851–69. London: Sage.

Denzin, N.K. and Lincoln, Y.S. (2000) *Handbook of Qualitative Research*. Thousand Oaks, CA: Sage.

Gray, D.E. (2004) *Doing Research in the Real World*. London: Sage.

Griffiths, M. (1998) *Education Research for Social Justice*. Buckingham: Open University Press.

Guba, E.G. and Lincoln, Y.S. (eds) (1994) 'Competing paradigms in qualitative research', in N.K. Denzin and Y.S. Lincoln (eds) *Handbook of Qualitative Research*. pp. 105–17. Thousand Oaks, CA: Sage.

Haraway, D.J. (1991) *Simians, Cyborgs and Women: The Reinvention of Nature*. New York: Routledge.

Harding, S. (1987) *Feminism and Methodology: Social Science Issues*. Bloomington, IN: Indiana University Press.

Harman, J. (2005) *Using Science to Create a Better Place; Understanding the Social Context of the Environment Agency's Work*, Available at: www.sharedpractice.org.uk/Downloads/Literature_%20 Review.pdf [accessed 31 July 2007].

Hartsock, N. (1997) 'Comment on Hekman's "Truth and Method": feminist standpoint theory revisited – truth or justice?', *Signs* 22(2): 367–75.

Hill Collins, P. (2000) *Black Feminist Thought: Knowledge, Consciousness, and the Politics of Empowerment*, 2nd edn. New York: Routledge.

Jarvis, P. (1998) *The Practitioner Researcher: Developing Theory from Practice*. New York: Jossey-Bass.

Kemmis, S. and McTaggart, R. (2000) 'Participatory action research', in N.K. Denzin and Y.S. Lincoln (eds) *Handbook of Qualitative Research*, 2nd edn, pp. 567–605. Beverly Hills, CA: Sage.

Kincheloe, J. and Berry, K. (2004) *Rigour and Complexity in Educational Research*. London/ New York: McGraw Hill/Open University Press.

Messick, D., Darley, J.M. and Tyler, T.R. (2001) *Social Influences on Ethical Behavior in Organizations*. New Jersey, London: MEA Publishers.

Murray, D. (1997) *Ethics in Organizations*. London: Kogan Page.

Robson, C. (1993) *Real World Research: A Resource for Social Scientists and Practitioner Researchers*, 2nd edn. Oxford: Blackwell.

Sprague, J. and Kobrynowicz, D. (2004) In S. Nagy Hesse-Biber and M.L. Yaiser (eds) 'A Feminist Epistemology', in *Feminist Perspectives on Social Research*, Oxford: Oxford University Press.

4

Privilege, power and politics in work based research

Key points

In this chapter, we discuss power and politics and how they can be recognized and, where appropriate, used, mitigated or confronted by you, the researcher, by virtue of your privileged position. We discuss how power and politics affect the context, form and outcome of research and how you can mange these dynamics within your workplace studies. We close the chapter by looking at the notion of care for the researcher as your main priority.

The growth in significance of work based learning has rapidly increased acceptance that learning is not so much a function of an educational site as of location and time. Specifically, work has become a recognized location for learning (Beckett and Hager, 2002; Billet, 2001; Boud and Garrick, 1999). Work, rather than disciplinary knowledge, becomes the content and context that shapes learning, resulting in new skills or new insights in the workplace and the activities of work. As Barnett (2003) points out, this is a significant shift from traditional knowledge clustered in disciplines towards the legitimatization of workplace-based knowledge.

This change in the production, validation and communication of knowledge is having a profound influence on the meaning of learning and is de-institutionalizing knowledge (McIntyre and Solomon, 2000), so the site of knowledge production has moved into the workplace. Even provision from the academy is becoming modularized, pre-packaged and distributed both virtually, online and in classrooms, and more emphasis within the curriculum is being focused on the notion of professional practice and preparation for work. This new politics of the curriculum has been embraced by governments worldwide as a social as well as an economic imperative to stimulate economic growth and prosperity. The politics of power, ownership and purpose of knowledge has consequently moved to influences outside the academy – not necessarily a bad thing. The transfer of power has not always been accompanied by a deep understanding of the nature of university education or a complementary desire to be held accountable for the power now exerted over the academy. Indeed, learning agreements in work based learning are a way in which this power is manifestly shared, and we discuss related issues in Chapter 6.

Work has become a multi-disciplinary site for knowledge creation through a combination of pragmatism, practice and the 'gifting' of opportunity. These are mostly in the pursuit of goals of someone other than the person creating the knowledge. In the workplace, this may be an employer looking to improve business efficiency or to find new markets for products. In the academy, it may be to further work on shaping the curriculum, where the goal is the accumulation and practice of skills and knowledge for successful performance in the workplace. Driven by the power of governments to fund and by employers to employ, this shift is a fundamental change from the search for knowledge for its own sake to a performativity model of knowledge, created to satisfy instrumental criteria of relevance and speed.

Accompanying this shift came a number of new challenges for researchers. The power relationship between lecturer and student might once have been confined to the institution, apparent in assessment and review, but ring-fenced within the context of 'formal study' this is no longer true. The politics of learning had also been an issue for the institution, affecting the student indirectly in terms of course selection and content. Discipline infighting was a matter for the academics. Irritating though this might have been, the course curriculum was set by the institution or awarding boards and the assessment was clear and usually made in ignorance of students as individuals. With the continued pace of change and the increased economic and thus political power bestowed on industries and institutions to develop work-relevant skills programmes, there is a different and potentially more invasive power. This changes the policies of learning in and for the workplace, both in terms of who controls the curriculum and for whom research is undertaken. This chapter is concerned with these changes in the politics and power relationships of work based research. (For a fine discussion of the issues of power and politics as they refer to work based learning, see Zemblyas, 2006.)

The range of issues faced by insider-researchers is indicated by a participant in a professional Doctorate programme below.

My current role as Superintendent Engineer within my organisation has direct bearing on the planning, implementation, execution and final certification of this project over the vessels that are entrusted under my care and responsibility. My role carries a considerable amount of influence and power since I am the first

(Continued)

(Continued)

point of contact in shore management from the vessel. I have full budgetary access and control; however, these projects deal with hard facts of engineering and structural anomalies of the vessel, hence there is no room for influencing the acquisition of data collection, since independent inspectors have their own mandate of what they would like to observe in relation to the vessel's steel structure and machinery. My role here is to facilitate this process.

Qualitative research in general has few things to say about power and political relationships between researchers and the researched. In this context, ideas about relationships come mainly from the literature on ethics in research and do not deal directly with these dual relationships. There are two notable exceptions. One is May (2003), whose focus is power and subjectivity where inquiry is a mode of surveillance over subjects – the use of subjective data to extend corporate control. The second is Ryan (2007), who discusses the limitation of external ethical controls when dealing with insider-researcher practice. However, what the literature does mainly address is the dynamics between the two and guiding principles on how to treat participants, providing some examples of relationships that cross the boundary between what is helpful and what can harm.

The most salient issue when looking at questionable relationships between researchers and participants is power. A number of feminist researchers have noted the inherent power differential in this context and advocate researchers studying only those with the same or higher level of social power so that their relationship is balanced, rather than one of authority. As we will see later in the chapter, achieving this balance is difficult. And it is not the only challenge which emerges in the selection, use and development of qualitative research methods. This means that researchers need to be conscious of their methods and of their origins. In an editorial of *Qualitative Health Research*, the then editor Janice Morse made an appeal we echo that, as a researcher, you should think 'on the politics of methodological development and consider your role seriously, active or passive, in the development of qualitative methods' (2006: 4).

Politics, however, is often regarded as a fact of life in organizations. The premise that every organization is composed of people who have varied task, career and personal interests (Morgan, 1998) allows us to understand an organization as a political entity. 'The idea of politics stems from the view that, where interests are divergent, society should provide a means of allowing individuals to reconcile their differences through consultation and negotiation' (p. 149). Pfeffer (1981) defines organizational politics as 'those activities carried out by people to acquire, enhance, and use power and other resources to obtain their preferred outcomes in a situation where there is uncertainty or disagreement' (pp. 4–5). In this sense, the meaning of politics in an organization is conceptualized as the exercise of power to negotiate different interests among members while maintaining one's interests in certain organizational issues.

Hardy and Clegg (1996) present two different perspectives on organizational power: the functionalist perspective and the critical perspective. The functionalist perspective indicates that power is exercised during the decision-making arena as a part of a deliberative strategy to achieve intended outcomes, and it is also used to control access to the decision-making arena and hence to ensure compliance through decision. On the other hand, and from the critical perspective, 'power is conceptualized as domination, and actions taken to challenge it constituted resistance to domination' (Hardy and Clegg, 1996: 626). Critical theory asserts that the dominant group in an organization attempts to exercise power to manipulate discourses of an organization on behalf of itself. By doing so, it can keep on imposing its own interests on the dominated and reproduce its privileges over them.

Who speaks for whom?

In an interesting piece of work, Jensen (1997: 25) explores a series of questions relevant to the power and politics of work based learning. He asks, 'Who speaks and why?', 'Who speaks for whom?' and 'To whom is one speaking?' His analysis requires one to question the motivation of the research being undertaken, the reasons for doing it and the contribution it can make. In this sense, it is a moral requirement to have an understanding of what drives the research. Is the power of taking control of the research, or the research subject, about the politics of influence the research might reveal? Or it is about reinforcing stereotypical images and positions of those being researched? In the workplace, where participants might be vulnerable to the economic power concentrated in the employer or even in an organized union, researchers must look inward to see what they are personally trying to gain from the research and how are they using the subjects to achieve this.

This requires a personal honesty and response to the second set of questions about on whose behalf the researcher is speaking. All too often, academy-based researchers hide their motivation, claiming neutrality for their research methods, and speak on behalf of science, truth or some other abstract and questionably defined notion. Work based researchers act on behalf of someone, and this needs to be declared both to participants for their agreement to join the research and to those who read the research, to understand what is being offered. These are personal politics and power issues and, although they cannot be removed from real world research, they should not be covered up. Certainly, there is a need in all research to respect others in more than careless rhetoric, but the scope to be deceitful is wider and the potential benefits greater in work based learning than in academy-based research.

The next discussion concerns the politics of research, action research and power embedded in the research methods commonly used by work based researchers: the interview and action research.

Politics – action research

Action research, by its very nature, is a collaborative endeavour and action researchers need to be prepared to work the political system. It often brings the challenge of balancing interdependence between researchers and their subjects or co-researchers. Moreover, throughout the research activities, as a researcher, you need to retain credibility and integrity. The key is to assess the power interests of the relevant stakeholders to the research and take a stand. You are not required to accept a role that makes you a tool for any unfair, unethical or illegal activity to benefit the gate-keepers who allow the research to take place.

It is clear that when action research is involved, there is potential for role ambiguity and conflict, and you need to make this explicit so that the authority invested in the action research does not become one of power exerted over those collaborating in the research. Action research within an organization, for instance, requires an understanding of the macro- and micro-politics of the organization and the research project's declared and latent purposes. Moreover, if action research is intended to change practice, whether personal or organizational, it is likely to encounter resistance. It may even be considered a subversive exercise by many of those directly or indirectly involved in the process. You need to recognize and incorporate this reality into the action research process. Its perceived subversiveness may derive from its methods of emphasis: listening, questioning and reflecting on activities that have gained their credibility through workshop practices or which maintain some power relationship in the organization.

Even the basic idea of action research – to liberate ideas, find solutions and allow informed choice – might rankle among many with whom the research is taking place. In this sense, action research is political and, accordingly, needs to be politically astute. This may involve a range of strategies and tactics which allow both the activity of action research to take place and at the same time develop and maintain relationships to reduce resistance. This second aspect involves, according to Coghlan and Shani, 'intervening in the political and cultural systems, through justifying, influencing and negotiating, defeating opposition and so on' (2005: 533–46). But this is never easy, and often requires a type of tactical knowledge of the likely outcomes of political machinations. Macfarlane, in his book on researching with integrity, illustrates this point with a short case study. In it, a researcher overhears a plot by certain members of an international project to reduce the influences of a co-chair who they think has been rude to them. The researcher keeps quiet, not informing the plotted-against co-chair, having decided that to inform the person would disrupt the research project more than not telling them. Indeed, this sort of tacit political knowledge did contribute to the project's successful completion. Macfarlane states that, while the 'language of research may speak of "collaboration" there are frequently tensions between powerful, ambitious, or egoistic personalities that can come to the fore' (2009: 134). Visser (2003) makes the point that insider–outsider boundaries are highly unstable and are

Table 4.1   How to deal with politics

1. Understand both the surface and the deep meaning to the main stakeholders of the research and its findings.
2. Informally come to understand the context in which the research is to take place. Talk to those in the workplace and informally appreciate the issues, frustrations and tensions in evidence even before the research is undertaken.
3. Come to terms with your political agenda in carrying out the research and determine how far you are prepared to be manipulated by the research site politics.
4. Be confident of the outcome of the research and the use to which it is to be put; try not to be the bullet in someone else's cocked gun.
5. Accept the political context of all research and thus appreciate that your intention may not be the same as that of your research participants.
6. Engage in the politics but retain your integrity, credibility and dignity.

subject to the dynamics, personalities and politics of how one's position is understood through time and space. This is reinforced by Soobrayan, who argues that the main research instrument in qualitative research is the researchers themselves, and concludes that 'ethics, truth and politics of research is consequently a deliberate exercise in taking risks, making choices and taking responsibilities' (2003: 107/8). Table 4.1 indicates six ways of dealing with politics in work based research.

Power – the interview

As Davison (2004) suggests, at the outset, researchers may enter a research encounter not expecting to cause distress to participants in the research process. She states that the methodological literature on qualitative research 'consistently endorses the advantages of close relationships with respondents which will enhance rapport and enrich research findings' (2004: 381). The research methods selected for any research study can affect the likelihood of sparking revelations that cost both researcher and researched, especially methods that emphasize emancipatory collaboration and empowerment yet are more invasive, for example phenomenologically grounded interviews, covert ethnography and some action research. Further, in being an interested researcher, there is an implicit ethical danger of appearing more like a personal friend or, as an insider-researcher, quite the opposite.

Interviews have become a sensitive and powerful method of investigating subjects' public and private lives in qualitative research. However, they are regularly employed for independent participants, failing to recognize the interdependency of the engagement. Although the qualitative interview is often considered emancipatory, it is not without power issues. For instance, although friendship, trust and empathy may facilitate the interview, its main purpose may be to glean unguarded confidences. Wray-Bliss (2003) has spoken of the research interview as domination and, although not meant to reify the relationship of research to one of victim and researcher, such terminology does offer the chance to reflect on its power dynamics. As Kvale suggests, its use may be to create a 'fantasy of democratic relations [which] masks the basic issue of who gains materially and symbolically from the research and where claims of participation disguise the exertion of power' (2006: 482).

Discussion on the asymmetrical power relationship of the interview is under-developed in the literature on interviews. Briggs (2002) reviews its form, suggesting that the interviewer has control over what is said, how it is said, how it is recorded and how it is subsequently represented and encoded as knowledge. Following Kvale (2006), Table 4.2 briefly outlines some of the

Table 4.2   Key power dynamics and forms of relationship in research interviews

The interviewer rules the interview
The interview becomes a one-directional questioning event. The research often determines the time, place and topics, poses the questions, critically follows up the answers and then closes the conversation.

The interview is a one-way dialogue
The roles are clear, the interviewer asks the questions and the interviewee answers them. To challenge the authority of the interviewer in the process of the interview may even be considered impolite.

The interview is an instrumental dialogue
The interview is never intended to be a dialogue with the interviewee, but is clearly a means to an end for the interviewer. The interview is an instrument for providing the narratives and texts needed for research goals and interests.

The interview may be a manipulative dialogue
The interview may have a hidden agenda for the researcher, one that they do not wish the interviewees to know about, as they might frame their answers accordingly.

The research interview may follow a more or less hidden agenda
The interviewer may want to obtain information without the subject knowing what they are after.

The interview as monopoly on interpretation
Differing from true dialogue, where an interpretation can be developed through engagement with the purpose of finding such an interpretation, interpretation in social research is usually the researchers' privilege. They are the ones who assign to the research what the interviewee really meant and frame it in their own theoretical scheme.

The power asymmetry may not be one-sided. Consider the following situations:

Counter-control
Interviewees may opt not to answer questions or to deflect them. They may seek to go beyond the proffered relationship and try to turn the interview into a counselling session, or they may even withdraw from the interview. The different counter-strategies depend on the context and the type of interview subject.

Table 4.2   *(Continued)*

Membership research
The interview transcript and the interviewer's interpretation can be given back to the interviewee for checking. However, there may be real issues directly related to the value of the interviewee's interpretation in this approach. The interviewee might not accept any critical or sensitive interpretation and there may be issues of the interviewee's competence to understand any theoretical issues which arose. Indeed, Kvale (2006) argues that few researchers let their subjects have the final say on the interpretation made and what goes into a report.

key power dynamics and offers for reflection forms of relationship for work based researchers, like you, considering this research instrument.

A precondition – an ethic of care

Noddings states that 'caring involves, for the one caring, a "feeling with" the other' (2003: 30). She then theorizes caring as a three-phased social process consisting of engrossment, empathy and disposition to act on behalf of another. In this sense, caring is a learned process and one which can be incorporated in the training of researchers. Crigger (2001) has shown how this might be done with nurses in their practice and we will address how this might be done in Chapter 5. The basis of caring is, for Noddings as it is for Heidegger (2000), an engrossment with another, the process of setting aside one's own self-concern in order to be free to empathize with the other. This leads researchers to make decisions regarding their research which dissolves the participant/object divide in unengaged research. The impact of the research is imagined, and empathy determines the researcher's actions. This might certainly compromise at least one of the stakeholders to the learning contract but, as Noddings proposes, where possible, we should 'ideally, be able to present reasons for our action/inaction which would persuade a reasonable, disinterested observer that we acted on behalf of the cared-for' (2003: 23). She goes further, to accept the argument that, while others might disagree and so behave differently, in itself this is no reason to reject action. These acts of caring are not without anxiety, for they require you to anticipate and, where possible, lessen the burden on the cared-for. Thus, caring is more than a superficial clarification of one's actions by means of a voluntary consent form; it is the reframing of the research project as a mutual activity which has personal consequences other than the research report and which has its own legitimacy.

For someone like yourself who possesses the discretionary powers of the researcher, caring requires a form of existential trust that transcends the social roles bestowed by others. Participants offer up their vulnerability, revealing themselves in their authenticity, stripped of the protection of these roles. It is involving, not observational. When we care for an individual, we care for them as part of being as a whole, thus recognizing all beings in harmony and so becoming authentic ourselves. Caring carries a moral obligation. Baier takes this position when she considers that, in moral trusting, 'one leaves others the opportunity to harm one ... and also shows one's confidence that they will not take it. Reasonable trust will require good grounds for such confidence in another's goodwill' (1995: 235). If this trust is proven to be misplaced or misunderstood, specifically in relation to a highly cherished aim, contemplating even a small risk to the expected outcome may prove intolerable. If you accept the offered trust, you are in a privileged and powerful position; you are trusted not to use your authority to manipulate and exploit the trustee.

For parties to trust each other, they have to assume the motives are bene-volent and this has a resonance with the popular feminist meaning of caring. The emphasis can be 'biological' (Noddings, 2003), psychological (Gilligan, 1995) or on trust (Baier, 1995; Gibbs, 2004; Held, 1995), but at its core is a recognition of the integrity of the researcher and the researched. The application of care is not a sentimental approach to research; it is about how researchers can best meet their caring responsibilities. As Smeyers summarizes:

> Caring will always create moral dilemmas (because the needs for care are infinite) and will furthermore pose moral problems that arise out of the particular location in which people find themselves in various contexts of care. Still, it might make human societies more moral as it can serve as a critical standard and it puts moral ideals into action. (1999: 246)

It is from this perspective that we propose that work based researchers – indeed, all researchers – approach their obligation of being researchers. This may be more familiar to work based researchers than those from less applied traditions.

We advocate that parties to the learning contract agree, through their existential trust, to explore the research problem with a caring disposition, recognizing the legitimate claims that such an approach can make. We suggest that the relationship between caring and knowing is complex and involves a constant reflective process, but one which the students develop in their transcendent self as well as in their competences as a researcher. It is one where the participant and object of knowledge are merged, where traditional empirical epistemologies do not hold exclusive claims to truths, and where intellectual argument does not objectify the participant through rationalization and determinism. An ethic of care realigns the notion of power in a traditional research relation and is critical to eliminate the potential for exploitation in work based projects (Gibbs, 2004).

Firstly, you will want to undertake research with which you feel com-fortable. As an insider-researcher carrying out research in your own organizations or communities of practice, you may have concerns about interviewing your colleagues. For example, you may feel uncomfortable asking difficult or controversial questions or making someone junior feel compelled to answer questions (see Merriam et al., 2001). In addition, although protection of the individual seems to be paramount in most ethical guidelines, consideration must be given also to cases where the powerful are being researched. Questions arise about whose interests will dominate and who owns the research process and output. In this instance, the notion of trust embedded in an ethic of care is obvious. It must, however, be a deep existential trust for a specific other, where the interests of the researched and the consequences of the research engagement are the researcher's important concerns. See, for example, MacCorraidh's work with part-time adult learners in Belfast: 'Participants were kept fully informed of my intentions and progress and I took a sensitive approach throughout the enquiry ...' (MacCorraidh, 2004).

Secondly, the investigative methods of particular organizations and work situations may tend towards a particular style or mode. For example, artists may favour ethnography and historical methods, while people in financial management might prefer quantitative approaches. Practitioner-researchers such as yourself who are insiders and concerned with ethics of being-in-the-world, and of care, have to consider the appropriate approach and methods to fit in with both professional/work requirements and the issues of their ethical stance.

Thirdly, there is the university's requirement to take full account of ethical considerations of how apt the approach and methods are. These may run counter to the ethics of being, or feel inappropriate, unduly instrumental or difficult to acknowledge. For example, the university must consider for whom it is beneficial and whether there is any detriment to people (individuals, communities of practice or members of organizations) or other living creatures. It must also consider the economic implications, such as feasibility and whether the research will in some way bring about financial gain and, if so, whose interests will be served. In addition, it should consider whether the research is sustainable – for example, whether it will cause any detriment to the environment. This should not, however, be problematic since many ethical issues in research derive from the principle, shared with the British Psychological Society, that 'the investigation should be considered from the standpoint of all participants'. We would simply change this to 'the standpoint of care for all participants'.

The questions addressed in this chapter concern researchers working as insiders collaboratively with colleagues. In such a situation, you are likely to need not only recourse to textbooks on research and research ethics, but a sense of what it is like to be an insider-researcher from the perspective of other insiders. Understanding of others and the human qualities needed for a successful ethics of research needs you to be respectful, sensitive and imbuing confidence with openness, democratic sensitivity and a feel for the micro-politics of a situation, amongst other understandings and nuances of understanding. These, we argue, can only be acquired through real life participation and understanding of care for others.

Discussion questions

1. Consider the various influences on you as an insider-researcher. List them as those within your control and those outside, and then discuss how they might affect your research.
2. Issues of power can change the reception of your research. How you can best prepare to manage these issues?
3. How can understanding the politics of your workplace be used to improve your research outcomes?
4. What are the main ethical issues related to power and politics?
5. How would you control and plan to ameliorate your influence on research participants?
6. Discuss why workplace researchers should care about anything other than their research outcomes.

References

Baier, A. (1995) *Moral Prejudices: Essays on Ethics*. Cambridge, MA: Harvard University Press.

Barnett, R. (2003) *Beyond all Reason: Living with Ideology in the University*. Buckingham: Society for Research into Higher Education and the Open University Press.

Beckett, D. and Hager, P. (2002) 'Life, work and learning: practice in postmodernity', *International Studies in the Philosophy of Education* 14. London and New York: Routledge.

Billet, S. (2001) *Learning in the Workplace: Strategies for Effective Practice*. New South Wales: Allen & Unwin.

Boud, D. and Garrick, J. (eds) (1999) *Understanding Learning at Work*. London: Routledge.

Briggs, C.L. (2002) 'Interviewing, power/knowledge, and social inequality', in J.F. Gubrium and J.A. Holstein (eds) *Handbook of Interview Research*, pp. 911–22. Thousand Oaks, CA: Sage.

Coghlan, D. and Shani, A.B. (2005) 'Roles, politics and the ethics in action research design', *Systemic Practices and Action Research* 18 (6): 553–46.

Crigger, N. (2001) 'Antecedents to engrossment in Noddings' theory of care', *Journal of Advanced Nursing* 35 (4): 616–23.

Davison, J. (2004) 'Dilemmas in research: issues of vulnerability and disempowerment for social worker/researcher', *Journal of Social Work Practice* 18 (3): 379–93.

Gibbs, P. (2004) *Trust in the University*. Amsterdam: Kluwer Academic.

Gilligan, C. (1995) 'Hearing the difference: theorizing connection', *Hypatia* 10: 120–7.

Hardy, C. and Clegg, S.R. (1996) 'Some dare to call it power', in C. Hardy, S.R. Clegg and W.R. Nord (eds) *Handbook of Organization Studies*, pp. 622–41. London: Sage.

Heidegger, M. (2000) 'Letter on humanism', in D.F. Krell (ed) *Basic Writings*, pp. 213–25. London: Routledge.

Held, V. (1995) 'The meshing of care and justice', *Hypapia* 10: 128–32.

Jensen, R. (1997) 'Privilege, power, and politics in research: a response to "Crossing sexual orientations"', *Qualitative Studies in Education* 10 (1): 25–30.

Kvale, S. (2006) 'Dominance through interview and dialogues', *Qualitative Inquiry* 12 (3): 480–500.

Macfarlane, B. (2009) *Researching with Integrity: The Ethics of Academic Enquiry*. London: Routledge.

May, C. (2003) 'Where do we stand in relation to the data? Being reflexive about reflexivity in health care evaluation', in J. Latimer (ed) *Advanced Qualitative Research for Nursing*, pp. 17–31. Oxford: Blackwell.

McIntyre, J. and Solomon, N. (2000) 'The policy environment of work-based learning: globalisation, institutions and workplaces', in C. Symes and J. McIntyre (eds) *Working Knowledge: New Vocationalism in Higher Education*. Milton Keynes: Open University Press.

MacCorraidh, S. (2004) 'How can I improve my practice so that students spend more time communicating with myself and with each other in the target language?' Available at www.jeanmcniff.com/qub.html.p.s. [accessed 30 September 2009].

Merriam, S.B., Johnson-Bailey, J., Lee, M-L., Kee, Y., Ntseane, G. and Muhmad, M. (2001) 'Power and positionality: negotiating insider/outsider status within and across cultures', *International Journal of Lifelong Education* 20 (5): 405–16.

Morgan, G. (1998) *Images of Organization.* Thousand Oaks, CA: Sage.

Morse, J.M. (2006) 'The politics of developing research methods', *Qualitative Health Research* 16 (3): 3–4.

Noddings, N. (2003) *Caring: A Feminine Approach to Ethics and Moral Education.* Berkeley, CA: University of California Press.

Pfeffer, J. (1981) *Power in Organizations.* Cambridge: Ballinger.

Ryan, A. (2007) 'Ethical issues', Ch. 14 in C. Seale, G. Gobo, J.F. Gubrium and D. Silverman (eds) *Qualitative Research Practice*, pp. 239–47. Los Angeles, CA: Sage.

Smeyers, P. (1999) 'Care and wider issues', *Journal of Philosophy of Education* 33 (2): 233–51.

Soobrayan, V. (2003) 'Ethics, truth and politics in constructivist qualitative research', *Westminster Studies in Education* 26 (2): 107–23.

Visser, G. (2003) *Researcher Positionality and the Political-temporal Contingency in a Post-apartheid Research Environment.* Available at: www.lse.ac.uk/Depts/geography/rp59.pdf

Wray-Bliss, E. (2003) 'Research subjects/research subjections: exploring the ethics and politics of critical research', *Organization* 10 (2): 307–25.

Zemblyas, M. (2006) 'Work-based learning, power and subjectivity: creating space for a Foucauldian research ethic', *Journal of Education and Work* 19 (3): 291–303.

5

Gaining access for the insider-researcher: issues, practices, audiences, ethics and gratitude

Key points

In this chapter, we look at the issues of negotiating access to the research site and people to be involved in the research process. We note that special groups may have more stringent moral and legal access requirements and you must satisfy yourself that you have complied fully with these requirements. This special consideration includes people in the care of others and/or who may be deemed unable voluntarily to agree to participate in any research.

Gaining access to research participants may not seem particularly problematic. You simply ask those you want to participate to take part, don't you? Well, no. There are many issues that range from politeness, through ethics, to legal requirements which must be considered in planning and gaining access. For instance, issues related to access vary between organizations and with the form of your position, in work based studies, and include the research methods to be used and the power relationship of the research's sponsor to the community being studied.

For the researcher to access the participants might seem a simple, practical matter: simply asking the authority figure in charge of the workers – manager or director – and giving the reassurance of confidentiality to all participants, presenting a summary report to the individuals in authority and limiting disruption to work flows should be sufficient. However, this instrumental approach to access is fraught with problems for it ignores the nature of the community with which you are going to engage and how that engagement will be undertaken. Further, the individual in authority may not exist, or be readily identified, in communities developing as a result of social or geographical proximity or from a common vulnerability. These might be communities of children, those with learning disabilities or those experiencing social exclusion due to sex, ethnicity, age or physical disability.

The difficulty can be both logistical and epistemological, as this example illustrates.

I felt that I would get more information about how managers *think* about this topic, what their belief systems are, and what they feel their skill level is by conducting a first-hand conversation with them versus having them independently complete an online survey.

Getting to all of their direct reports, on the other hand, would require a different approach due to the scope, the time it would take, and, most importantly, the sensitivity surrounding the confidentiality of their responses. Keeping in mind 'fit for purpose', I needed to make sure I would get as much participation as possible and as much honesty and candour. The environment was already pretty vulnerable following the impact of the credit crisis. Little did I know when I crafted this approach that there was 'more to come' in terms of how deeply the firm would be impacted by the acquisition of X.

Moreover, an organization is a dynamic and complex place and researchers, both insiders and outsiders, might be treated with suspicion and might not always be welcome, particularly if asking what may be perceived as sensitive and awkward questions about managerial actions. It may be sceptical about the role of outsider-researchers and so may not value academics both for what they can contribute and what their motives are. Studies have noted that organizations deny access because academics fail to provide answers about what, how and why they will carry out a specific study and whether this study will be of any value to the company and the managers themselves. However, access may also be problematic when, by becoming an insider-researcher, the context of one's normal relations to the community as a practitioner/employee/manager is changed by virtue of taking on the role of researcher in one's workplace.

The issue of gaining access to organizations is one of the many problems facing researchers aiming at in-depth, qualitative case study research, since considerable time is often spent on this task (Patton, 2002; Shenton and Hayter, 2004). This is compounded by pressure to use time effectively, and it may be harder to gain time for interviews than to find time for respondents to complete questionnaires; these are likely to be much easier to arrange than loosely structured interviews and observations, but may not be ideal from your research design perspective. Compromise will be called for, as discussed later.

If the research focuses on sensitive topics – redundancies, staff morale and change (mis-)management – it can be even more difficult to enter organizations, either your own or others'. To be successful, your methodology requires a deep understanding of entrenched phenomena which may be invasive and personal, and may deal with people or positions vulnerable to the outcome of your research. Your report may adversely affect their working environment and your research method may lead you to become absorbed in the issue for the community you join, changing your remit and leading you to ask yourself if you are still researching or are now advocating.

These are some of the issues that, on first thought, might not occur to you as you determine how best to gain access to the community you are to study. This chapter will address the difficulties experienced in gaining access to research participants in order to develop evidence-based policy and practices. It is constructed in five sections. The first deals with issues surrounding the nature of community, especially the idea of a community of practice. The second section deals with gaining access and considers the best use of gatekeepers, stakeholders, snowballing and advertising, and the third discusses research design and methodologies. The fourth is a discussion on the ethics of care and includes the issues of dignity, respect, empathy, benevolence and trust, and how these might be especially important when the research community is made up of special audiences. These comprise not just your workplace colleagues, but those vulnerable communities of patients, children, the socially disadvantaged and foreigners. Finally, the fifth section considers sharing knowledge and the researchers' duty of gratitude when leaving the research site. The issues of access will be reviewed in relation to the methodologies used, such as observational participation and in-depth interviews.

What is a community?

What is a community? In general, a community has an identity which reflects itself and separates it from other communities. The nature and value of community networks has been called 'social capital' by social theorists such as Bourdieu (2005) and Putman (2001), and this notion helps to emphasize the real value communities possess for their members. Putman, in his important study into the alienating effects of modern social life in America, *Bowling Alone*, discusses the notion of social capital as a feature of social organizations such as networks, norms and trusts which facilitates coordination and cooperation for mutual benefit. The dynamics of these interactions, even in small communities such as workplace groups, not only bring strength to the community but act as a barrier to new members joining on a permanent or temporary basis. A community's main infrastructural strength comes from its:

- *tolerance* – an openness to others, curiosity, perhaps even respect, a willingness to listen and learn, but with caution about integration
- *reciprocity* – in the short run, there is altruism; in the long run, self-interest
- *trust* – the confident expectation that people, institutions and things will act in a consistent, honest and appropriate way (or more accurately, 'trustworthiness' or reliability) is essential if communities are to flourish.

In the workplace, whether this is formal or not, the functions of this infrastructure have been identified by Wenger (1998) as communities of practice, and it is to them we now turn.

Communities of practice

The features of communities – networks, norms, trust, reciprocity and tolerance – are all features of a derivative of the general study of community evident in 'communities of practice', which comprise the chief of those with which work based learners such as yourself will engage. The term 'community of practice' was coined relatively recently, but the phenomenon to which it refers is age-old. The concept has proved to provide a useful perspective on knowing and learning.

The term is most associated with Wenger (1998), who states that a community of practice is formed by workers engaging in a shared domain of activities. Such groups might be artists clustered into an artistic community, a group of engineers working on a similar problem, or a group of skilled and semi-skilled workers and novices in a garage. For instance, work with apprentices has shown that it is more complex than that they simply learn from journeymen and more advanced apprentices. Not always intentionally, more generally group members learn from each other about themselves, the skills required to do the job and how to achieve the corporate goal.

There are three distinctive characteristics of a community of practice. These are: domain (a shared competence that distinguishes members from others), community (the development of its social capital as discussed above) and practice. This third characteristic is perhaps the most investigated by work based researchers into the shared practices of that community. These are often embedded in specific equipment, experiences, stories, ways of addressing both each other (nicknames, for example) and outsiders. The bonding of the community that this repertoire of activities and entities creates may not always be apparent to the members; indeed, the more it is absorbed, the more 'natural' is the behaviour and the more difficult it is for members to reflect and reveal them.

As work based researchers, negotiating access to communities in whose practices you are interested and having them trust you beyond superficial functions and processes is as difficult, if not more, than gaining the actual permission to begin insider research. This type of access is called cognitive access, and is at the level of the individual. It requires more from the researcher personally, establishing credibility with participants which transcends the ascribed authority of the permission-granting gatekeeper. Such personal qualities of empathy, dignity and respect for others cannot be pretended, as members of communities of practice have knowledge of people they accept into their community (for research or other purposes) which is not simply propositional, but dispositional and embedded. To try and fake this or to speed it up can be counterproductive to the research aim.

In addition to remaining as open as possible and challenging my assumptions, I needed to ensure I had support for this project. My sponsor, the CEO of my organization, definitely supported the project. It was my peers and the remainder of the senior management team that I needed to convince. This called for me to be seen as a subject-matter 'expert' for this work. If an organization hires an external vendor for such a project, the consultant would be met with a degree of credibility and authority. In my case, I needed to be seen as the expert in this study and its grand champion. If I didn't achieve either, then the research would not yield the desired change, but merely a report that might be seen as interesting, one that would just gather dust once the initial discussions were completed. I was so aware of this when I did the initial presentation to my peers, my fellow senior vice-presidents. I included so many quotes from the literature that I spent so much time proving I had deep knowledge of the subject matter, culture, that I missed the opportunity to connect all the pieces of the project for them. I recognized this and the next presentation to the remainder of the senior management team was much stronger and the context didn't get overshadowed by my need to prove my knowledge. This area was enhanced greatly by completing the research methodology. This process forced me to put together a detailed outline of the process, resources and expectations, that I was able to answer questions with confidence and provide a thorough overview.

In addition to supporting the project, I needed to make sure this group was engaged. The outcome of the studies would serve as a foundation for coaching them on their behaviour as leaders. If I had not gained their interest and trust at the start, I would not have been able to move forward with the steps beyond the data analysis.

Facilitating access

The following example puts into practice the points we discuss in the preceding paragraph.

According to Okumus et al. (2007), there are three types of access. First, there is formal access, which refers to achieving an agreement between the organization and the researcher on specific terms of engagement. This can be contractual, as in a learning and research agreement, and will include what, when and how empirical data are collected and what might be the return to the organization, for instance, a report.

The second form of access, personal access, concerns getting to know the relevant executives, managers and individuals.

The third involves fostering an individual rapport with participants and developing a good understanding and collaboration between managers and the researcher. These three forms approximate those refined by Gummesson (2000), who defines these three different access types as:

- physical access, which means the ability to get close to the object of the study
- continued access, which refers to maintaining an ongoing physical access to the research setting
- mental access, which refers to being able to understand what is happening and why in the investigated settings.

More colloquially, we combine these and propose a four-stage access model of 'getting in', 'getting on', 'getting out' and 'getting back'. According to Robson (2002), this derivation is the model most often referred to in the methodology literature. For the 'getting in' stage, as a researcher, you are expected to be clear about your objectives, and the time and resource requirements. It is advised that existing contacts are used, that respondents' reservations about time and confidentiality are dealt with positively, that non-threatening language is used when explaining the nature and purpose of the study, and that a final executive report is offered. Once access has been gained, it becomes necessary to re-negotiate in a non-evaluative and non-partisan manner. Your personality, your interpersonal skills and particularly your interviewing skills will play an important role at this stage. The best strategy for 'getting out' is agreeing on a deadline for the closure of the data collection process. It is also essential to manage the process of withdrawal to keep open the option of returning for further fieldwork.

Table 4.2   Checklist for negotiating access

---

1. Establish contact details for individuals from whom it is necessary to get permission.
2. Prepare an outline of the study.
3. Clear any necessary official channels by formally requesting permission to carry out the study. Permission may be needed at various 'levels'.
4. Discuss the study with 'gatekeepers' (for instance, managers or head teacher). Go through the study outline (purpose and conditions, including consent and participation). Attempt to anticipate potentially sensitive issues.
5. Discuss the study with likely participants. Go through the study outline with a group or with individuals, depending on circumstances.

Be prepared to modify the study in light of these discussions (for example, timing, treatment or sensitive issues).

Source: Robson (2002: 379)

Techniques for engaging with participants: gatekeepers, snowballing and advertising

In effect, organizations are gatekeepers and it is important to understand the reasons why they will or will not open the gate. Here are some of the usual concerns:

- information held is confidential
- promises have been implied or given
- enabling research takes up staff time and often requires space, like a desk for the researcher.

An organization may recognize the power of acting as gatekeeper to a desirable set of research data or contact addresses. In particular, it may have its own research agenda or policy towards research and, to be accepted, any proposal from a researcher may have to fit into this context. The organization may wish to influence:

- the aims and structure of the project
- the method
- the precise location, and, possibly
- the report arising from the research.

As a researcher, you need to be aware of these issues and be prepared to compromise on the first three. The final element, the actual representation of your research findings, is your ethical responsibility to yourself and to the participants and should not be compromised. The main discussion on access to research subjects is discussed in Chapter 7.

For vulnerable groups such as children, patients and the socially under-privileged, or where the existing data are confidential, overcoming the first hurdle may require formal presentations, committee decisions and formal acceptance. Indeed, in many cases where human subjects are involved, you may need to satisfy policy and moral gatekeepers prior to the physical gate-keepers. These are most often evident as the ethical committees of the organizations to be investigated and of the universities on whose behalf the work is undertaken.

Once access is secured, you need to recruit participants. Recruitment may follow strict requirements determined by the precepts of the research design or, more likely, the majority of participants in a community of practice if your project is a case study. Voluntary participation must be assured and participants may not come forward on your request, despite the authority of the gatekeeper. Indeed, the power of the gatekeeper may adversely affect their willingness to engage deeply with the investigation. That said, gatekeepers who can identify willing participants are the best starting point in settings unfamiliar to you, such as in more anthropological studies.

Once you have worked with one or two members of the community and established your credentials, the network of the community can have a snowball effect. The participants themselves endorse the project and your role in it. This technique of word-of-mouth recruitment, provided it fits the research design or the compromises it involves are manageable, is the best way of gaining cognitive access; how participants become willing to help the research is worthy of its own investigation.

You may find it effective to make people aware of the investigation when your study is more quantitative. Advertising for participants and ensuring their anonymity can provide sufficient numbers to permit the use of questionnaires within the rubric of a survey design.

Selecting research methods and implications for access

The epistemological claims you want to make from the research, the appropriateness of the methods to enable such claims, and the willingness of the community to subject itself to the methodologies, all influence the validity of the research itself. (Issues of power are discussed in Chapter 4.) Unless all parties are able to negotiate their position throughout the research process regarding shifts in power and purpose, the research gift may be inappropriately given and accepted, leading to ingratitude and reparation owed for harm to participants. Indeed, you have a moral imperative only to accept that which is reasonable for the research engagement, taking and using no more than the research remit requires.

In many cases, where the engagement of the researched is restricted to the completion of a simple, non-invasive attitudinal or behavioural questionnaire, offering a 'thank you' is both good manners and, in many circumstances, a proportionately grateful response for the time spent and information given by the respondent. However, such a response cannot be generalized; if the questionnaire is, for example, about restructuring processes, working relations or assessment of personal contribution to corporate objectives in the work context, it requires more from the researched. Their responses may be influenced by the power relationships with the practitioner. Moreover, if the method of data collection is by interview, especially if unstructured, there is considerable potential for gleaning information that is costly to the researched and potentially valuable to you, yet beyond the remit of the project. In such circumstances, as a researcher, you have a moral dilemma over the use of the gifted data.

You might ensure that the gift as now offered is indeed intended, but the actual utility of this excessive gift may not be realized until the information is analysed. In these circumstances, your duty of non-malfeasance and fidelity would direct you not to use the data in your research without prior confirmation that the information, as given, which led to the conclusions beyond the initial agreement with the researched, has permission to be used. This is especially important if any potential consequences for the organization might have a negative impact on the researched when revealed through your research.

Within the neo-liberal nature of work, it seems plausible that the benefits and costs may be unequal and, as Bridges warns, anyone contributing to such research and expecting fair recompense 'would be naïve to assume that such debts might be repaid' (2001: 379). In these circumstances, both you and the participant should understand the nexus of power within the workplace and be familiar with the power dynamics that render the research engagement viable. However, the freedom to ascertain acceptability remains inequitable. It begs the question of how gratitude can be an adequate response to the structural power inequities that form the background to workplace research. Here, power is either overt, in the sense of the relationship between you, as the workplace researcher, and the participant, or covert, disguised by the choice of research methods or attempts to replace existing relationships with those of researcher and researched. Such ambiguity could create complexity and confusion which might distort the epistemological nature of the inquiry and impact the *habitus* of the working community.

McLaughlin (2004) has described these situations as creating 'issues of identity, power, status, language and communication' (2004: 133) and these may be further compounded through the research methodology used and the claims and uses made of any research findings. Because of the location, moreover, any researcher's claim of neutrality is problematic, however sincere, given your colleagues' prior experience of you, the power relationship between you and also the power conferred upon you by the organization. For instance, offers of anonymity for the participant may lack credibility, given the pragmatism of the workplace community and its knowledge of your veracity. Thus, as a workplace researcher, you have to deal with their reflexive engagement both as worker and as researcher, which could lead to incommensurate views of truth and, more generally, issues of personal power and potential exploitation.

Insider research engagements represent a form of cooperation between participant and researcher which, as Standish has described, has a 'taken for granted idea of data' (2001: 498). 'Givens' can be solicited: 'Can you give me a moment of your time?' or 'Please give me an interview'. However, they must not be obtained through theft or deception or for purposes of exploitation. This is not always easy to avoid for, as Davison (2004) suggests, you might well commence a research encounter not expecting to distress the participant but end up doing just that. She states that the methodological literature on qualitative research 'consistently endorses the advantages of close relationships with respondents which will enhance rapport and enrich research findings' (2004: 381), but careless or deliberate selection of research methods can affect the likelihood of revelations that cost both you and the participant more than either can afford. This may be especially true of methods that emphasize emancipatory collaboration and empowerment yet which are invasive, for example, phenomenological ground interviews, covert ethnography and aspects of action research.

For the workplace-researcher, the period of the engagement extends from before the data-gathering period until after the project is completed. Located as you are on the spot, a workplace-researcher experiences the change you are yourself researching. In collaborating with your working community, you need to consider fully the ambiguities that your role may represent to other members and the potential this creates for harm. In this context, the role of the practitioner as an insider-researcher occupies a unique place in the continuum of personal relationships between researchers and participants. It poses a series of novel ethical and practical considerations, possibly different from those of the outsider-researcher. Indeed, Bridges recognizes that most of the time, researchers are 'inviting the generosity of their participants and perhaps there is something more ethically elevated in responding to such generosity with a true spirit of gratitude' (2001: 379). Of course, issues of gratitude do arise throughout the research process, including during reporting, and gratitude is dealt with in more deal in the following section.

An ethic of care

At the end of the previous chapter, we spoke of care and as the actor who possesses the discretionary powers of the researcher, your caring requires a form of existential trust that transcends social roles configured through the power of others where those who trust you offer up their vulnerability, to reveal themselves stripped of the protection of their social roles and status. It is involving, not observational. When we care for an individual being, we care for them as part of humanity and thus recognize empathetically ourselves in them. It carries a moral obligation. Baier takes this position when she considers that in moral trusting, 'one leaves others the opportunity to harm one ... and also shows one's confidence that they will not take it. Reasonable trust will require good grounds for such confidence in another's goodwill' (1995: 235). If this trust is proven to be misplaced or misunderstood, then your contemplating even a small risk to an expected outcome, specifically in relation to a highly cherished aim, may prove intolerable.

In such a vulnerable state, those who accept the trust offered are in a privileged and powerful position. You are trusted not to use this authority to manipulate and exploit the trustee. Trusting of this type assumes benevolent motives as a necessary condition for parties to trust each other. The application of care is not a sentimental approach to research; it is about how researchers can best meet their caring responsibilities. As Smeyers summarizes:

> Caring will always create moral dilemmas (because the needs for care are infinite) and will furthermore pose moral problems that arise out of the particular location in which people find themselves in various contexts of care. Still, it might make human societies more moral, as it can serve as a critical standard and it puts moral ideals into action. (1999: 246)

It is from this perspective that work based practitioner-researchers, indeed all researchers, approach their obligations. This may be a more familiar position for work based practitioner-researchers such as you than for those from less applied traditions.

As an insider-researcher, you need to undertake a reflection on your own intent as well as your skills to be able successfully and harmlessly to undertake such research (see Ch 4).

Leaving the site – gratitude

Leaving a research site may be difficult. You may well have made friends, built relationships and actually been inducted into the community of practice you were studying. Moreover, personal relationships may change as a consequence of the research findings you reveal, leading to feelings of guilt, manipulation and deceit, or joy, pleasure and satisfaction.

Throughout this chapter, we have proposed or implied that to understand and respond to these feelings, we should clarify the form of the workplace-researcher's relationship with participants within the complex work based location by classifying both parties' obligations. This obligation is one of gratitude. Your practical consideration must be relevant to your community, yet you yourself must remain distanced. Judgements have to be made in a complex array of interwoven micro-political, social and economic issues which include your recognition that you are distancing yourself while retaining privileges not afforded to outsiders. Furthermore, as a group member, you may experience concern over your future, for success in the research project may enhance your social, cultural and economic capital, leading to promotion beyond the research group. For these reasons, it seems appropriate to suggest that gratitude is due for the participation and the data. Gibbs (2009) has proposed that this is the appropriate response from researchers in workplace studies to their participants for the following four reasons:

- Gratitude is something given and received outside a contractual relationship.
- It assumes possession of the 'given' is in the hands of the giver, indicating something in the workplace not owned by an employer who can demand its delivery.
- It recognizes the autonomous agency of the giver, independent of their role and status in an organization.
- It places an obligation, a contra-organizational power, on the researcher towards the participant.

Such a stance requires that any potential harm you anticipate is made plain and, where harm might occur, a different form of research engagement selected. The research might be undertaken as a commercial consultancy, where the commissioner of the research and the application of its findings are evident to participants, whose own perspective and engagement with you may well change. It might not prevent participants offering views leading to their dismissal, but it would be done voluntarily with this possibility made plain. This does not nullify the argument regarding gratitude; rather, it clarifies it as one of many forms of moral response appropriate for you, from which you have a moral obligation to choose.

It would be inappropriate in the conclusion of this chapter to offer you a list of standard answers to such intricate issues. The aim is to raise these issues for consideration by workplace-researchers and others who may be involved. Such a discussion accepts that research protocols and methodologies which were developed outside the context of work to reveal a notion of truth may fail if transferred to the workplace and used to influence change in organizations from within. Developing a contextualized foregrounding which is a morally robust approach to workplace-research may disturb traditional notions of epistemological truths, but if we avoid this issue, we hide behind convention and evade our moral responsibility. Of course, this humanistic position is contestable, but within a credo of lifelong learning, it at least raises issues worthy of discussion concerning personal development, not workplace servitude.

Successful research is planned research, and we close this chapter with a draft outline strategy worthy of consideration when planning research and the role of access in its implementation.

A strategy for access

- Allow yourself sufficient time – physical access may take time – weeks, or even months to arrange, so plan ahead. Where the intended participants are not the same people who grant you physical access, you may well have to wait for longer. Once you have physical access, then comes the hard part – gaining cognitive access! This is access to the data that you need your participants to share with you, in order to understand their social reality.
- Use existing contacts and develop new contacts – the use of known contacts will depend on your choice of research strategy and the approach you are going to undertake. This is where gatekeepers may be critical to your success.
- Provide a clear account of the type of access required and its purpose – a clear account of the requirement and establishing your creditability will be vital in order to gain cognitive access.
- Overcome organizational concerns – concern might be expressed over the amount of time or resources that will be involved. There may be sensitivity about the topic, the confidentiality of the data and the anonymity of the organization and individual participants.
- Highlight possible benefits to the organization – a discussion which allows the organization to think through the implications of the project will allow

(Continued)

(Continued)

you to find ways in which the project can provide your participant with something of value from the project in terms of exchange of information and ideas. Often access is dependent on a report of the findings. It might be prudent to devise a simple contract to make clear what has been agreed.

- Use suitable language – use straightforward language (or 'clear') appropriate to the nature of the people you are contacting.
- Establish credibility – just because you have been granted entry into an organization, you should not assume that those whom you wish to interview are prepared to cooperate.

Discussion questions

1. What are the main issues in securing access to vulnerable communities?
2. For what should researchers be grateful?
3. What is the relationship between research method and access? Do you need to be more concerned about using some research methods than others? What impact does this have on your research findings?
4. What are the ways of attracting research participants and when would you use them?
5. What are communities of practice? Do you belong to any?
6. At what levels do gatekeepers operate for insider-researchers in work based research involving multiple stakeholders?

References

Baier, A. (1995) *Moral Prejudices: Essays on Ethics*. Cambridge, MA: Harvard University Press.

Bourdieu, P. (2005) *The Logic of Practice*. Cambridge: Polity Press.

Bridges, D. (2001) 'The ethics of outsider research', *Journal of Philosophy of Education* 35 (3): 371–86.

Davison, J. (2004) 'Dilemmas in research: issues of vulnerability and disempowerment for social worker/researcher', *Journal of Social Work Practice* 18 (3): 379–93.

Gibbs, P. (2009) 'Gratitude in workplace research: a Rossian approach', *Journal of Education and Work* 22 (1): 55–66.

Gummesson, E. (2000) *Qualitative Methods in Management Research*. London: Sage.

McLaughlin, C. (2004) 'Partners in research: what's in it for you?', *Teacher Development* 8 (2–3): 127–36.

McNiff, J. (2004) *The Professional as Researcher*. A module on the Ed.D programme at Queen's University, Belfast. Available at: www.jeanmcniff.com

Merriam, S.B., Johnson-Bailey, J., Lee, M.-Y., Kee, Y., Ntseane, G. and Muhamad, M. (2001). 'Power and positionality: negotiating insider/outsider status within and across cultures', *International Journal of Lifelong Education* 20 (5): 405–16.

Okumus, K., Altinay, L. and Roper, A. (2007) 'Gaining access for research: reflections from experience', *Annals of Tourism Research* 34 (1): 7–26.

Patton, M. (2002) *Qualitative Research and Evaluation Methods*. London: Sage.

Putnam, R. (2001). *Bowling Alone: The Collapse and Revival of American Community*. New York: Simon & Schuster.

Robson, C. (2002) *Real World Research*. Oxford: Blackwell.

Shenton, A. and Hayter, S. (2004) 'Strategies for gaining access to organizations and informants in qualitative studies', *Education for Information* 22: 223–31.

Smeyers, P. (1999) 'Care and wider issues', *Journal of Philosophy of Education* 33 (2): 233–51.

Standish, P. (2001) 'Data return: the sense of the given in educational research', *Journal of the Philosophy of Education* 35 (3): 497–518.

Wenger, E. (1998) *Communities of Practice, Learning, Meaning and Identity*. Cambridge: Cambridge University Press.

6

Learning contracts/agreements and intellectual capital

Key points

This chapter discusses the role, value and purpose of learning contracts or agreements. It is in two sections. The first concentrates on a discussion of the notion of a learning contract. It concludes that, although their use is widespread, their form, if not their usage, is currently without much cohesion. This section closes with a discussion of how you can develop a personal learning agreement.

The second section deals with how these contracts release social and intellectual capital both for you and your employer. This discussion is based on the various forms of capital identified by Bourdieu and concludes by contextualizing learning agreements in the field of work based studies.

SECTION 1

Everyone appears to be a winner from WBL; the student, the university, and the corporate organisation. (Gustavs and Clegg, 2005: 10)

Background

There is currently an emphasis on learning and employability as central drivers of economic growth and this is well documented in the European Communication *Making a European Area of Lifelong Learning a Reality* (European Commission, 2001). The rationale is that organizational success is predicated on investment in human capital; individuals' employment and their broader social status is dependent on continuous learning. The goal of autonomous learning as preparation for being-in-the-world-of-change has clear advantages for individuals and society. Tompkins and McGraw declare rather inspirationally that the challenge for academics is leading 'students to the wisdom of their own minds and setting them free on their own learning' (1988: 172). In this context, the contract's explicit function is to facilitate access for the work based learner to resource and support from the university and an employer, to deliver an outcome that increases the cultural capital of both employer and employee (Garnett, 2000). Yet the very notion of combining education and the workplace is problematic. Tasker and Peckham (1994), Barnett (2000) and West (2006) claim that academic and industrial values are incommensurable and that it is only with mutual respect that collaboration can be fruitful. As Evans et al. describe, 'the workplace is a site in which antagonistic relationships are expressed' (2006: 6).

The introduction of learning contracts was intended to reflect organizations' obligations to enable students to flourish, to recognize non-traditional learning that has taken place and to offer specific, personalized learning routes for individuals to engage with the world of credentials. The intent was to encourage through certificated credentials the development of social capital in those who had been excluded from its accumulation. Indeed, learning contracts have been used in UK higher education since the 1970s, originally as a means of agreeing individually negotiated programme components such as independent study modules and work experience modules (Caffarella and Caffarella, 1986; Closson, 1996; Gibbons and Phillips, 1979). Even in these earlier times, there was a range of approaches including the structuring of entire programmes in the pioneering School of Independent Study at the University of East London.

Learning contracts

Essentially, a learning contract's origins are drawn from the work of the American adult educationist and administrator, Malcolm Knowles (see Table 6.1).

Knowles' skill lay in putting the idea of self-direction into packaged forms of activity that could be taken up by educators and learners. He popularized these through various books and courses. His five-step model in his practice-based book, *Using Learning Contracts* (Knowles, 1986), is still pertinent today. It involves:

- diagnosing learning needs
- formulating learning needs
- identifying human material resources for learning
- choosing and implementing appropriate learning strategies
- evaluating learning outcomes.

Table 6.1   Leading figures in learning contracts

Professor Malcolm Knowles

Malcolm was perhaps the central figure in US adult education in the second half of the twentieth century. In the 1950s, he was the Executive Director of the Adult Education Association of the United States of America. He wrote the first major accounts of informal adult education and the history of adult education in the USA. Furthermore, Malcolm Knowles' attempts to develop a distinctive conceptual basis for adult education and learning via the notion of andragogy became widely discussed and used. He was Professor Emeritus of Adult and Community Learning at North Carolina State University at the time he wrote *Using learning contracts* (Jossey-Bass, 1986). *Source*: www.infed.org/thinkers/et-knowl.htm

Professor John Stephenson

John was educated at Barrow Grammar School and the London School of Economics and is Emeritus Professor and Professor of Learner Managed Learning at Middlesex University. He was responsible for the groundbreaking negotiated learning centre in the 1970s and 1980s at North East London Polytechnic (now the University of East London), which has became the inspiration for much of the higher education accredited work based learning in the UK. He has held many influential positions in epoch-forming organizations, for instance Capability and UfI, and written influential texts such as his book on learning contracts and his widely read *Capability and Quality in Higher Education,* with Mantz Yorke. *Source*: www.johnstephenson.net/jsfullcv.htm

Professor David Boud

David has been involved in research and teaching development in adult, higher and professional education for over 30 years and has contributed extensively to the literature. He is currently Professor of Adult Education at the University of Technology, Sydney. Professor Boud is interested in how people learn and what can be done to foster their learning. This has taken him to a variety of settings in adult, higher and professional education and prompted an examination of many practices and processes. He has published extensively and is widely regarded as a leader in learning in the workplace. *Source*: www.education.uts.edu.au/ostaff/staff/david_boud.html

For Knowles, 'contract learning is, in essence, an alternative way of structuring a learning experience: it replaces a content plan with a process plan' (1986: 39).

In the UK, pioneering work on learning contracts was undertaken by John Stephenson at the University of East London (see Table 6.1). Stephenson and Laycock (1993), in another practically orientated text, marked the move from a pedagogical approach where the teacher is in complete control to one which emphasizes cooperation, autonomy and experiential learning. Their definition, taken from their important collection of practical examples, is seminal. They state:

> Learning contracts are agreements negotiated between students and staff and, where appropriate, employers, regarding the type and amount of study to be undertaken and the type and amount of assessment or credit resulting from this study. (1993: 17)

They balance and emphasize the students' needs and obligations in this process. For instance, they suggest that learning contracts help students like you reflect, collaborate and develop skills and confidence, own their studies and recognize the roles of different stakeholders. In response, you need to be explicit about setting your learning goals and then justify them, turn them into a plan and address issues such as the level of performance required.

Following these pioneers are many contributors. These include Anderson, Boud and Sampson (1996). They describe a learning contract as needing to contain clear learning objectives and assessment criteria for the programme's expected standard, a process that is appropriate to the level of programme, and agreement about the types of evidence to be produced. Their definition builds on Knowles' work and describes a 'learning contract' as typically:

> a formal written agreement between a learner and a supervisor which details what is to be learnt, the resources and strategies available to assist in learning it, what will be produced as evidence of the learning having occurred and how that product will be assessed. (1986: 163)

Lyons and Bement (2001) add the need to show that the programme is coherent from an individual's perspective and has integrity and balance. They comment that the learning contract plays a central role in meeting quality criteria and quality assurance requirements within higher education. Osborne et al. (1998) describe this type of work based learning programme as being particularly valuable in more open curricula where the programme (or a significant part of it) is built around the experience, context and work focus or aspirations of the learner.

Perhaps the most influential current figure involved in work on learning contracts is David Boud. Championing autonomy as a goal of education, he has supported the notion of negotiated and contracted learning as an individual-centred approach to learning, amongst others including group-centred and project-centred approaches. In a recent paper, David discusses the positive aspect of learning contracts which embrace the concept of negotiated learning. It is worth quoting at length his and Carol Costley's thoughts:

> In order to accommodate independent projects within conventional course structures, basic frameworks are established around what is termed a learning contract or learning agreement. These commonly take the form of open templates in which students propose goals and objectives, learning activities and assessment processes (Anderson et al., 1996). Plans are negotiated with a staff member and approved by a university panel or individual as being appropriate in content. The place of advising in this is threefold. First, to orient students to create an environment where they are comfortable with the idea and resources to identify projects and develop plans; second, to undertake one-to-one negotiation of the plan with the student; third, to assist the student in judging whether the plan is complete. The entire pool of supervisors (and other academics and practitioners) could provide a resource of expertise that students could draw upon for specific needs in the execution of any particular plan. (Boud and Costley, 2007: 122)

Other contributors to the debate include Doncaster (2000), Stephenson and Saxton (2005) and Gibbs (2009). All describe how learning contracts are used in work based learning and suggest changes or modifications to the original work.

One size does not fit all

Learning contracts for work based learning programmes can take various forms and, Anderson et al. argue, it would be 'misleading to talk about a learning contract as if there were only one model to follow' (1996: 222). In the workplace, learning contracts provide a means of formalizing what is otherwise often an informal and sometimes ad hoc process of learning. (See, for instance, Lee et al., 2000.) Many organizations are already using personal development plans or equivalents as part of their employee and organizational development processes. Cunningham et al. (2004), Megginson (1994) and others support the use of learning contracts to formalize self-managed workplace learning and to focus employees on learning objectives that can be reported and reflected upon. The contracts often have no link to formally accredited activity, although they offer a common language and structure to bring together organizational, professional (including CPD), personal and academic objectives and requirements.

Garnett (2000) discusses organizational involvement in learning agreements for university-accredited work based learning programmes and indicates that, for the agreement to work properly, the employer needs to be an active partner. He also comments that the culture of the work organization will have a significant effect on the learning agreement and the resulting programme, which needs to be understood and managed by university staff.

In summary, according to Lester (2007), there are three developments worth noting in the use of learning contracts for negotiated work based learning programmes:

- A trans-disciplinary approach, where prior as well as planned learning is included in the contract, facilitating a programme that is more coherent and developmental for the individual and, potentially, the work organization (Doncaster, 2000; Osborne et al., 1998).
- The extension of negotiated WBL to doctorate level (Costley and Stephenson, 2008) has resulted in a different focus to learning contracts which, while retaining the essential aspects described above, also become research and development proposals often based on professional activity.
- An increasing use of technology to help learners put together learning contracts, most notably in the Learning through Work system (Stephenson and Saxton, 2005).

Not without their detractors

The literature on learning contracts is confused and definitions are varied. The early convention was the use of the term 'contract', more assertively in the form of 'learning contract' or 'contracted learning' as the methodological manifestation of the contestable notion of andragogy (Knowles, 1986). More recently, the term 'agreement' has been substituted and carries a less legal tone whilst maintaining the same formal framework. For instance, Stephenson and Laycock (1993), Anderson et al. (1996), Boud and Solomon (2001), Rhodes and Shiel (2007) and Lester (2007) all use both terms interchangeably.

Laycock and Stephenson (1993) address the semantics of learning contracts in the opening chapter of their seminal work by denying that they are contracts at all. Knowles recognizes the legalistic connotation of contract (1986: 38) and introduces a more generic term: 'contractual learning'. However, in doing so, he replaces the recognizable and assessable transmission of meaning that is 'contract' with an unknowable notion of knowledge acquisition. (It is unknowable, as how can you determine what will be learnt? Learning is a personal ontology.) This mechanical, non-humanistic approach is emphasized when he declares, 'in the world of the future we must define the mission of education as to produce competent people' (Knowles, 1986: 18–19). These inconsistencies point towards an inappropriate use of the term 'contract' for autonomous, emancipatory learning.

Other definitions remove the centrality of the learner, with Anderson et al. stating that a learning agreement is a 'negotiated agreement based upon both the learning needs of the individual undertaking the contract and the formal requirements of the course involved' (1996: 4). For Moore, it is 'important to enable the learner to construct their own learning in the workplace which meets their individual needs and those of the organisation' (2007: 167). These last two definitions show greater transparency in the relationship of the parties to the contract, giving equal prominence to the complementary needs of university and employer.

As originally conceived, the learning contract is intended to reflect institutions' obligation to enable the student to flourish but, as Doncaster argues, they are also used in 'forwarding the interests of their organisation' (2000). Nikolou-Walker and Garnett (2004) also support this view, arguing that the distinctive feature of work based learning is the relationship between an external organization and an educational institution. This is based on 'satisfying the need of the external organization in return for revenue to the educational institution . . . *in which* learners have some contractual relationship with the external organization' (2004: 298, my italics). These observations suggest that the recipient of the outcomes enjoys a disproportionate benefit and risks exploiting students. Moreover, in an educational context, the issue of academic honesty may be compromised when making presentations of outcomes to employers.

Thorne and Wright suggest that '[H]onesty and openness is not always realistic in such programmes' (2005: 398) and this determines relations between the parties and the outcomes.

Developing a learning agreement or contract

The following general principles are based on the precepts outlined by the UK Quality Assurance Agency for Higher Education (QAA, 2007) for work based and placement learning. Each ought to be addressed in any learning agreement for which the university is responsible and together form the basis of a learning contract. They include:

- Awarding institutions are responsible for the academic standards of their awards and the quality of provision leading to them, and must have in place policies and procedures to ensure that their responsibilities, and those of their partners involved in work based and placement learning, are clearly identified and met. All partners providing work based and placement learning opportunities must be fully aware of their related and specific responsibilities, and learning opportunities provided by them should be appropriate.
- Awarding institutions must ensure that work based and placement learning partners are provided with appropriate and timely information prior to, throughout and following students' work based and placement learning.
- Learning outcomes are clearly identified, contribute to the overall and coherent aims of their programme and are assessed appropriately. Awarding institutions must have effective policies and procedures for securing, monitoring, administering and reviewing work based and placement learning that are updated regularly.
- Students are informed of their specific responsibilities and entitlements relating to their work based and placement learning, and this information is made available in a timely manner to give support and guidance prior to, throughout and following their work based and placement learning.

To contextualize the QAA precepts into a learning agreement, it is useful to turn to Anderson et al. to reiterate their claim that there is 'no one model of a learning contract suitable for all purposes' (1996: 17). However, there is some benefit in utilizing the model broadly suitable for a range of educational settings, found in Chapter 3 of Anderson et al. (1996). This eight step model is as follows:

Step 1: Establish the relevant learning needs

These needs may take several forms. They might be:

- stated needs – to increase my skills in marketing
- real needs – to gain a better job to impress my partner
- unstated needs – to increase my self-esteem

- delight needs – to be recognized beyond my current position in the firm, to surprise others with my accredited ability, or to redress previous educational slights
- secret needs – to be the intellectual, scholar or person to which my own consciousness, or my social status, declares I should not aspire.

Of course, these needs must be tempered by what is possible for you, the student, to learn and, indeed, what you should learn – gang warfare might satisfy some of the above! To determine these learning needs, detailed personal consideration needs to be given to the purpose of the learning and then revealed to you. This might be done through a literature search, workshops, course materials, research project outlines and discussion with those with a stake in your learning. These include the university, the employer and your family and friends. Such an holistic approach to identifying evident as well as latent learning needs will ensure support, focus and direction when structured learning begins.

This first stage is clearly the most important, for it sets up both the epistemological and ontological issues for you to address. Spending insufficient time at this stage leads to poorly defined objects and learning outcomes, and ultimately to dissatisfaction. Remember: a learning agreement is, or ought to be, a negotiation. The more assured you are, the more likely it is that others can provide the experiences needed to reveal the learning and offer the necessary evidence to secure accreditation.

Step 2: Refine the learning objectives

This step follows naturally from Step 1, when the general needs of the learning programme are refined into realistic objectives. This realism is required not only of your ability and competency but of your resources, and these may be provided by the workplace. Moreover, the form and content of the objectives helps the university understand more fully its obligation to you and the process. Clear objectives lead to clear monitoring, more successful completion and happier, more fulfilled, learning.

Objectives should reflect your perceived needs and be achievable in the time and with the resources available. Ambiguous objectives often arise from unarticulated needs and hence have some value in making these needs evident, but then the objectives need to be re-assessed to ensure that the overall aims of the learning contract are met; that is, the academic award is achieved.

For example, a set of learning objectives might include:

- understanding the source of data used to formulate the company accounts
- investigating how the company's ethical policy was constructed and how it is implemented
- preparing a report on my own teaching practice in respect of second language teaching in my class
- making suggestions to the Board on how it might improve waste disposal.

Step 3: Identify the resource and learning strategies

This is a critical stage. You, the learner, need to understand where information can be accessed, the requirements of the access and the effort involved. The information may range from company accounts to the most obscure academic journal. Decisions and iteration may need to be made to the learning contract when the actuality of the resource requirement is made evident. For instance:

- The accounting process may be considered confidential and a matter of commercial sensitivity.
- The ethical policy was not created, but adopted, and has never been implemented (an interesting issue, but full of politics so better left alone).
- No one else is willing to help, and the literature on the subject is currently inaccessible.
- Suggestions to the Board need to go through 'channels' and it is by no means certain that they will arrive.

This is not to say that in these circumstances the objectives necessarily need to be changed, but that further negotiation will need to take place. This will release resources for you to place the learning experience which, as we have suggested, can be achieved by involving stakeholders from the very start. According to Anderson et al. (1996), the best way is to develop a plan which includes what to look for, who to talk to and how to locate data and priorities. This certainly seems efficient and sensible.

The approach to data collection and dealing with understanding issues will be confronted and resolved in different ways, depending on how you learn. Learning can be through experience and discovery, and through doing and reflecting, and includes learning by copying, by experiment, by problem solving and opportunity taking. If your individual learning style can be collaboratively discussed and resources provided to accommodate this style, the learning experience will prove more successful. However, your preference may prove impossible to accommodate and you must be prepared to investigate other learning styles to reach a compromise with the needs of the other parties to the contract.

Step 4: Determine what is to be produced

This separate step needs to be integrated into the process from the beginning. The learning agreement will offer outcomes both in learning and in the forms of production which will provide evidence of the learning. It is important that what is achieved is sufficiently important to carry the evidence to assess the award's academic learning outcomes and also to satisfy the other parties to the agreement. Too much is unachievable; insufficient fails to win academic recognition. Tri-partite discussions are clearly best, remembering that the outcomes from all parties need not be congruent. That is, the major exercise for the employer may contain within it a small, ring-fenced piece of work that simultaneously satisfies the needs of both the university and your accredited learning.

Written outcomes typically consist of a phrase beginning with an active verb (with or without an adverb), the object of the verb, indicating on what you are acting, and a phrase that indicates the context or provides a condition. For example:

Critically evaluate the new EU regulatory developments, especially in relation to X's marketing practices.

Step 5: Determine the criteria of assessment

Determining the criteria requires a collaborative approach, where the pragmatic issues of the workplace are blended with the formal assessment criteria of the university. An overriding criterion in the workplace might be what works but, without the opportunity critically to discuss processes and to contextualize them in the relevant literature, for the university this may be inadequate. Of course, this is not necessarily true and, after enlightened discussion, relevant forms of assessment might be found which satisfy all parties. This is particularly pertinent where the learning contract centres on artistic endeavour, as aesthetic criteria are difficult to articulate readily. However, assessment strategies enable judgements to be made about whether and how the presented work complies with the pre-determined methods of making those judgements. In this sense, these need to be known beforehand and include discussions on the form of assessment: written or oral exams, self-assessment, written report, assessment of outcomes or of the employer and university.

Step 6: Review the learning contract

Once all these activities have been undertaken, what is left may bear little resemblance to the contract's original intention. The review process helps you to see the original needs in a structured format to decide if this is indeed something to which you want to commit. This is a time to reflect and engage with the learning contract to consider changes which, it may now be clear, have an impact on every aspect of the contract.

Step 7: Carry out the contract

Get on and do it! To be successful, clear objectives are required but also clearly defined lines of communication to the support services provided. These will be within the university and hopefully in the host organization, through mentors.

Step 8: Self-assess and submit

You need to reach a state where you are comfortable with what has been achieved, and ensure that it is easy for the assessor to see the achievement clearly. This should not be made difficult; the onus is on you to present the experiential learning, in the desired format of the university, in an interesting and assessable way.

Suggested content of a learning contract

Student information section

Employer information section

University section

Learning outcomes

Authorizing signatures

Resources and methods

Documentation of learning

SECTION 2

Social/intellectual capital: the substance of the learning agreement

A candidate was a voluntary member of a committee of her professional body. The committee was supportive of her research in a related area as it had the potential to provide real value for the membership in general and specific help with their remit. No financial support was given to the candidate but the committee provided access to some resources such as an online survey instrument and individuals offered help in the data analysis. Everything went well until it became clear that the candidate could benefit financially from the research by developing a commercial offer from the results. Ownership of the intellectual property became an issue for the committee and it was clear that this had to be sorted before the research went ahead. After some discussion and a visit by the candidate's advisor, an intellectual property agreement was drawn up allowing both parties to use the results of the work with the other's agreement, which would not be unreasonably withheld. Although it seemed at first to be unnecessarily formal to have such an agreement, the result was an increased sense of ownership and commitment to the work from all sides. Everyone relaxed and looked forward to the results!

In the context of knowledge economies, there has been a blurring of the role played by the form of knowledge that depends on a binary distinction between creator and user, as the above example indicates. This is the central premise in Gibbons et al.'s (1994) notion of distinctive 'mode 2' knowledge. This is the form of knowledge which is produced and valued outside the university and which is not discipline-based. The significance of 'mode 2' knowledge is reflected in the growth of interest in the business literature in knowledge management (Quintas, 2002) and intellectual capital, for instance Edvinsson and Malone (1997), Stewart (2004), Ulrich (1998), Burton-Jones (1999) and Hislop (2005). The emergence of this perspective has created tensions in institutions which may have profited from decoupling these forms of knowledge. Amongst these are universities who may have seen their mission as pursuing knowledge for its own sake, but are now recognizing and actively embracing a more explicit economic role in the creation and transfer of knowledge (see Ch 8).

In this context, Garnett (2001) has argued that Stewart's (2004) sectioning of intellectual capital into three distinct forms – human, structural and consumer – acts as a useful framework for the analysis of the 'impact and value of university facilitated work based learning to organizations working in partnership with the university' (2001: 78). Garnett argues that in the past universities have concentrated on human capital. This has the potential to be transformed through employment into organizations' structural capital, and their changing missions and models mean that they share a responsibility to enhance the practicality of institutional learning. (Eraut calls this 'ready-to-use' – 2004: 248). He clearly points out that applying knowledge through and for work, rather than simply at work, 'challenges the position of the university as the sole validator and evaluator of high level knowledge' (2001: 79).

Bourdieu's notion that cultural capital is institutionalized within educational qualifications and his discussion of the cost of transforming this capital into economic capital under certain circumstances are appealing. They tie in with the idea of intellectual capital and its application to work based studies developed by Nikolou-Walker and Garnett (2004). The forms of capital identified by Bourdieu are economic, cultural and social, each of which contributes to the field of the study of a specific aspect of social life. Within it are structures that maintain it, such as institutions, authorities and activities through which individuals transact. This field is not fixed in time and space; by dynamic engagement with its populations, it is changed by them and changes them in ways that reflect the weight of capital each brings to the engagement. The way this cultural capital is employed is greatly influenced by the habitus that has shaped the form of actions the individual can perform.

As Smith (2003) points out, whether habitus can be mediated through formal organizations as well as in the identity of individuals or not, it seems reasonable to accept that Bourdieu's positioning of educational accreditation is consistent with the notion of cultural capital. This is because it depends on the perceived value of the award's functionality rather than its content. Degrees from different institutions are ostensibly of equal standing, but are attributed different cultural, and ultimately economic, capital.

Cultural capital has three forms: the *embodied* state, that is, in the form of long-lasting dispositions of the mind and body; the *objectified* state, in the form of cultural goods (pictures, books, dictionaries, instruments, machines and so on); and the *institutionalized* state. This type of objectification must be set apart because, as will be seen in the case of educational qualifications, it confers entirely original properties on the cultural capital which it presumes to guarantee. It is this third form of social capital that forms the basis of our analysis, linking the field of higher learning with the habitus of the agents which populate it.

Social capital, in Bourdieu's approach, consists of all actual or potential resources linked to being part of a durable network of more or less institutionalized relationships of acquaintance or recognition. It is a personal asset that provides tangible advantages to individuals, families or groups that are closely connected. The direct transmission of economic capital remains one of the principal means of reproduction, and the effect of social capital ('knowing the Clearing admissions officer' or the 'old school/ college/university network') tends to moderate the effect of academic sanctions.

Bourdieu is clear that the worth of educational qualifications never functions perfectly as currency. He sees the credentialization of education as a form of legitimate symbolic violence by powers: 'they impose meanings and to impose them as legitimate by concealing the power relations which are the basis of its force, adds its own specifically symbolic force to those power relations' (Bourdieu and Passeron, 1990: 4). Credentials thus give the illusion of fairness but, through the traditional modes of delivery and accreditation, as van Zanten suggests, give a 'strong legal, political and pedagogical legitimation to the process of social reproduction' (2005: 673). As Bourdieu and Passeron say, credentials 'are never entirely separable from their holders: their value rises in proportion to the value of their bearer, especially in the least rigid areas of the social structure' (1990: 29). This fixing of the market is performed by those who have inherited power and intend to retain it.

Compared with social capital, intellectual capital is more grounded in practice and relies less on the habitus of accredited learning than its functionality. As providers of educational awards, we create difficulties for ourselves in work based learning with these concepts of intellectual capital, which emerge from different but interrelated social practices.

For the most part, the literature relating to work based learning describes application of knowledge in the sense of workplace activity and adoption of workforce norms and identities (Blaka and Filstad, 2007; Garrick and Rhodes 2000). It also acknowledges the concept of 'tacit knowledge', or what Nikolou-Walker (2007) terms 'unconscious knowledge', embodied in the learner mainly as specific or generic workplace skills. This concept leads to a perspective that, in a knowledge-based economy, knowledge is necessary to economic development in terms of human capital, intellectual capital or structural capital (Jessop, 2006). These ideas are developed in discussions concerning learning organizations (Nikolou-Walker, 2007).

Stewart (2004) argues that it is intellectual capital which is the true measure of the wealth of an organization in the new knowledge economy. The importance attached to the concept of intellectual capital is indicative of a revolutionary shift from the company as a place of production to a 'place for thinking'. At one level, this could be thinking to improve what is already being done, or at a deeper level to bring about a fundamental change in what is being done. The economic importance attached to knowledge and learning has impacted upon and challenged the role of the university (Barnett, 2000), and the rise of the 'corporate university' is a measure of the extent to which higher education institutions are losing influence (Jarvis, 2001). Although Garnett (2001) has highlighted that university work based learning has the potential to contribute directly to the intellectual capital of organizations, the role of university courses in the 'knowledge age' is instead typically still seen as developing the individual for employment.

Stewart (2004), and Edvinsson and Malone (1997) agree that intellectual capital is a combination of three components. These are:

- Human capital – this originated in Becker's work (1964, 1993) and is concerned with knowledge and capabilities of individuals and groups of workers. A key task for management is to reveal and capture the tacit knowledge that is in evidence in individual practice but defies traditional codification. In summary, it is knowledge contained within an organization which, when liberated, represents the company's competitive advantage.
- Structural capital – this is the means by which an organization captures, develops, codifies and shares knowledge so that it can be effectively applied. It is critical to intellectual capital, for it functions to create a structure that supports human capital and also recognizes the overall importance of customer capital. Structural capital's significance is outlined by Stewart (2004), who includes not only technologies and inventions, but strategy and culture, structures and systems, organizational routines and procedures. Central to structural capital's value to the organization is the help it can give individuals to develop their personal knowledge, store and transmit the information derived from it and access information provided by others.
- Client capital – this is the system and process by which the organization taps the human and structural capital of clients' organizations such as suppliers, partners and customers. It is of central importance to the company's worth.

The relationship of these three forms of capital is explained by Harris, who suggests that 'once an organisation becomes aligned and balanced in these three foundational components, it is able to create the best possible financial capital (value)' (2000: 24). The *International Journal of Learning and Intellectual Capital* carries useful articles on the value and form of organizational intellectual capital (see www.inderscience.com/browse/index.php?journalID =86&year=2007&vol=4&issue=4).

Garnett (2001) argues that work based programmes offer the employer two opportunities. One is to develop an individual member of staff, and another, through the work based project, is to focus university critical thinking upon project work with potential to contribute to the intellectual capital of the organization. This is done by developing the individual learner, but also by contributing to the development of the structural capital of the organization. Not all intellectual capital is automatically valuable to an organization; it is only valuable if it helps to deliver the organizational objectives. Once intellectual capital value drivers are identified, they can be utilized via a learning contract, first to make them manifest and second to engage them in the successful development of the organization. An appropriate approach is to make use of partnership agreements with organizations, and learning contracts with individuals, to negotiate and define learning pathways which integrate work based and academic learning.

Garnett (2001) states that work based learning offers the opportunity to create a process for recognizing, creating and applying knowledge through and for work rather than simply at work, and thus challenges the position of educational institutions as the sole evaluators of knowledge. For Garnett, as educationalists, we need to explore how we codify the knowledge, both explicit and implicit, so it may be used effectively. He and Nikolou-Walker conclude that work based learning appears not only to be an imperative for individuals and their employers, but for universities as they 'seek continued relevance and funding in the twenty-first century' (2004: 297). This has some support from Hodkinson et al., who claim it is 'possible to theorise and explain individual workers' roles in workplace learning' (2004: 11). A discourse such as this, with the goal of developing intellectual capital, might be used to explore an individual's learning in employment practices in a proposed new field. Our proposed new field is one of a mediating discourse between employment and education governed by the influence of learning contracts.

Summary

This chapter has discussed the role of learning contracts, both as a way of identifying learner achievements to be codified in academic accreditations and awards, and in order for them to become more readily available to a company's structural capital. In doing so, the simplistic notion of a contract has been questioned, suggestions have been made on the form and context of the contract, and the issue of distinction of the university and the workplace has been investigated on the basis of intellectual capital.

Discussion questions

1. What advantages do learning contracts bring to learning?
2. Is it possible for the learner, university or employer to be exploited by learning contracts? If so, how? What might be done to ensure fairness?

3. Who holds the power in learning contracts? Is this appropriate and fair?
4. How do learning contracts differ from traditional lecture-based learning?
5. Could organizations such as unions benefit from learning contracts, or only individuals?
6. What are the social and educational implications of learning contracts, and can they work for all learning situations?

References

Anderson, G., Boud, D. and Sampson, J. (1996) *Learning Contracts: A Practical Guide*. London: Kogan Page.

Barnett, R. (2000) *Realizing the University in an Age of Supercomplexity*. Buckingham: The Society for Research into Higher Education and Open University Press.

Becker, G.S. (1964) *Human Capital*. Chicago, IL: University of Chicago Press.

Becker, G.S. (1993) *Human Capital: A Theoretical and Empirical Analysis with Special Reference to Education*. Chicago, IL: University of Chicago Press.

Blaka, G. and Filstad, C. (2007) 'How does a newcomer construct identity? A socio-cultural approach to workplace learning', *International Journal of lifelong Education* 26 (1): 59–73.

Boud, D. and Solomon, N. (eds) (2001) *Work-based Learning*. Buckingham: SRHE and Open University Press.

Boud, D. and Costley, C. (2007) 'From project supervision to advising: new conceptions of the practice', *Innovations in Education and Teaching International* 44 (2): 119–30.

Bourdieu, P. and Passeron, J.C. (1990) *Reproduction in Education, Society and Culture*. London: Sage.

Burton-Jones, A. (1999) *Knowledge Capitalism*. Oxford: Oxford University Press.

Caffarella, R.S. and Caffarella, E.P. (1986) 'Self-directedness and learning contracts in adult education', *Adult Education Quarterly* 36: 226–34.

Closson, R.B. (1996) 'The learning society: how shall community colleges respond?', *Community College Review* 24: 3–18.

Costley, C. and Stephenson, J. (2008) 'Building doctorates around individual candidates' professional experience', in D. Boud and A. Lee (eds) *Changing Practices of Doctoral Education*, pp. 171–86 London: Routledge.

Cummings, T. (2004) 'Organization development and change: foundations and applications', in J. Boonstra (ed.) *Dynamics of Organizational Change and Learning*, Chichester: Wiley.

Cunningham, I., Dawes, G. and Bennett, B. (2004) *The Handbook of Work-based Learning*. Aldershot: Gower Publishing.

Doncaster, K. (2000) 'Learning agreements: their function in work-based programmes at Middlesex University', *Education and Training* 42 (6): 349–55.

Edvinsson, L. and Malone, M.S. (1997). *Intellectual Capital: Realizing your Company's True Value by Finding its Hidden Brainpower*. New York: HarperBusiness.

Eraut, M. (2004) 'Informal learning in the workplace', *Studies in Continuing Education* 26 (2): 247–73.

European Commission (2001). *Making a European Area of Lifelong Learning a Reality*. Available at: www.bologna-berlin2003.de/pdf/MitteilungEng.pdf [accessed 2 October 2008].

Evans, K., Hodkinson, P., Rainbird, H. and Unwin, L. (2006) *Improving Workplace Learning*. Abingdon: Routledge.

Garnett, J. (2000) 'Organisational cultures and the role of learning agreements', in D. Portwood and C. Costley (eds) *Work-based Learning and the University: New Perspectives and Practices* (SEDA Paper 109, pp 59–66.) Birmingham: Staff and Educational Development Association.

Garnett, J. (2001) 'Work based learning and the intellectual capital of universities and employers', *The Learning Organization* 8 (2): 78–81.

Garrick, J. and Rhodes, C. (eds) (2000) *Research and Knowledge at Work: Case Studies and Innovative Strategies*. London: Routledge.

Gibbons, M. and Phillips, G. (1979) 'The case for negotiated learning contracts', *NASSP Bulletin* 63: 55–60.

Gibbons, M., Limoges, C., Nowotny, H., Schwartzman, S., Scott, P. and Trow, M. (1994). *The New Production of Knowledge:The Dynamics of Science and Research in Contemporary Societies*. London: Sage.

Gibbs, P. (2009) 'Learning agreements and work-based HE', *Research in Post-Compulsory Education* 14 (1): 31–41.

Gustavs, J. and Clegg, S. (2005) 'Working the knowledge game? Universities and corporate organisations in partnership', *Management Learning* 36 (9): 9–30.

Gustavsen, B. (2004). 'Theory and practice: the mediating discourse', in P. Reason and H. Bradbury (eds) *Handbook of Action Research*, London: Sage.

Harris, L. (2000) 'A theory of intellectual capital', *Advances in Developing Human Resources* 2: 22–37.

Hislop, D. (2005) *Knowledge Management in Organizations*. Oxford: Oxford University Press.

Hodkinson, P., Hodkinson, H., Erans, K. and Kersh, N. with Fuller, A., Unwin, L. and Senker, P. (2004) ' The significance of Individual Biography in Workplace Learning', in *Studies in the Education of Adults* 36 (1): 6–26.

Jarvis, P. (2001) *Universities and Corporate Universities*. London: Kogan Page.

Jessop, B. (2006) 'Cultural political economy, the knowledge-based economy, and the state', in B. Andrew (ed) *The Technological Economy*, pp. 144–66. London: Routledge.

Knowles, M.S. (1986) *Using Learning Contracts*. San Francisco, CA: Jossey-Bass.

Laycock, M. and Stephenson, J. (1993) *Using Learning Contracts in Higher Education*. London: Kogan Page.

Lee, T., Fuller, A., Ashton, D., Butler, P., Felsted, A., Unwin, L. and Walters, S. (2004) *Learning as Work: Teaching and Learning Processes in the Contemporary Work Organization*. Learning as Work Research Paper No 2. Leicester: The Centre for Labour Market Studies, University of Leicester.

Lester, S. (2007) 'Professional practice projects: APEL or development?', *Journal of Workplace Learning* 19 (3): 188–202.

Lyons, F. and Bement, M. (2001) 'Setting the standards, judging levels of achievement', in D. Boud and N. Solomon (eds) *Work-based Learning: A New Higher Education*, pp. 167–83 Buckingham: SRHE/Open University Press.

Megginson, D. (1994) 'Planned and emergent learning: a framework and a method', *Executive Development* 7 (6): 29–32.

Moore, L.J. (2007) 'Ethical and organisational tensions for work-based learners', *Journal of Workplace Learning* 19 (3): 161–72.

Nikolou-Walker, E. (2007) 'Vocational training in higher education: a case study of work-based learning within the Police Service of Northern Ireland', *Research in Post-Compulsory Education* 12 (3): 357–76.

Nikolou-Walker, E. and Garnett, J. (2004) 'Work-based learning: a new imperative', *Reflective Practice* 5 (3): 297–312.

Osborne, C., Davies, J. and Garnett, J. (1998) 'Guiding the learner to the centre of the stakeholder curriculum: independent and work based learning at Middlesex University', in J. Stephenson and M. Yorke (eds) *Capability and Quality in Higher Education*, pp. 85–94. London: Kogan Page.

QAA (2007) 'Work-based and placement learning', in *Code of Practice for the Assurance of Academic Quality and Standards in Higher Education,* Section 9. Available at: www.qaa.ac.uk/academic infrastructure/codeOfPractice/section9/placementLearning.pdf [accessed 15 September 2008].

Quintas, P. (2002) 'Managing knowledge in a new century', in S. Little, P. Quintas and T. Ray (eds) *Managing Knowledge*, pp. 1–14. London: Sage.

Rhodes, G. and Shiel, G. (2007) 'Meeting the needs of the workplace and the learner through work-based learning', *Journal of Workplace Learning* 19 (3): 173–87.

Smith, E. (2003) 'Ethos, habitus and situation for learning: an ecology', *British Journal of the Sociology of Education* 24 (4): 463–70.

Stephenson, J. and Laycock, M. (eds) (1993) *Using Learning Contracts in Higher Education*. London: Kogan Page.

Stephenson, J. and Saxton, J. (2005) 'Using the Internet to gain personalized degrees from learning through work: some experience from Ufl', *Industry and Higher Education* 19 (3): 249–58.

Stephenson, J. and Yorke, M. (1998) *Capability and Quality in Higher Education*. London: Kegan Paul.

Stewart, T. (2004) *Intellectual capital.* London: Nicholas Brealey.

Tasker, M. and Peckham, D. (1994) 'Industry and higher education: a question of values', *Studies in Higher Education* 18 (2): 127–36.

Thorne, A.A. and Wright, G. (2005) 'Developing strategic alliances in management learning', *Journal of European Industrial Training* 29 (5): 383–404.

Tompkins, C. and McGraw, M.-J. (1988) 'The negotiated learning contract', in D. Boud (ed.) *Developing Student Autonomy in Learning*, pp. 172–91, New York: Nichols.

Ulrich, D. (1998) 'A new mandate for human resources', *Harvard Business Review* 51: 125–34.

van Zanten, A. (2005) 'Bourdieu as education policy analyst and expert: a rich but ambiguous legacy', *Journal of Education Policy* 20 (6): 671–86.

West, P.W.A. (2006) 'Conflict in higher education and its resolution', *Higher Education Quarterly* 60 (2): 187–97.

7

Developing a methodology

Key points

This chapter will take you through the principles of developing and justifying the methodology for your project. How and where the methodology section of your project fits into the whole project is shown in Chapter 11. The need arises because it is important to show how a project has been undertaken. To gain valid and usable results, you need to research a project properly or, as often stated in research texts, with 'rigour'; that is, the work reflects that you have an understanding of research, and how to carry out research and analyse and evaluate data. The 'methodology' is how you approach the whole business of undertaking the project and is more than a set of research methods and a project plan: it also embraces the philosophical, conceptual and contextual perspectives from which the project is being taken forward, along with justification for using the chosen approach in the situation in which you are working.

Your methodology should emphasize the creativity of your work based research project's design. As a relatively new field of study, work based learning is still creating and understanding the contribution of its research methodologies to new forms of knowledge generated by merged sites of knowledge production and use. Work based research is therefore also about furthering our knowledge and understanding of work based research methodologies.

Methodology includes the development activities that take place while carrying out the research and can include the processes of change in day-to-day professional practice, following the completion of the research. It is highly likely, therefore, that you will already be using methodologies in your work, even if you have not thought through all the implications of the idea of a methodology. Most work based projects combine the research and the development aspects of methodology, as they take a researching approach to real-life issues and developments while also being located within your professional practice. This means that it is unlikely that you will be able simply to take a textbook methodological approach and apply it to your project: your methodology will need to grow out of your position within your work setting, your professional and organizational context, your practical and ethical constraints, and the purpose and aims of the project.

Constructing a methodological framework

A methodological approach is followed by the construction of a method-ological framework and can be seen as starting at a conceptual or philo-sophical level and working down, through principles for research and action, to specific data-gathering and practical actions. Many research text-books use a sequence similar to that below, adapted from Grix (2004), though usually focusing purely on knowledge- and data-gathering rather than including action:

Ontology	The nature of being/of reality: what is there to be known? Your own situation in the world and how you perceive it is likely to inform your ontological position.
Epistemology	The nature of knowledge: how do we know what there is to be known? Your ontological position is likely to inform the way you view knowledge, and what knowledge is important and salient to particular research questions you may wish to ask.
Methodology	How can we go about acquiring knowledge and making changes? The way you understand and select knowledge is likely to inform the methodology you construct for your project work.
Methods	What techniques and processes are appropriate for acquiring knowledge and creating change? The methods you use are part of the methodological framework that you will construct. Particular methods are associated with particular methodologies; however, in this book, we point out that you may not be able to use an existing 'ideal type' methodology from research textbooks.
Focus of attention	What sources of data are relevant and accessible: where, to whom or what should interventions be applied? As well as your own position regarding the construction of a methodology, you will have practical and time constraints that may also affect how you do this.

The topic and aim of the project

Prior to thinking through the above sequence for your methodological framework, you may need to make a critical evaluation of your own point of view or ideology behind the project aim. You may consider that you need to discuss why you have chosen a particular project as a topic of research with particular aims and objectives. For example, one work based project sought to find out why people chose to smoke in a particular area of a building and how they might be encouraged not to smoke. The work based researcher did not like smoking and had concerns about people's health. However, a different project might have been identified such as finding out from a broad range of workers in this particular company what lounge areas they would like. To examine why you have chosen a particular project helps you, to some extent, to state something about your ideology, your values and what you find important. For example, in social science research, from which we draw heavily, researchers may state that they are taking a feminist or neo-Marxist perspective; the reader then knows that the person undertaking the research holds particular views and can bear these in mind when contemplating how the work has been constructed and then evaluated.

Your approach to the project

As well as the research topic itself, your chosen approach and methods also underpin your point of view or ideology which in turn is often based upon a particular set of values that you may take for granted. Not only are you working within your own point of view or ideology, but within particular discourses, often associated with particular professions, work situations and cultures. You should therefore have a sense of your own ontological and epistemological perspective and state this, along with any dominant positions within the professional, organizational or civic communities in which you work. In terms of methodology, the implication is that this provides the philosophical starting point for how you construct your methodological framework. While having particular perspectives described here as ontological and epistemological does not dictate a particular kind of methodology, it is important to explain in as much detail as possible why you have decided to undertake specific research and why you have decided to undertake it in a particular way. This will entail explanations related to values and judgements as well as a practical and theoretical rationale. Abridged examples of methodologies can be found in Chapter 10.

The difference between methodology and methods is often least well understood. Methods, sometimes called techniques or tools, such as questionnaires, interviews and focus groups have to be justified within the whole methodological framework. At face value, there are some obvious connections between some set methodological approaches (although none are completely prescribed) and specific methods – for instance, a post-positivist approach may use methods such as controlled trials, and a phenomenological approach is likely to use methods such as discussions-as-interviews – but the reality can be more complex. Working from, for instance, an interpretive perspective where qualitative rather than quantitative methods are more likely to be used does not mean that survey-type research that produces quantitative data is ruled out. It has implications for the way that surveys are approached and designed and, in particular, the way that resultant data are interpreted. Writers such as Holliday (2002: 18) dispute the association of particular methods with particular methodologies. Holliday writes about 'the fluid picture' and shows that methods and methodologies are no longer considered linear. Crotty (1998) addresses the merging of theoretical perspectives and shows their development.

Paradigms

To understand better the connection between values, ideology and philosophical thinking and the methodologies that researchers use, the following explanation about the broad paradigms from researcher communities may be helpful.

A 'paradigm' is a deep-rooted set of perspectives that includes an ontological and an epistemological position and a set of values for operating in the world. In the natural sciences and some technological professions, there is usually a dominant paradigm within each major field; only when its key assumptions are successfully challenged is it replaced by a different paradigm (a good source on this is Kuhn, 1968). In the social sciences and many professional fields, paradigms often exist together as competing schools of thought, sometimes harmoniously and sometimes giving rise to disputes and contestation. Rather than displacing earlier paradigms in the way described by Kuhn, newer paradigms can become overlaid on older ones so that features of both co-exist. An example of this is the way that the idea of 'profession' is constructed, with at least four co-existing paradigms: an ancient, learned one; a pre-industrial trade model; an industrial-era technocratic model; and a late twentieth-century, reflective–interpretive paradigm. This evolutionary approach to paradigms is described by Tornebohm (1974).

Various ways of classifying major paradigms have arisen in the social sciences. Sometimes a rather crude 'positivist' and 'anti-positivist' division to illustrate major paradigms is adopted, while at others a number of key schools of thought are considered. Two approaches are summarized here, the first drawing on Guba and Lincoln (2000) and the second on Burrell and Morgan (1979). Guba and Lincoln describe five major research paradigms, summarized below.

Positivism

A positivist approach treats reality as objective and knowable. From a research viewpoint, it seeks to verify hypotheses and establish natural laws, adding to a growing stock of knowledge. The researcher is regarded as objective and external to the research; value-based issues are rarely raised. Methodological approaches are generally quantitative and technical in approach, favouring methods such as experiments, trials and surveys. There is a strong notion of replicability in positivist research (the same results should be achieved by different researchers undertaking the same research).

Post-positivism

Post-positivistic approaches share many of the characteristics of positivism though, while they treat reality as objective, they regard it as not perfectly knowable. The emphasis therefore moves to testing rather than proving hypotheses: non-falsified hypotheses are considered to be the best available knowledge, potentially subject to amendment. Methodological approaches may be quantitative or qualitative, and in some post-positive approaches, the researcher is viewed as an interested intellectual; value-based issues can contribute to how the focus of the research is decided.

Critical theory

Critical theory regards reality as being shaped over time by a wide range of social and cultural values, with knowledge subject to individual and cultural construction. It tends to seek historically located, structural insights geared towards critique of the status quo, education to address ignorance and misapprehensions, and emancipatory action. Methodological approaches favour dialogue and dialectics, and can include emancipatory action research as well as more quantitative approaches.

Constructivism

Constructivist approaches regard reality as being individually and socially derived, with knowledge an individual construction that nevertheless can be subject to consensus. The researcher is generally regarded as an involved participant who seeks to give voice to the experiences and perceptions of the other participants. Methodological approaches favour dialogue and hermeneutics, and there is a strong drive towards achieving authentic reflections of participants' subjective reality.

Participatory paradigms

Participatory approaches start from the premise that reality, and knowledge of reality, are co-created from a mutual understanding that arises from lived experience. Participatory research is essentially a collaborative activity by a community of enquiry or practice which may be led by a facilitator, but never involves a 'researcher' carrying out research on others. Participatory research is generally geared towards action, which may be in the form of artistic or other expression, changes to the community of enquiry, or wider social or cultural changes.

Burrell and Morgan group social science approaches into four major paradigms, depending on their view of knowledge (subjective to objective) and their view of society, effectively whether they are concerned with describing the status quo or with creating change. The objectivist paradigms tend to take a structural view of societal phenomena (they are concerned with institutions, major concepts, classes of things and generalizations), while the subjectivist ones focus more on individual actors and how they construct and interpret situations.

While its approach may be useful, it is worth noting that this work is now 30 years old and does not take account of newer approaches such as radical feminist phenomenology or participatory research. Figure 7.1 is taken, with minor changes, from Burrell and Morgan (1985: 29).

Several points need to be made about these representations of paradigms. Firstly, there is more to considering paradigms than deciding where in either Guba and Lincoln's or Burrell and Morgan's models to fit your own perspective. Most personal paradigms will be more specific than those described, and they may not fit with all the characteristics of any one model. It is also perfectly possible to have a coherent world view that cuts across more than one textbook paradigm. The main point is that your paradigmatic approach needs to reflect your genuine belief and it needs to be coherent.

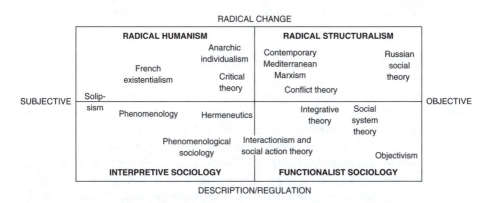

Figure 7.1   Burrell and Morgan's framework for social science paradigms (Reproduced with kind permission from Burrell, G. and Morgan, G. (1985) *Sociological Paradigms and Organisational Analysis*. Farnham: Ashgate.)

Secondly, paradigms do not have to be completely exclusive. Two ideas illustrate this. First, Znaniecki (1934) uses the concept of a 'humanistic coefficient', normally represented by a series of concentric circles, to describe how frames of reference can legitimately change, depending on what is being considered. In the central circle are the physical aspects of the natural world, on which most observers agree; moving towards the outside, there is increasing room for individual perception and interpretation, until the outer ring contains the purely subjective. Using Znaniecki's model, it would be appropriate to work from a positivistic or post-positivist scientific paradigm in the central ring, and decreasingly so in successive rings. Second, research by Kitchener and King (1981) shows how our view of knowledge changes as we develop greater epistemological maturity. In early childhood, we simply accept knowledge for what it is and, as we develop, we tend to adopt first an absolute view of knowledge (favouring a positivistic approach), then favour a more subjective view, and finally (if we get that far) look for the most accurate and complete representation without expecting it to be completely true or to lack gaps: we seek out 'maps that work' rather than ideal representations.

Thirdly, a distinction can be made between the kind of philosophical, scientific or sociological paradigms described above and our day-to-day operating paradigms or perspectives. Deep-rooted values and ways of seeing things tend to change only slowly or in response to major events, while values and perspectives that influence everyday practice can change as a result of gaining new knowledge or understanding different viewpoints; we can move to a different standpoint fairly easily. Rather than regarding paradigms as rigid towers that extend from an ontological level through to methods and practices, this view suggests that, while we have certain values and perceptions that are fairly constant, others are much more flexible and context-dependent.

Finally, the way that paradigms are represented here is only one way of seeing things; there are other perspectives, some of which can be found in texts mentioned below, for example Arbnor and Bjerke (2009).

Considering a methodological approach

Methodology consists of principles for acquiring knowledge or for creating change, or both, and some actual methodologies used in work based projects can be found in Chapter 10. Methodological approaches are more operationally focused than the paradigms discussed above, although some reflect a particular paradigm, or effectively represent paradigms in their own right, and others can be approached from a variety of different perspectives. Methodologies are sometimes described as being quantitative or qualitative, though many approaches lend themselves to gathering and using both kinds of data, depending on what is appropriate in particular situations.

Some widely used methodological approaches relevant to work based projects are briefly described below. These tend to cross into and borrow from each other so that, for instance, action research can contain elements of grounded theory, critical theory, phenomenology and experimental research. Soft systems methodology has much in common with action research and draws variously on phenomenology, grounded theory and statistical research, while also being presented as a case study. Case studies can involve a wide mix of methodological approaches. It should also be noted that many 'standard' methodological approaches derive from the social or natural sciences and are not specifically geared to creating action, so work based approaches will normally need to build on and adapt textbook methodologies.

Examples of methodologies

The following are some examples of distinct methodologies that have been used in constructing a methodological framework for a work based project.

Phenomenological approaches

Phenomenology is in essence a philosophy or paradigm rather than a specific methodology, but especially in its later North American form has given rise to a particular approach to research and action that, rather than seeking external realities, puts aside existing preconceptions and theories and aims to gain a deep understanding of individuals' perceptions. Phenomenological approaches are powerful for understanding subjective experience, gaining insights into people's motivations and actions, and cutting through the clutter of assumptions and conventional wisdom. They are particularly good at exposing limitations in current thinking, action or policies, developing widened or alternative perspectives and testing complex systems. Phenomenological research is often associated with discussions-as-interviews, but phenomenological principles can be used to inform a wide range of approaches to research and practice including ethnographic studies, case studies, action research and interview-based studies.

Hermeneutics

This is in origin concerned with the understanding of texts, both at the level of the meanings conveyed and through attempting to get below the surface by understanding the perspective and context from which the text is produced. Subsequently, this has developed to encompass forms of expression other than texts – from discourse and interview records to artefacts, events and organizational systems. Additionally, it now encompasses more dialectic and interpretive forms of research in which the meaning of a text, artefact or event is seen as a product of the interaction between the author's meaning and the reader's or observer's interpretation. Central to hermeneutics is the idea of a conversation, either literally or with a text or context, in which reality is explored and understanding developed.

Grounded theory

This is an inductive approach to research and understanding in which, rather than starting from a hypothesis or theory about a situation, theory is seen as growing out of data and incidents as they are collected and observed. As with phenomenological approaches, the researcher or actor starts by suspending any assumptions about the situation. The aim is to produce meaning and interpretation that has value in the context being studied rather than to seek theories or truths that can be generalized. Grounded theory is sometimes associated with *theoretical sampling*, a technique that allows a consistent sample to be built up and re-focused during the progress of the research without reference to statistical sampling techniques. Although generally regarded as a qualitative methodology, it has also been used quite widely with quantitative and particularly statistical data collection methods.

Action research

This aims to make changes or improvements in a situation through a cycle or set of cycles of investigation, action and reflection, while at the same time reporting it in a way that is useful both to the project in hand and potentially to outsiders. Stemming from the work of Kurt Lewin in the 1940s, action research was originally a means of assisting people to move forward through enquiry into issues in their own lives. It has become widely used as a methodology for practitioner and collaborative research as it provides a straightforward way of taking a researching approach to practice or change. Most forms of action research follow a cycle of four stages: planning, acting or creating change; observing and data gathering; reflecting; and decision making. The 'plan–do–study–act' cycle used for business process improvement is a form of action research and similar principles are used in soft systems methodology. Ethical issues need careful consideration in action research due to the potential effect of changes on participants.

Soft systems

Developed by Peter Checkland (1999, Chekland and Poulter, 2006) and his colleagues at Lancaster University as a process methodology for addressing problems in human and organizational systems, this is not specifically a research methodology, although it shares many characteristics with action research. It has also been used both as a research approach to practical issues and as an overarching framework to draw together different strands of research in order to inform action. A similar cycle or sequence to action research is used, although there is more emphasis on assessing the situation in which intervention is thought necessary, building a detailed and multi-dimensional picture and defining the key processes that need to take place within the system.

Survey-based research

The basic principle of much survey-based research is to take a sample for study from an overall population and, through the use of statistical methods, to make inferences that are representative of the population as a whole. Surveys typically need a good understanding of what is to be researched in order to be able to frame research questions and design data-collection instruments effectively, although they can lend themselves to more qualitative approaches.

Ethnography

This is a broad methodological category within which different methods, normally qualitative, can be employed. Its main principle involves going into (or being in) 'the field' and collecting primarily unstructured data through methods such as observation, discussions and interviews to explore and illustrate a social situation. Ethnography is sometimes conflated with participant observation, where the researcher is also a full or partial participant in the situation being studied (an insider or participant researcher), although it is possible to undertake ethnographic research as an outsider. Ethnography is potentially a useful approach to research in a situation where the researcher already plays an active part (for example, within an organization or community of practice) or can be seconded into an active or observing role.

Case study research

Not a methodology in itself, this is an approach that can draw on a variety of methods (qualitative and quantitative as appropriate) to assemble a single case or small number of cases. Its purpose is to investigate and present an example in a way that is of use beyond its face value, for instance to draw out points that have potential for wider application or to illustrate problems in policy or practice. A case study approach can be used to present projects and sequences of actions as well as specifically researched instances, giving it particular relevance to writing up practice so it is of wider value and interest. Case studies aim to illustrate and describe particular instances or episodes in a way that has relevance to other examples, rather than either presenting them as unique, or assuming that the findings may be generalized.

Bricolage

This describes an approach to research that combines multiple perspectives and methodologies in order to gain a better understanding of real-world situations. It goes beyond multi-method research, moving away from 'textbook' approaches and developing appropriate methods to fit and essentially grow out of the situation in hand. A central principle of *bricolage* is that it aims to respond to the complexities and contradictions of live contexts and those living and working in them without seeking to impose a particular approach to gathering or analysing data; it has been described as anarchic and acknowledging the subjectivity of any research process, but also demanding a deep knowledge of a wide range of approaches and techniques.

Developing a methodological approach

Developing a methodological approach for a work based project involves rather more than selecting paradigm *a* and methodology *b*, and choosing methods *x*, *y* and *z*. Building on your understanding of your position, you will probably have located reasonably well the standpoint from which you are working. You may find, for instance, that your perspective and how you go about things suggests, for example, a post-positivist or structuralist paradigm, or lies in the constructivist/phenomenological spectrum. Alternatively, your perspective may not fit particularly well with established paradigms, but you are able to describe your ontological and epistemological starting points and your essential values.

The next step is to consider how your perspective fits where you will be working and what your project is setting out to achieve. Different paradigms and ways of thinking are effective for different things; for instance, if your project involves both technological and people-related aspects, you may find that you need to work from a natural sciences perspective for some aspects and a more reflective, subjectivist one for others. Similarly, in undertaking a major organizational change, it is likely that a structural or systems perspective will be needed alongside a more participatory one. Alternatively, if you want to challenge a policy or set of practices and come up with something that is rooted in the experience of the people who live or work in a particular situation, you will need to take a perspective capable of penetrating assumptions and system structures. While you are not being asked to contradict your core values, a major work based project is likely to require more than one perspective.

This more grounded consideration of perspective leads into the development of an appropriate methodological approach. Depending on the nature of the project, it may be possible to work within a specific (or dominant) methodology, but real-life projects typically combine aspects of more than one methodology, or can be seen from different methodological perspectives. As an example, a project to develop a new way of working might be construed principally as an action research project, but could also draw on aspects of soft systems methodology and adopt approaches from grounded theory or experimental research; when written up, it might be treated as a case study.

In developing your methodological approach and framework, the following framing questions might be considered:

- How would you explain your methodological approach and the principles underpinning it?
- Is the methodological framework you are developing coherent with your personal position?
- How does it fit with the context and purpose of the project?
- Is the approach likely to be effective in terms of what you are setting out to do?
- Will your approach be appropriate for the data you want to collect or support the action you want to take?
- Are any ethical issues likely to be raised when you start to apply your methodology? Some ethical matters can be managed at the level of methods, but major issues can arise because the ethical implications of a particular methodology (such as adopting a purely structural approach to change, or the capacity of a participative project to raise unrealistic hopes) have not been thought through in advance.
- Can you write a persuasive justification for your approach? Are there other approaches that you could take, and would they be more or less effective?

Finally, you will need to show that your methodology is capable of being both valid and robust. How these terms are defined is slightly different, depending on the research tradition that you are using. Essentially, validity refers to the fitness-for-purpose of the approach in relation to what you are aiming to achieve, the context in which your work is taking place, and your perspective or standpoint.

Robustness, reliability or rigour (the term usually depends on the research tradition, itself often dependent on the subject discipline) concerns the extent to which your findings or decisions will follow from the methodology and the data with which you are working. In natural science traditions, there is an assumption that research should be replicable, that is, different researchers using the same methods should produce the same or comparable results. In action-based and interpretive traditions, robustness is more likely to be achieved through making the methodological and decision-making process visible, so that it is clear how particular conclusions and decisions have been reached. In both sets of traditions, you will be looking to ensure that a sufficient or representative range of data is captured for what you want to do or illustrate. You also need to ensure that the data can be analysed and interpreted consistently. As far as possible, the research should not contain hidden sources of bias, for example that you do not design a project to validate a particular theory or model by looking only for supporting data.

Methods for data collection

The methods chosen to collect data and information from the field should be methodologically coherent, practically and ethically feasible, and capable of providing the type of information that you need. This is where it is important to consider the depth and extent of data that you want to collect: for instance, to what extent do you want to be able to comment on *how much* and *how many*, and how deeply do you want to explore perceptions and insights from the field? The descriptions below outline some key methods of data collection that can be used in work based settings without attempting to describe their application in detail.

Before exploring specific methods and tools, it is worth noting that many methods lend themselves to use in ways that range from pre-structured to more open. Structured approaches – where data categories are determined in advance, for instance through tick-box questionnaires, structured interviews or observation checklists – allow easier analysis and greater comparability of data, and are more amenable to quantitative analysis; they often work well where it is desired to use a statistically representative sample in order to draw an inference about a population as a whole. Their disadvantage is that they are relatively inflexible, do not lend themselves to exploring depth of information, and effectively impose the researcher's structure and perspective or meaning on the respondents or participants. Open approaches – such as discussions-as-interviews and open written responses – can avoid these restrictions and produce a much greater depth of information, but they require much more time to analyse, they are less amenable to quantitative analysis, and it is often not possible to draw from them conclusions about overall populations. Clearly, it is possible to combine both approaches, either within one method (for example, open and more structured questions) or by using multiple methods in one project.

An issue that can occur in any situation where participants are aware that they are involved in research – but particularly in questionnaires, interviews and experiments or focused observations – is the 'response effect', where participants tailor their responses (consciously or otherwise) to what they think the researcher is expecting. This can be made worse by poor design or the use of a particular method (such as including leading questions in a questionnaire or interview), but can also occur when the participant knows the researcher (for example, as a work colleague) and has some knowledge or suspicions about their agenda or viewpoint. Reducing 'response effect' is partly a function of the way that research tools are designed and researcher–participant interactions conducted, but there are situations which will mitigate against using particular methods.

Interviews

Interviewing is a widely used research technique that can be adapted to work in a wide range of situations to gain information about people's perceptions, experiences or preferences. Interviews can be conducted face-to-face, on the telephone or, in some cases, through online 'chat'. It is possible to use structured interviews to produce easily compared answers, semi-structured interviews where open questions can be followed by more structured ones, and discussions-as-interviews with no pre-set questions and where discussion progresses around a broad theme agreed between researcher and interviewee. At all levels of structure, one of the advantages of interviews over questionnaires is that they allow the researcher to explore areas of ambiguity and seek clarification; the main disadvantage is the length of time they occupy, and the fact that the interviewee's identity cannot be kept hidden from the researcher (unless third-party interviewers are used).

Structured interviews are sometimes described as questionnaires administered verbally, although there are some important differences. The interviewer is able to ask questions in sequence without disclosing later questions, and it is slightly easier – and less confusing to the interviewee – to branch off in different directions according to the answer to a previous question. Structured interviews are generally recorded on a proforma that resembles a questionnaire and may contain space for short, written answers, use tick boxes, yes/no or numerical responses, or have multiple-choice answers. The design of schedules and questions for both structured and semi-structured interviews has much in common with questionnaire design, covered below.

Semi-structured interviews tend to use a schedule of questions in the same way as structured interviews, but allow more open verbal answers which are either written down by the researcher on a proforma or, ideally, recorded. They give participants more latitude in responding in their own words, but can also be focused using specific questions in response to a general answer. Both semi-structured and structured interviews can be carried out by telephone, although the former are more time-consuming and typically require advance notification.

Unstructured interviews are generally discussions around broad themes agreed in advance between researcher and interviewee and carried out face to face. Their direction can be influenced by the interviewee as much as the researcher. They do not have preset schedules, although it is usual to have a brief, written explanation as part of the agreement with the participants. Sometimes they are undertaken as a sequence, either over time for longitudinal research or simply to provide more time and allow the researcher to consider what was discussed in one session before going on to the next. It is usual to record and transcribe unstructured interviews, and provide a copy of the transcript(s) to the interviewee for checking;

sometimes a final session can be used to go over and discuss matters arising from the transcript, although discussion from this will need to be recorded and noted separately. Unstructured interviews are good for revealing deep information and understanding, but require a high level of skill on the part of the interviewer and are also very time-consuming to conduct and analyse.

Questionnaires

The questionnaire is another widely used research tool often associated with survey research and with short-term evaluations, though capable of more qualitative use. Questionnaires can be highly structured with closed questions only (that is, yes/no, multiple-choice or numerical answers), allow for short, written responses, or pose more general and open questions with room for fairly lengthy responses. Closed-question questionnaires are the easiest to analyse statistically, but limit responses to the categories the researcher has included. Open questions require at least some qualitative analysis, even if ultimately they will be reported quantitatively. A fairly common option for large-scale questionnaires is to aim for the majority of questions to be easily analysed, but to include enough open questions to allow for answers that cannot be accommodated by any of the standard categories.

Questionnaire design is less simple than it may initially appear. Some of the main points to consider are:

- Will the questions produce all the data needed?
- Are the questions clear and unambiguous, or could they be misinterpreted in any way?
- Are the questions neutral – that is, do they avoid giving the impression that they favour a particular answer?
- If there are pre-set categories for responses, do these cover all the main possibilities?
- Do they need an 'other' category and, if so, should this have an 'open answer' option to allow the respondent to explain further?
- Is the questionnaire straightforward to complete?
- Can responses be analysed in a straightforward way?

Before carrying out the main survey, it is usual to pilot the questionnaire with a small group to identify any problems in understanding or completing it, and to test the questions being asked. Piloting should also provide information about how easy and motivating the questionnaire is to complete, as well as how long it takes (this information can be given to potential respondents).

Depending on to whom and how they are circulated, questionnaires often suffer from low response rates; the highest rates tend to be achieved with internal questionnaires and those where potential respondents have a strong interest in the subject of the research. Response rates of five per cent are not atypical for postal questionnaires, and this needs to be taken into account when planning the number needed to yield a valid sample. If you make the questionnaires easy to complete and return and send out a prompt shortly before the closing date, this can improve the response. Email or online questionnaires are becoming popular and are generally quick and easy to answer, provided most potential respondents have Internet access.

Observation

Observation can cover a wide range of situations including specific instances (such as meetings, practitioner–client interactions, and performance of specific tasks), observation over given periods of time (for example, of traffic, interaction in a public place or the actions of a particular person), or longer-term processes by participant or non-participant observers (as in ethnographic studies).

You can record short-duration and specific-instance observation descriptively (or video-record for later coding and analysis) or, particularly if the same type of occurrences or interactions are expected to recur repeatedly, by means of a coding checklist you develop after a few pilot observations. Coding categories might cover, for instance, types of teacher–pupil interactions or types of vehicles and numbers of passengers. Observation records also need to consider what breadth of information needs to be captured, how unexpected categories are to be recorded, and whether the sequence and duration of events are important. These types of observations can yield both qualitative and quantitative information.

The kind of observation used in ethnographic studies (including some organizational studies) and in some types of action research projects may be less about observing specific instances, whilst these may still be relevant, than about noting down practices, occurrences and conversations over a period of time. This kind of research, often carried out alongside being an active member or temporary participant in the community or project being studied, can generate a vast quantity of notes and data that require your careful qualitative analysis and interpretation.

You often need to negotiate access with participants to perform observational research, and it raises issues of confidentiality in writing up, both at an individual level and where the inner workings of organizations are revealed.

Diaries, logs and notes

Diaries, logs and other forms of note-keeping can be grouped together as means of tracking unfolding or ongoing developments and using them for research purposes or to create an authentic narrative based on observations at the time. In practice, they can be combined with other materials such as notes of meetings and records of actions taken to provide a broad base from which to develop narrative. Diaries and logs can vary in their degree of structure from having a pre-designed structure (similar to an observation checklist), through unstructured and limited to observations, to including reflections and personal reactions. They can be kept by the (lead) researcher personally, by a group of researchers, or used as a research tool with participants who are asked to keep diaries or notes normally about something specific. Where participants are asked to keep diaries, the instructions or structures are critical in obtaining good-quality information.

Diaries and logs provide a useful source of data for analysing how a project or situation develops over time, although, like other generally unstructured material, they may require careful coding and qualitative analysis. They also require regular commitment from the researcher or participant.

Group-based methods

Most group-based methods can be considered as a form of interviewing which includes interaction between group members as well as with the researcher. The researcher also acts as a facilitator and chairperson to prompt discussion and keep the group on track. As well as discussion around key questions or themes, as with semi-structured and unstructured interviews, group sessions can allow the introduction of written material, artefacts, case studies and video or audio recordings for discussion. Capturing data from group discussions can be challenging, particularly if it is intended to identify who contributed what. Solutions include:

- video and audio recording
- having a separate scribe
- the researcher doubling up as note-taker (difficult in some contexts, successful in others)
- arranging for group members to record points on paper or computer (particularly where it is the outcome rather than the process that is important).

Open group-based methods produce different results from interviews due to the cross-fertilization (or contamination, depending on your viewpoint) of ideas that takes place, and it can be important to record the process used as well as the materials or ideas introduced by the researcher.

More structured methods can be used with groups, such as starting with questions that are answered individually (on paper or computer) before being opened to discussion. Another approach uses the Delphi technique, which aims to produce a decision about a particular issue through series of facilitator-managed cycles where initial responses are made to a question or issue, then discussed and commented on until a consensus is reached. This can lend itself to decision making in action research or soft systems projects.

Experiments

In its basic form, an experiment consists of a planned action, the results of which are recorded and analysed or reflected upon. This kind of simple experiment is widely used in small-scale action research projects and reflective practice to answer the question, 'What happens if I do *x*?' This kind of experiment works if the researcher is reasonably sure what would happen if *x* was not done, that the result is caused by *x* alone, and that it is not a singular occurrence.

In larger-scale experiments, these factors are often not known with any certainty, meaning that the experiment has to be designed to take them into account. This normally means:

- having a comparator ('control') situation or group where the action is not taken
- eliminating as far as possible any factors that could bias or confuse the results
- repeating the experiment enough times and, where relevant, with enough different variables to give reasonable confidence about the effects of the action, as opposed to those of random factors.

Experimental research involving people can involve considerable work to organize, and it can also raise ethical issues, particularly if telling people about the nature of the experiment (or even that they are part of one) risks changing their behaviour in a way that invalidates the experiment. On the other hand, experiments may identify factors that would be difficult or impossible to identify through more 'natural' forms of research.

Analysing data and information

The process of analysis is essentially about taking the captured raw data and summarizing into a form that is both accurately representative and provides meaningful information. In doing this, it is inevitable that detail will be lost and interpretations applied (whether these are formulaic interpretations employed in quantitative analysis or of the more individual type used in analysing qualitative data), so it is important to choose methods of analysis that are appropriate to the type of data and to the intended use.

The following descriptions are divided into qualitative and quantitative analysis, and focus on general principles rather than specific techniques. However, some data sets lend themselves to both forms of analysis. For instance, if you have a large number of unstructured interviews or essentially qualitative observations, emerging themes may sometimes be analysed quantitatively as well as qualitatively. Similarly, structured data collection methods often produce additional, freestyle data that are better analysed qualitatively.

Qualitative analysis

Qualitative data are generally characterized by volume and their relative lack of researcher-imposed structure. Part of its value lies in the context in which the body of data was generated, so it cannot be detached from who, when or where it was produced without losing some of its meaning. This generally means that qualitative analysis is involved and lengthy, something that needs to be planned into the project. The following is a general sequence for sorting and making sense of qualitative data, drawing on grounded theory and phenomenological research.

- Organize the body of data into a form in which it can be worked on. This may include having interviews transcribed or handwritten notes scanned on to a computer, or simply marking notes with identifiers such as participant, place and time. The main requirement for qualitative analysis is to be able to examine the body of data by theme (sometimes from more than one perspective), while still being able to examine it by participant or context. A qualitative analysis computer application can be useful, particularly if the volume of data is substantial, but data can also be manipulated in a database or word-processing package (or, for small amounts of data, a spreadsheet).
- Start to 'code' the data. Coding means identifying key categories that sum up what is being said or what has been observed; initially, relevant text can be highlighted or marked. Once a few sets of notes or transcripts have been examined, it is useful to start paraphrasing the key categories and comparing texts to identify what is being expressed in common. Coding involves striking a careful balance between comparing texts and remaining faithful to individual accounts, and also between using categories that suit your purpose and interpretation and ones that are 'native' to the accounts or observations.
- With many kinds of material – particularly interviews, long, written responses and multiple observations – there will be a point where no new categories emerge as more sets of notes or transcripts are examined. The categories are now 'saturated' and the next stage can be started.
- Identify key themes and strands within the data. These emerge from the coding and take the form of statements or theories that are grounded in the texts. Depending on your purpose, you are likely to emphasize some themes more than others; an extensive qualitative study is likely to produce a multitude of themes, some of which are not particularly relevant to the focus of your study.
- Use these themes to engage in a dialogue with the original texts: what was said or observed about theme A? How does participant X view or approach it? How does it appear in context Y? This dialogue phase enables you to re-examine the original sources and draw out the depth of the statements or observations, as well as allowing you to identify further contextual information. This will typically result in a set of notes for each participant or context organized by theme, and a set of themes organized by participant or context.

Quantitative analysis

Quantitative data may have been collected in a form ready for numerical analysis (for example, in an online questionnaire or pre-coded for analysis in SPSS or a spreadsheet), or it may first require coding or organizing into categories. Coding for quantitative analysis means numbering each category so that responses can be fed into the software in a way that allows the data to be manipulated. For small quantities of data where limited analysis is to be performed, coding and counting can be done manually, but a spreadsheet or statistics application becomes much more efficient as the quantity of data and desired complexity of analysis increases.

If you want to analyse essentially qualitative data quantitatively, you need first to identify key categories as described in the preceding qualitative section. These can then be treated quantitatively, as above.

A basic level of analysis simply examines the data set as a whole, for example providing totals and percentages for each response or observed instance, and basic measures such as the mean, median and inter-quartile range. In much quantitative research, more depth is required through cross-tabulation; that is, identifying how responses or instances relate to other responses or instances. This enables questions to be answered such as, 'How does the proportion of respondents giving a positive answer to question A vary with age, gender and job type?' Cross-tabulation is made much easier with data in an electronic format.

To draw inferences from the significance of levels of response or occurrence, or to relate survey data to overall populations, more detailed statistical analysis is needed. The type of analysis and the statistical model you use must be appropriate to the data set and the purpose of the analysis; for instance, some pre-programmed statistical analyses assume that populations are distributed normally, and will produce misleading results if the actual distribution is, for instance, hyperbolic or Mandelbrotian.

Evaluating and interpreting data and information

Between analysis and writing up, there is a further stage of evaluation and interpretation that identifies what is worth including and what its meaning is in the context of the project or study.

Evaluation assesses the value of the information for the purpose required. An evaluation of a body of analysed data will often ask whether it is relevant, valid and robust. Just because it has been collected and analysed does not mean you are obliged to present it: it needs to be relevant to the project or research, even if only confirming something that was already thought to be true or stating that the findings are inconclusive. The questions of validity and robustness could lead you to reject some results as being too unreliable or lacking in validity to be worth reporting, or to comment that they are tentative.

Interpretation is an important part of the research and reporting process, as it gives meaning to the data. It is essentially the process of attaching significance to the results and, if appropriate, theorizing from them and considering their implications. Particularly in qualitative research, interpretation starts as you code, but the more explicit interpretation that occurs afterwards brings you, the researcher, clearly into the 'frame' of the research as interpreter, expert and theorist. This interpretive aspect is often also present in quantitative studies, particularly if you present the results in the form of an argument or to inform action.

The process of interpretation involves developing a dialogue between the emerging findings, your own theories and expectations and perhaps those of your community of practice, clients or stakeholders, and existing material such as published and emergent research.

Discussion questions

1. How is the body of data relevant and significant, and to what/whom?
2. How does it compare with expectations, with existing practice, with published or other research?
3. What does it confirm, support, challenge or disprove?
4. What if any theories do you have about it?
5. What are its implications (relevant to the project and, perhaps, beyond it)?

From this, you can start to 'make sense' of the findings for writing up or as a basis for practice.

There are a few common pitfalls of interpretation for you to avoid. These include:

- reporting findings out of context to give them unsupported meanings
- assuming that the characteristics of the sample are those of the population as a whole
- assuming that findings are general when the methodology does not support this
- extrapolating to produce unsupported conclusions
- making assumptions based on false logic (such as assuming that, because 40 per cent of school leavers go to university, there is a 40 per cent chance that a particular school leaver will do so).

References

Arbnor, I. and Bjerke, B. (2009) *Methodology for Creating Business Knowledge*, 3rd edn. London: Sage.

Burrell, G. and Morgan, G. (1985) *Sociological Paradigms and Organisational Analysis*. London: Heinemann.

Checkland, P. (1999) *Soft Systems Methodology in Action*. Lewes: Wiley.

Checkland, P. and Poulter, J. (2006) *Learning for Action: A Short Definitive Account of Soft Systems Methodology and Its Use*. Lewes: Wiley.

Crotty, M.J. (1998) *The Foundations of Social Research: Meaning and Perspective in the Research Process*. London: Sage.

Grix, J. (2004) *The Foundations of Research*. London: Palgrave Macmillan.

Guba, E. and Lincoln, Y. (2000) 'Paradigmatic controversies, contradictions, and emerging confluences', in N. Denzin and Y. Lincoln (eds) *Handbook of Qualitative Research*, pp. 163–88 London: Sage.

Holliday, A. (2002) *Doing and Writing Qualitative Research*. London: Sage.

Kitchener, K. and King, P. (1981) 'Reflective judgment: concepts of justification and their relationship to age and education', *Journal of Applied Developmental Psychology* 2: 89–116.

Kuhn, T.S. (1968) *The Structure of Scientific Revolutions*. Chicago, IL: Chicago University Press.

Tornebohm, H. (1974) *Paradigm in the World of Science and the Theory of Science*. Goteborg: Goteborg University.

Znaniecki, F. (1934) *The Method of Sociology*. New York: Farrar and Rinehart.

8

Collaborative research

Key points

The relationship between researcher and researched is a central question in research, and a particular issue in work based research. The question raises a number of issues for the researcher concerning subject, object and the research process itself. Feminist research, in particular, by exploring the implications of gender for the research process has alerted us to the positioning of the researcher in the research, the danger of generalization, the importance of subjective knowledge, the relationship between the public and the private, reason and emotion, the reality of social inequality, power relationships and reflexivity. However, less attention has been paid to research and the research process from the point of view of the researcher who forms and enters collaboration with co-researchers.

Collaborative research is a common mode of enquiry at undergraduate and postgraduate level, when learners work in pairs or groups on a joint assignment or project. A thoughtful and reflexive approach to research requires you to fully recognize and report the reality, dynamism and implications of inter-researcher relationships. It is a failure of much reported research that the challenges of the research process itself are frequently glossed over in the interests of presenting a superficially coherent and orderly account of research enquiry. The reality, however, is invariably far removed and, as we shall suggest in this chapter, you must pay as much attention to the complexity and challenges of collaborative research as to the undoubted benefits.

We start by exploring what we mean by collaborative research, and then look at the benefits and limitations. We identify some of the key issues for researchers seeking to collaborate, and present a typology of collaborative research that will be helpful to researchers in locating your own research and considering future collaborations.

Collaborative research

The first distinction we must make is between research that involves collaboration between researchers, and research that involves collaboration between a researcher and those being researched. Both types of collaboration can legitimately be termed 'collaborative' and there are some common issues. However, the first type of collaboration, that between researchers, we shall describe as 'researchers collaborating' and only the second type, that which involves collaboration between researchers and researched, shall we describe as 'collaborative research'. This distinction will ease description and understanding, but the principal reason for making this distinction is to differentiate between cooperation, which we take to mean joint working on a project without necessarily having shared values and objectives, and collaboration. The latter term we understand as a more powerful term, often signifying a common or a shared values orientation and a deeper level of involvement and engagement in the process and outcomes of the research. It is this richer and, by implication, more significant model of collaborative research that has potentially significant benefits for the quality and impact of work based research. However, it may also bring a range of complexity, complication and difficulty to the process and practical organization of research on the one hand, and matters relating to ethics, power and authority on the other.

Researchers collaborating

The benefits of researchers collaborating are many, but there are pitfalls and issues stemming principally from tensions between the members of the research team themselves at a personal or professional level, or from differences of how to approach research and of the interpretation of research data. As an insider-researcher undertaking work based research projects, you will frequently organize into teams of two or more members. The advantages of this mode of organization include:

- sharing research tasks
- capitalizing on different skills and strengths in the team
- taking on a bigger project than would otherwise be possible
- enabling members to specialize in one or more aspect of the research
- utilizing established and previously successful working groups.

We will not go into detail here about the specific benefits of these advantages for work based research. We encourage our own learners to organize and group together to carry out work based research, and in the majority of cases all goes well and the outcome is enhanced as a result of the joint approach. However, it is important to be aware of the main possible pitfalls.

The primary reason that group projects fail or meet problems is when personal differences intervene and get in the way of successful team working.

Groups will often allocate different roles to each member, and it is typically when these roles are not fully accepted, are unclear or when, for whatever reason, the role is not carried out properly that problems surface. And clearly, in the case of a time-constrained academic project when each member is being individually assessed, the consequences of partial group performance are potentially serious. The best prevention is to ensure that the precise roles and responsibilities of each member are written down and clearly agreed, and that there is a system of monitoring individual performance. This way, any problem areas such as non-delivery of an aspect of the work, may be quickly identified and a remedy put in place. Groups need to trust and motivate each other, but equally must be prepared to take prompt and decisive action if one member does not pull their weight.

Gender roles and expectations can intervene in the allocation and adoption of roles and responsibilities in the group. De facto, teams tend to be all male or all female, but mixed gender teams can be a positive benefit, especially when dealing with gender-related research topics. The aim here is for members to be aware of gender as a potential issue for the team and to be open to and supportive of how this aspect is approached by the group. Teams can come across tension between the hierarchical requirements of a research project (especially when, as is usually the case, the project is being assessed) and the myth of an academic community operating in a democratic model. Whilst all members may feel that they should have an equal input into and influence on the outcome of the project, organizational requirements may lead to one member taking a lead role, or some roles being more influential than others. The question of power relationships within research teams is an important one, and the best advice is that teams should be sensitive to this aspect of their group, and seek advice from tutors and others if they feel there is an unhelpful imbalance existing or becoming apparent. The following discussion of collaborative research addresses this issue in detail. For one of the few frank (and therefore most revealing) discussions of power in research teams, you could read Colin Bell's (1977) account of the Banbury restudy.

The benefits and disbenefits of collaborative research

The primary focus of this chapter is research that involves collaboration between researcher and researched. The first issue that arises is the question of what counts as 'collaboration' and 'collaborative' when applied to work based research. In thinking about this question, you may find it helpful to remember that many practitioners of collaborative research maintain that the overriding rationale for the approach is that it is ethically constructive, in that it elicits data and analysis that are shared, multi-dimensional and grounded in participants' lived experiences. The extent to which these features lead to greater richness of data and analysis is largely dependent upon the closeness of the relationship between researcher and researched.

Take the case of a researcher–subject relationship in which you, as the researcher, share the aims and objectives of the research with the subject, and enable the subject to comment on the research process, research questions, data collected and so on. At this level, there is sharing of information and process, but it is questionable how much input and influence the subject has on you or the research itself. Now take the case of a researcher–subject relationship in which you involve the subject in decisions about the aims, objectives and research process and so on, so that the subject has influence, autonomy and agency as a participant in the research project.

The key distinction between these two cases is that in the second, fuller involvement, there is a very different ethical and power relationship between subject and researcher. It is tempting for researchers only to pay lip service to a collaborative model of research. It involves giving up some power, introducing potential for tension between different agendas, a threat to the accomplishment of the intended research objectives and, ultimately, if agreement or consensus cannot be achieved, the possibility of failure. Alongside greater risks, however, lie greater rewards. Exponents of the second, more democratic model of collaborative research, argue force-fully that transferring power to research subjects helps to ensure that data and analysis are not imposed autocratically by researchers pursuing their own agenda and prioritizing institutional, academic or private ends.

We do not want to suggest that collaborative research is necessarily complicated, complex or difficult to set up. Collaboration can arise naturally and easily, especially in circumstances where you are currently, or have recently been, a participant in the research setting. In such cases, there can be shared trust and respect between professionals or practitioners, sharing of a common language, culture and values, and a genuine commitment to enable all participants to have an authentic voice that is faithfully recorded and represented in the research report. A further benefit of this mode of research is that genuine knowledge exchange can occur in which researchers and researched contribute equally to understanding the research environment and bring different perspectives to bear in a fruitful and productive way. Given that researchers are sometimes accused of maintaining an artificial divide between the academy and the real world, collaborative research may certainly contribute to narrowing the gap and creating a positive benefit through the meeting of diverse viewpoints.

There are certain circumstances where collaborative research may be the only way in which a research project can be achieved, for example in the case of hard-to-research closed spheres and private systems. These contexts might include emergency services, prisons, health environments and research with disaffected or excluded individuals and groups. In these circumstances, formal ethical approval is usually required and you would in many cases be denied access unless a comprehensive and genuine commitment is made to fully involve gatekeepers and/or the subjects of research in determining the shape, content and direction of the research. You need to be aware, however, of a potential disbenefit: where the researcher's agenda is hijacked or undermined by this process and it becomes impossible to complete the research as planned, or at all. This can be a high-risk research environment, and the risks should be fully assessed and managed and mitigated accordingly.

There is a strong tradition of user and carer involvement in research in the field of health and in particular mental health and social work. Wallcraft et al. (2009: 144), in a discussion on employing paid service users in work based research, identify nine key principles for overcoming barriers to success and maximizing the benefits of the collaboration:

- personal commitment
- inclusion
- clear communication
- respect
- education/training
- effective hiring practices
- individualized attention
- supportive infrastructure
- additional resources and project flexibility.

If we replace 'effective hiring practices' with 'specific and agreed objectives', then we have a comprehensive and workable set of principles to guide all types of collaborative research design.

The indisputable strength of collaborative research derives from the inclusion principle – taking the widest sense of the term to embrace a shared language and conceptual framework, creating a shared space for collaborative research. As Miller (1994) argues, such a framework is created by listening to each other, sharing expectations and exploring barriers to learning within the research group.

You should be aware of particular issues relating to corporate sponsorship of research, in which the sponsoring organization or company seeks to address particular issues and problems towards its own corporate objectives. There are strong influences currently emanating from government, and mediated by higher education and research funding councils, towards encouraging and promoting models of research that engage more closely with business, commercial and private sector interests. Universities have a vested interest in engaging with this agenda to access funds to supplement hard-pressed research budgets. There are other good reasons why universities should ensure that their research leads to more effective knowledge transfer and exchange. Corporate sponsorship of research may be set to become more prevalent as governments try to find ways of limiting their education spending, and many in academia regard this trend as a lifeline to protect research teams and budgets.

However, there is no such thing as a free lunch. Corporate bodies across the private and public sectors may sponsor a piece of research carried out by the university, but in return expect a high degree of compliance in meeting their interests, objectives and desired outcomes. Sometimes such sponsorship may be in the form of matched-funded bursaries for post-graduate research studentships, and at other times such studentships may be funded fully by the external organization. The external partner will almost invariably wish to have a decisive say in the design of the research to be carried out to ensure that it meets its own corporate interests. This involvement by a corporate body can be seen as a legitimate way of ensuring that the external partner's interests are fairly represented, given their financial investment. All too often, though, the involvement is seen by the researcher on the ground as unwelcome interference. Clearly, each case is different, but it is undoubtedly the case that some external partners in research risk jeopardizing the independence and integrity of sponsored research through over-enthusiastic influence over research direction and activities. From your perspective, the only protection available is a carefully drafted research contract which specifies – and limits – the involvement of external partners, and provides for a mediation process in cases of disagreement.

The benefits of collaborative research

We would argue that the full benefits of collaborative research can only be realized when there is full participation and involvement of all parties in the whole research process, and there is a different understanding and distribution of knowledge and power from that in traditional research processes. Many of the historical debates on truth in social scientific research spanning many decades have centred on how different research traditions and paradigms have addressed the question of knowledge and understanding of the real world. Such debates continue, and have led to sharp divides between positivist and interactionist approaches to research design, methodology, data gathering and analysis, and impact hugely on how research is interpreted and utilized for policy and practice.

A participative approach becomes problematic of course when the research subjects are junior in status to the researcher and we must acknowledge that, due to the pervasive power inequalities that exist in organizations, 'power sharing' of the kind we are suggesting here may be difficult, if not impossible, to achieve in such cases. Where this is so, the researcher should at all times be open and thorough in exploring and explaining the issues of power in the research setting, so that the reader can make an informed evaluation of the data presented.

Collaborative research sits squarely within an interactionist research paradigm, in which the researcher claims that to understand the micro-dynamics of social situations, you should respect the context of research by involving the subjects of research in the whole process. In this way, subjects' own understanding and perspectives drive the research agenda and direction, not the researchers'. To be more accurate, collaborative research is seen at its most powerful under the following conditions: when the research agenda is jointly negotiated by researcher and researched, when – and this point is crucial – there is as equal a distribution of power (control over research decisions) as possible, and when the limitations to this sharing are fully explored and explained to research subjects. Subjects are not only fully informed, but are equal participants in the research process. Their authentic voice can be present in the research, not only through their reported responses, but through their contribution to the design and progress of the research project itself.

Such a model can fully meet philosophical objections to research on sensitive issues, for example social settings involving those who may be vulnerable, have low status, or are in any sense outside mainstream society. Many classic sociological studies have developed their insights precisely through following this collaborative style of research that gives higher involvement and participation to participants in the study (see, for example, Whyte's (1955) participant observation of street corner society, Hargreaves' (1967) analysis of social relations in a secondary school, and Cicourel's (1976) study of juvenile justice). Essentially, such research will lead to discourse that speaks of 'researching with', rather than 'researching on', gaining the trust of participants and emphasizing the shared nature of both the research agenda and process. A key element of this form of research is that your own stance is sublimated more than in traditional research, and a variety of perspectives – yours and your subjects' – are allowed to inform the aims, objectives and direction of the research.

Collaborative research can have a direct impact on enhancing the quality of research, particularly through incorporating practitioner perspectives. When researching work based settings, it is vital that you acknowledge the existence of different practitioner viewpoints. These differ not only between managers and managed, but also between sub-groupings and individuals who may be differentiated by gender, age, social class, length of service, status, work role, contract and so on. In addition, there may be more subtle differentiating factors that may be invisible to the external researcher, but lived out daily by participants. Collaborative research has the potential to uncover both anticipated and unanticipated dimensions of work based settings and to bring off a more faithful portrayal of underlying realities. Many seminal studies of the workplace rely heavily on inside knowledge gained through direct observation of the workplace setting, and are therefore highly reliant on employer cooperation in facilitating such access – see, for example, Taylor's (1947) classic work on time and motion, Roethlisberger and Dickson's (1939) study of human relations at work, and Trist and Bamforth's (1951) research on high-performance work systems. Note, however, that cooperation is different from collaboration; in these studies, there was minimal involvement of employers or employees in the research process. This point is developed later in the chapter.

Learners carrying out work based research are often advised to avoid projects that might encounter some of the barriers to access and ethical approval mentioned above. This advice is generally sound, given the restrictions of time and other resources at your disposal. However, where you, as a work based researcher, are researching your own workplace, access can sometimes be easier to negotiate even where the work setting is a sensitive one. The participant or practitioner work based researcher often has insight into any potential research problems and access to strategic context that suggests certain lines of research the organization may find beneficial. That said, some work based environments, for example hospitals, care homes, prisons, schools, government offices and certain sensitive private sector organizations, can present you with insurmountable obstacles to access unless a collaborative approach is negotiated. In health environments, for example, research proposals typically have to pass severe ethical scrutiny by bodies set up for this purpose before the research can proceed. Similar requirements are in place in all universities where research is originated and the procedures are designed to protect the subjects of research. Presenting a collaborative research model certainly does not guarantee that ethical approval is given, nor that the relevant managers will authorize the level of access that the research may require. A research proposition that privileges practitioners' and/or participants' perspectives is, however, more likely to be successfully negotiated than one that does not incorporate a collaborative approach.

Most work based learning projects stem from courses offered by a university. One of the reasons for the significant growth in work based learning and research in universities is that one of their purposes is to promote knowledge transfer with public and private sector organizations. Collaborative work based research represents a highly effective way of achieving knowledge transfer. Our definition of collaborative research, involving a common or shared values orientation and a deeper level of involvement and engagement in the process and outcomes of the research, gets to the heart of knowledge transfer.

Recent years have seen higher levels of engagement between universities and the business sector and much of the progress in this area has been through projects that are jointly developed and where there is a high level of collaboration between academic and commercial interests. In this context, whether the joint projects are short or long term, a collaborative research model is invariably a pre-requisite to effective knowledge transfer. This must be two-way to be effective, hence many people prefer the term 'knowledge exchange' to describe the interaction. The benefits for universities and public and private sector organizations include breaking down the barriers between academy and practice, and avoidance of over-theoretical research. This increases the likelihood of practical application and implementation where practitioners gain insight from researchers and vice versa.

A summary of the benefits of collaborative research

Collaborative research:

- avoids inappropriately imposing researchers' perspectives onto subjects
- allows a variety of perspectives on a common research issue, problem or question
- is informed by practitioner perspectives and thus improves the quality of research
- accesses hard-to-research closed spheres and private systems
- promotes knowledge exchange, leading to change, innovation and growth
- avoids over-theoretical research, increasing likelihood of practical application and implementation
- breaks down barriers between academy and practice
- encourages practitioners to gain insight from researchers and vice versa
- directly addresses ethical issues of consent, power and exploitation that are problematic for non-collaborative work based research
- respects the context of the research
- provides the authentic voice of participants
- is democratic.

The disbenefits of collaborative research

There are a number of drawbacks to collaborative research which need to be carefully weighed against the benefits outlined above. Perhaps the most important, from the point of view of you as an insider-researcher, is that collaborative research is high maintenance and time-intensive. A sole researcher who plans, designs and carries out their own research project is, in the main, reliant only on themselves for the timely achievement of the project. Careful planning can minimize disturbance to the planned schedule of tasks. However, involving other practitioners in the design and accomplishment of the research immediately adds several layers of complication and complexity to the research process, which can impact negatively on the timing, direction and the very accomplishment of the research project. The maintenance of good personal relationships between members of research teams, especially when teams are spread across two or more organizational cultures, is both challenging and time-consuming. For these reasons, we have to treat collaborative research as high risk and high reward.

We have noted above the danger that sponsorship of research can, in varying degrees, influence, distort or hijack the research agenda. This is a serious matter for researchers and those who sponsor research. It is vital that protection is afforded to both parties to do everything possible to ensure that different research aims can be assimilated and accommodated. A research contract is always needed to set out the responsibilities, obligations, objectives and liabilities of all parties to the research, including a process for mediation in the event of disagreement. Underlying this document is the need for you to ensure, wherever possible, that there is a clear understanding of the relevant issues on all sides and that a basis of trust is established to allow open and frank discussion of potential pitfalls and possible solutions.

If this sounds a tricky business, that's because it is. Achieving a balance of interests can involve delicate negotiation around issues of power, politics, personalities, funding, research careers and corporate influence – a heady mixture under any circumstances! Some examples of potential areas of disagreement in research that is sponsored may be helpful.

Example 1

Researchers are invariably under pressure to publish their research to meet the need of their employing university to achieve positive results in national research assessment exercises. Sponsors often have different publication needs, for example for internal dissemination and corporate conferences, which may not coincide with the researcher's typically longer timescale. For example, this may be three to six years for a doctoral programme.

Example 2

Sponsors may be keen to identify the practical implications of research involving their organization, and to develop further aspects of these. Researchers may need to focus more specifically on theoretical frameworks and the constructs underlying practice. These two objectives may be complementary, but, equally, have the potential to be in tension and to pull the researcher in different directions.

Example 3

Researchers carrying out research towards a university qualification need to take on board the views of their director of studies and/or supervisors in relation to the progress and direction of their research. The agendas of these advisers may be quite different from the agenda of corporate managers and/or mentors. And the larger the team(s) involved in shaping the research, the greater number of different viewpoints there can be.

One of the disbenefits of collaborative research is shared with all forms of applied research and arises from prevailing currents of academic elitism. This is the notion that applied research has lower status than traditional research where the research remains external – in many senses of that word – to the research site and subjects. This view has its origins in research paradigms that lay claim to a discourse populated by terms such as theoretical, scientific, objective, pure and independent. By contrast, applied research, embracing collaborative research as the ultimate exemplar of the approach, is described using terms like practical, social, subjective, applied and interactive. In certain university subject disciplines and research environments, these views are still to be found and there is a danger that the researcher who carries out applied and/or collaborative research may find their career adversely affected vis-à-vis colleagues who pursue more 'acceptable' research avenues.

A summary of the disbenefits of collaborative research

Collaborative research can:

- be high maintenance and time-intensive
- mean that corporate funding hijacks the research agenda
- involve an inappropriate balance of practical and theoretical aspects
- put strain on personal relationships
- lead to pressure on you, as the researcher, to publish and the timing may not suit the organization's timescale
- mean that there is inequality due to status/level of team
- undermine your 'objectivity'
- mean that having large teams increases the range of vested interests
- mean that your career as an academic may be blemished (there is a low status of applied research in some disciplines)
- lead to difficulty in maintaining the relationship with the host organization.

A typology of collaborative research – the intervention continuum

Based on this account of the collaborative research approaches available to the work based researcher and their benefits and disadvantages, it is now possible to offer a tentative typology of collaborative research (see Figure 8.1). This typology is constructed along a continuum of intervention with low intervention described as 'detached' research, which has little or no involvement of the subjects of research and whose sole output is research publication with little or no perceived benefits for the research site organization. At the other extreme of the continuum, action research requires high involvement by subjects and carries a key objective of organizational change.

Researchers and organizations may use this typology to assess the relative and potential utility of proposed research to the organization. It is therefore a tool that can assist researchers in persuading organizational managers to allow high levels of access and involvement of their staff in return for the greatest benefit of research to the organization.

Research that involves little or no involvement of research subjects is here termed 'detached'. The research involves no collaboration in the sense used in this chapter, that is, signifying a common or shared values orientation and a deeper level of involvement and engagement in the process and outcomes of the research. The primary research output is publication of the researcher's work as a conference paper, in a refereed journal or perhaps a book. There is no direct benefit to the organization being studied.

'Observational' research has a long tradition, particularly in social scientific research, involving varying degrees of 'participant observation'. Although this mode of research involves a high degree of involvement on

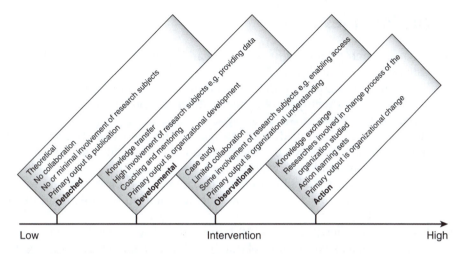

Figure 8.1   A typology of collaborative research – the intervention continuum

the part of the researcher in the research setting, which is required in order to gain access to the subjects and win the confidence of gatekeepers and subjects of research, there is limited collaboration as such. At the same time, the skilful researcher may generate useful organizational insights. These insights may themselves generate further research which may involve higher levels of collaboration.

'Developmental' research involves a much higher level of collaboration with research subjects; the case study is the primary example of this research mode. The research may involve specific continuing professional and personal development tools such as coaching and mentoring, and the primary aim of this mode of research is organizational development. Developmental research is frequently carried out by consultants and is therefore often commissioned by organizations that perceive they have a skills or knowledge gap to fill. University knowledge transfer programmes are frequently directed to this kind of organizational need.

The highest level of collaboration in research is exemplified by our fourth mode of research, – 'action' research. Like participant observation and case study, this has a strong research tradition, especially in the fields of education and health. The impetus for action research often originates in the organization itself, and typically involves and requires a high level of commitment from organizational managers to the research project. Organizational change and improvement is at the heart of action research and is also the key idea in the 'action research cycle' in which changes brought about by action research are themselves studied and evaluated through further research. The term 'knowledge exchange' is highly appropriate for this mode of research, since it gives equal weight to the knowledge brought by both the researcher and the subject of research into the frame of enquiry.

Discussion questions

1. What research topics might be particularly appropriate for researchers to collaborate in investigating?
2. How might some of the pitfalls of team working be overcome?
3. What might be the impact of gender differences and/or status in a team of researchers?
4. How close and developed does the relationship between researcher and researched need to be to count as collaborative? To what extent is a single 'voice' desirable and achievable?
5. Is involvement of the subject of the research in decisions about research aims, objectives, processes and outcomes a condition for collaboration? If so, to what extent?
6. How can the different interests of individuals who collaborate in a research project be balanced? (Think about the above examples of pressures to publish, the tension between focusing on theoretical and practical aspects, and the different agendas of university and outside work environments.)
7. What can be done to minimize the disbenefits of collaborative research?
8. Is applied research adversely affected by academic elitism?
9. Are there circumstances where applied research may be viewed more favourably?
10. Think of examples of detached, observational, developmental and action research.
11. Which of these best lend themselves to a university work based research project?
12. Which model(s) would be most attractive to an employer, and why?

References

Bell, C. (1977) 'Reflections on the Banbury restudy', in C. Bell and H. Newby (eds) pp. 47–62 *Doing Sociological Research*, London: George Allen & Unwin.

Cicourel, A. (1976) *The Social Organization of Juvenile Justice*. London: Heinemann.

Hargreaves, D. (1967) *Social Relations in a Secondary School*. London: Routledge & Kegan Paul.

Miller, W. (1994). 'Common space: creating a collaborative research conversation', in B. Crabtree, M. Miller, R. Addison, V. Gilchrist and A. Kuzel (eds) *Exploring Collaborative Research in Primary Care*, London: Sage.

Roethlisberger, F. and Dickson, W. (1939) *Management and the Worker*. Cambridge, MA: Harvard University Press.

Taylor, F. (1947). *Scientific Management*. New York: Harper & Row.

Trist, E. and Bamforth, W. (1951) 'Some social and psychological consequences of the longwall method of coal-getting', *Human Relations* 4: 3–38.

Wallcraft, J., Schrank, B. and Amering, M. (2009) *Handbook of Service User Involvement in Mental Health Research*. Chichester: Wiley-Blackwell.

Whyte, W. (1955) *Street Corner Society*, 2nd edn. Chicago, IL: University of Chicago Press.

A reflection on professional practice

Key points

This chapter considers what it means to reflect on professional practice. The connection between reflective practice and action research is made explicit, as is the distinction between reflection and reflexivity. A step-by-step guide to reflective practice is given which explains the key stages in moving from everyday observation to theorization.

Understanding the workplace

To understand work based research, it is necessary to understand the workplace. This will require you to be aware of and alert to the subtleties of the work setting. Not only this, but you will need an appreciation of the history, environment and culture of the workplace. The history will indicate how the industry arrived where it is; the dominant influences, forces, trends and values that have shaped the industry; and how it has responded (or not) to modernization, globalization and changes in the economic and social context in which the industry operates. The environment will indicate its relationship with other parts of the industry and with other industries; how successful it is in comparison with others; what its distinguishing features and unique selling points (USPs) are; and to what extent it has been influenced and reshaped by inter-professional agendas, workforce organization and re-organization, downsizing, mergers and takeovers. The culture will indicate a multiplicity of influences, the principal being the inter-personal, the psychological, the social and the political.

As well as history, environment and culture, we have to take into account the influence of the individual, the personal and the work based researcher.

This introduces the idea of 'agency', that is, the effect and impact of the individual person operating in the present. You will bring your own biography, history, experience and personality into the work setting. Thus, we can see that to understand work based research, we need to have a grasp of factors external to the organization, factors internal to the organization, and factors relating to you, the work based researcher.

It is good practice to acknowledge these influences, and in particular to acknowledge the influence that you, as a researcher, have on the work setting. This is the idea of reflexivity, or self-awareness. It means that you need to be sensitive to influences on you from outside the organization – your gender, ethnicity, social class, relationships and responsibilities, your own biography and psychology. These frame the lens through which you view the world, and observe and interact with colleagues and others in organizations. This awareness about the interaction between yourself and others – reflexivity – is at the heart of good qualitative research, and it is worthwhile reflecting upon the implications of this for your own work based research project. This chapter will help you to discover how, as an insider-researcher, you can make an original and worthwhile contribution to the literature in your chosen field using a reflective practice approach that will help you to write convincingly in a way that emerges from, but at the same time transcends, the work setting.

Practitioners, professionals and politics

Many work based research settings are populated by professionals who are regulated and influenced in their professional lives by sets of professional codes and practices. The term 'practitioner' has developed as a kind of quasi-professional concept, suggesting a mode of working that is characterized by thoughtful and reflexive action. For the work based researcher, how professionals and practitioners regard themselves and their work situation is a vital and rich source of data. A number of studies (for example Elliott, 1996, 1998) have found that practitioners and professionals, in the face of growing managerialism, the introduction of narrow and prescriptive occupational standards and the demands made by policy shifts towards increased accountability, find it necessary to affirm the territory of *their* expertise. This is frequently located in their subject or vocational background. Reflective practice is an enabling practice that makes such an approach possible.

The starting point of a reflective practitioner approach to work based practice and work based research is the recognition that, in order to be meaningful for the practitioner, conceptualizations of work should be grounded in practitioners' own understandings and experience of their working practices. It should equally reflect the range of these practices as well as their epistemological and ethical basis. It should reflect a phenomenological perspective towards organizations which recognizes the centrality of understanding individuals' orientations (Maslow, 1954) and that 'organisations are to be understood in terms of people's beliefs about their behaviour within them' (Greenfield, 1975: 83). It should also be capable of supporting theoretical and political opposition to attempts to redefine practitioners' shared values. Reflective practice requires a micro-political perspective that recognizes the different interests, biographies, careers, priorities, subjects, status and orientations of practitioners. It requires a moral and values orientation, since it is only through the 'grounding of our actions in our values that we can recognize the nature of the competing rationalities we face and find means of coping with them, whether as managers or those being managed' (Bennett et al., 1992: 15). It requires a political stance since it is centrally concerned with the development of a critical consciousness to a level where individuals can achieve a sufficient degree of social and political awareness to understand contradictions within society and work to transform it – what Freire (1972: 16) has termed 'conscientisation'.

The idea of reflective practice can be demonstrated to be at the centre of British philosophical discourse, from the seventeenth-century philosopher Locke's (1690) belief that appropriate knowledge and judgement are vital to well-informed rather than ill-informed understanding, to Mill's (1843) concern with the centrality of inferential thinking to the exercise of good judgement. John Dewey (1933) was the first to formally apply the idea to a work context (education). His definition of reflective thought is predicated upon its status as a conscious, voluntary and purposeful activity. Dewey believed that reflective thinking was an artistic rather than scientific endeavour which represented the ideal human mental state (1933: 29, 287–88) and acted as an antidote to a restrictive preoccupation with 'those things that are immediately connected with what we want to do and get at the moment' (Dewey, 1929: 159). In this respect, and to the extent that he understood human growth to be dependent upon both experience *and* reflection, Dewey's work was highly prescient of the reflective practice movement.

Laurence Stenhouse (1979) recognized the key role of reflective thinking for practitioners, arguing that what is learnt from comparative studies can 'tutor our judgement' (1979: 6). Donald Schön (1983) develops Dewey's notion of the essential artistry involved in the intellectual process of reflecting on action. It is the *creative* dimension of reflective practice which enables practitioners to deal reflectively with inconsistent or impractical demands, and which thus makes it such a powerful framework for understanding action in non-rational, unpredictable organizations.

A significant advantage of the notion of the reflective practitioner is that it provides a conceptual framework within which the complexities, tensions and contradictions of work can be explored, and at the same time a reference point against which the intrinsic value of practice can be judged. The potential for practitioners to inform and influence policy, and the process by which they make considered responses to political, cultural and technological change and devise considered strategies to contain or exploit both intended and unintended consequences, are also key issues which are given prominence within a reflective practice model.

In addition to the benefits at the level of practice, there are significant gains at the level of theory to a reflective practitioner model. Constructing reflective practice as an epistemology rather than a methodology frees it from the theoretical straitjacket of any single research tradition and opens up the possibility of exploring practice from a variety of perspectives. One major gain of this is that it achieves a defensible conception of theory as 'critical and systematic reflection on practice' (Pring, 1978). Another major advantage of this approach is that it can link practice with an important and influential body of literature, providing a theoretical and conceptual orientation which has the capacity to inform, improve and, perhaps most important at the present time, value practitioners' own reflective practice against the impositions of market-based policies at national and institutional level. Reflective practice embodies an approach to research that is distinct and well documented across a number of disciplines. It is particularly suitable for the work based researcher since its focus is the work based practice of the professional or practitioner. It is an approach that is particularly popular in the disciplines of education and health, however it is also well suited to interdisciplinary studies, and has been successfully applied in many other fields of study as varied as engineering design (Valkenburg and Dorst, 1998), social work (Yelloly and Henkel, 1995), management (Smith, 2001) and policing (Matthews and Pitts, 2001).

Probably the greatest exponent of reflective practice was Donald Schön, who described the process of thoughtfully considering one's own experiences in applying knowledge to practice while being coached by professionals in the discipline (Schön, 1983, 1987). In other words, it is the ability to think about what you are doing whilst you are doing it. This is understood as a key characteristic of professionals which enables them to apply experience to new settings and to make use of tacit knowledge, which is knowledge derived from practical experience and reflection. Schön understood reflective practice as a planned, conscious, purposeful and documented approach to research. In this, it is distinct from simple reflection or thoughtful action, but such activities may lead a practitioner professional to adopt reflective practice as a research approach.

In developing his ideas on reflective practice, Schön drew on his earlier work with Argyris on professional effectiveness in which the model of reflective practice was developed as a social process (Argyris and Schön, 1974). Reflective practice, whilst it produces a personal narrative account of the development of professional practice knowledge, needs to be given validity by reflexivity towards the methods and analytic processes of practice knowledge production. This approach to reflective practice can be seen in social science researchers' accounts of auto-ethnography, and is built into the model developed by Argyris and Schön. Knowledge generation and production within practice for particular audiences require processes of knowledge use, change and evaluation of practice outcomes from professional actions to be accessible as sources of data that can be evaluated by the reader and user of research.

One of the most useful aspects of reflective practice for the work based researcher is the notion of reflection-in-action:

> *Reflection-in-action* describes the process of working with, noticing and intervening to interpret events and the effects of one's interventions. For much of the time these factors are invisible and unconscious and, as Schön eloquently points out, they are part of the artistry of effective practice. However, in developing expertise of any kind it can often be helpful to become more deliberate and conscious of the process and aware of the decisions being made by others and ourselves. It is through exposing these decisions to scrutiny that the assumptions behind them can be identified and a conscious decision taken to act from a new perspective. (Boud, 2001: 12)

For the work based researcher, then, reflection-in-action is a powerful tool for uncovering otherwise hidden processes, decision paths and power relations in the workplace. It helps the researcher move beyond mere description to analysis. It could be argued that, if learning and change are core aspects of successful businesses, reflective practice becomes a core strategic tool for managers and executives in organizations of all types. Moreover, in everyday life, it could be further argued that the increasingly common practice of 'blogging' is a modern expression of reflective practice, albeit adapted for the platform of twenty-first century technology.

Reflective practice and ethnography

Ethnography has become a popular research approach in education, health and other fields of social science (see, for example, Barton, 2008). However, it has its origin in anthropology, where it is used to describe 'a picture of the way of life of some interacting human group' (Wolcott, 1975: 112). Both reflective practice and ethnography are strongly represented within the wider field of qualitative research approaches. There are very close connections between the two, and many would argue that reflective practice is ethnography in action:

> [Ethnography] is concerned with what people are, how they behave, how they interact together. It aims to uncover their beliefs, values, perspectives, motivations, and how all these things develop or change over time or from situation to situation. It tries to do all this from *within* the group, and from within the perspectives of the group's members ... Ethnographers thus try to rid themselves of any presuppositions they might have about the situation under study. They go into the 'field' to 'observe' things as they happen in their natural setting, frequently 'participating' themselves in the ongoing action as members of the organisation or group. (Woods, 1986: 4–5)

It is the twin aspects of uncovering a multi-layered reality from the subject's point of view and with the researcher participating in the organization that connects both ethnography and reflective practice so closely with both each other and with work based research. Observational research carried out by a participant is a very common form of enquiry in the social sciences, and is often referred to by the term 'participant observation'. All these terms are closely related and indeed overlap with each other, which should be reassuring for the work based researcher who will have a well-established body of research methods literature to draw upon in designing and carrying out work based research.

Theory building and conceptual frameworks

Reflective practice is an invaluable approach to thinking about theory building and conceptual frameworks. Many learners find theory building the hardest aspect of work based research to grasp. However, theories are simply models – ways of thinking about or categorizing knowledge about the world. A first step is to create a conceptual framework by narrowing ideas to some initial general constructs. Miles and Huberman amusingly call these concepts 'bins':

> Theory building relies on a few general constructs that subsume a mountain of particulars. Terms such as 'stress' or 'role conflict' are typically labels we put on bins containing a lot of discrete events and behaviours. When we assign a label to a bin, we may or may not know how all the contents of the bin fit together, or how this bin relates to another. But any researcher, no matter how inductive in approach, knows which bin to start with and what their general contents are likely to be. Bins come from theory and experience and (often) from the general objectives of the study envisioned. Laying out those bins, giving each a descriptive or inferential name, and getting some clarity about their interrelationships is what a conceptual framework is all about. (Miles and Huberman, 1994: 18)

You will sometimes see such general constructs referred to as 'categories'. Researchers use categories as one of their core tools for organizing, sorting and labelling the data gathered during the research process.

A good example of a data category is 'quality assurance'. Other examples are 'power', 'management', 'satisficing' (that is, doing just enough to comply but without heart or commitment) and 'motivation'. The characteristics of categories are that they are relevant to the research setting and to the problem under investigation; describe in a general way the individual components (events, actions and behaviours); bring together components in a purposeful way; and ascribe a generic meaning to otherwise isolated events or behaviours. They are normally recognizable in the relevant literature, although cutting-edge research may well develop new categories that go beyond existing taxonomies.

Codes and categories

The ability to carry out high-quality work based research relies on the process of organizing reflection-on-action into coherent data that can be communicated, understood, analysed, and related to other data. It is to the question of how to go about this process of organizing reflection that we now turn. To do this, we can think about reflection as a number of stages:

- observation
- experience
- purpose
- reflection-on-action
- coding
- categorization
- analysis
- comparison
- theorization.

We now have a working model of reflective practice, a model that takes us through the process of translating observations in the workplace into theory making. There are some points to note before we look at the model in detail. First, the model is a cycle because, having theorized to the end, we can continue to make further observations, reflect more on our own and others' experience, re-state our purpose and so on. Second, like any model, it is to be used, changed and made personal. There is no right and wrong model; they are all tools to use and adapt. Third, also like any model, it is an over-simplification of the real world. All social settings, workplaces included, are complex environments and our personal interaction and experience in them is also complex and multi-faceted. A model is merely a guide for thinking about the extremely complex process of capturing social reality for the purposes of a research project. You should acknowledge this clearly in your writing or run the risk of naive over-simplification.

Observation

Quite simply, observation is looking, reading, listening and being aware of your surroundings. It is noting what is interesting, strange, seemingly important or significant, amusing, shocking or telling. Many researchers find it helpful to use a workbook or a log to note their observations. Please note that at this point your observations will be relatively unstructured and disorganized – so much the better. It is tempting to focus on a specific line of research enquiry early in the project, but much better to let your obser-vations freewheel, as it were, to allow you fully to absorb the cultures, sub-cultures, mores, customs and power relationships of the workplace. Do this for a couple of days and you will have a kaleidoscope of observations that will be a rich source of ideas for possible research enquiry.

Experience

There is, it is said, no substitute for experience. This is true in research and especially for reflective practice. If you are an experienced professional or practitioner, you will have amassed a wealth of experience and understanding about your workplace which will provide a rich vein of topics for future enquiry. This also has its disadvantages, in particular the danger that you have become over-familiar with your work setting so, for example, fail to recognize the subtleties of power relationships in operation, or mis-read the dynamics of your own interrelationships with those senior and junior to you. However, one of the more powerful aspects of reflective practice is that it can help you to objectify your subjective experience through sensitizing you to your environment. This is what anthropologists describe as creating a 'strangeness' between yourself and the research subjects.

Purpose

It will be necessary to direct or connect your observational and experiential knowledge to a purpose. In your case, the purpose is to generate data for a work based research project, so this task must inform and direct your effort. Using your experiential knowledge and prior thinking about your work based studies in general, and about the project in particular, you will be juggling a range of potential issues and subjects. Just as the model as a whole is cyclical rather than linear, we have noted, so is this aspect of reflection. There will be interaction between purpose, observation and experience, and it is their frequent exchanges that will nudge you towards a shortlist of topics. Sometimes this process can seem like a whirlwind of confusing ideas, thoughts and blind alleys. 'Sleeping on it' is sometimes good advice. Some people find it helpful to write down some possible topics at this stage, while others prefer to approach this task with friends or fellow learners, and talk through potential possibilities and opportunities.

Reflection-on-action

Schön makes a distinction between 'reflection-in-action' and 'reflection-on-action'. The former is sometimes referred to as 'thinking on our feet', and refers to the ability – often associated with professionals – to draw on experience, understanding and judgement in order to deal with new and changing circumstances. The idea of reflection-in-action nicely encapsulates Schön's epistemology of practice which rejects technical–rational positivist explanations of how practitioners manage change in favour of an epistemology of practice in which the knowledge inherent in practice can be understood as artful doing. In encountering new situations, we draw on comparable memories and experiences to construct a frame or framework that guides our present actions and responses. Reflection-on-action describes the process of reflecting on experience after the event, drawing out lessons, implications and understandings that will inform future action.

Coding

Coding is the technical term for a descriptive label used to name observations, events and behaviours. An example is 'formal quality procedure'. Others might be 'quality in work conversations', 'customer quality concerns', 'management of quality', 'confusion about quality' and so on. Note that these codes *could* subsequently be grouped together under a single category of 'quality assurance'. However, it is best to group into categories later in the research process rather than sooner. The reason is that some codes may go into more than one category. For example, 'quality management' would obviously fit into a category of 'quality assurance' but, equally, obviously, would also fit into a category of 'management'. Equally, and perhaps confusingly, you may need to convert some codes into categories (see next paragraph)!

Categorization

Categories, as we have already noted, are constructs or 'bins' into which discrete events, actions and behaviours are placed for later analysis. Categories are necessarily broader and more general than codes, so 'winking' would be a code, whilst 'non-verbal communication' would be a category. But, as we have noted above, you may need to convert codes into categories. To take a trivial example, having decided that 'winking' is a code, you may come across distinct types of winking that signify different meanings, for example sexual, knowing, collusion, twitch and so on, that might justify elevating 'winking' from code to category. Categories map and differentiate the topic of the study. Often, categories can themselves be grouped into super-categories. For example, 'quality assurance', 'human resources', 'finance' and 'strategy' might all be grouped into a super-category called 'management'. Categories are creative constructs, and can help and inform the reflective process, in particular in thinking about relationships between events, actions and behaviours.

Analysis

Given a clear purpose for the work based project, and data organized into codes, categories and possibly super-categories, analysis is simply the description of relationships between the themes (categories) you have discovered. Analysis is critical, so it goes beyond description. This means it is essential to draw out implications and inferences from your data, exploring relationships, for example, between quality documents and quality in practice, and drafting emerging conclusions and implications which are further developed later in the study. Analysis is thoughtful and creative, so you have to link your themes to those in the literature, making judgements about the strength of evidence you have uncovered for particular trends and comparing this with what other researchers have found. It is well worth looking at the assessment criteria for your project, which will refer to analysis in some detail, as this is what differentiates high-quality work from the rest. At Queen's University Belfast, for example, a Masters level dissertation will achieve an A grade (70 per cent or above) only if it demonstrates:

- high-level analysis
- synthesis and evaluation of literature and topics/issues
- an evaluative approach evident in internal consistency of arguments and external criteria
- evidence of capacity to apply learning to this and other areas of experience
- flair
- originality and insight
- clear evidence of a high level of understanding and skill in undertaking and reporting a research process.

(Queen's University Belfast, 2007)

Comparison

Notice that in the assessment criteria above, reference is made to 'synthesis', 'evaluation' and 'other areas of experience'. This demonstrates the importance of comparison. You will need to locate your research findings and analysis in the context of other work based research. However, this is something that you will do early on in the research process at the point when you are formulating your topic. Looking at relevant literature is a good way of identifying a good topic and will help to ensure that your own study is relevant, topical and connected to other literature in the field. Another important comparison is with the sector or profession in which you work. Professions in particular rely on commonly accepted or tacit knowledge and understanding about the way the profession is followed and how professionals conduct themselves, communicated through training, professional development, common working practices and professional ethics and codes of conduct. Your research may confirm, question or undermine some or all of these forms of knowledge and customary practice, and you will need to be prepared to challenge accepted knowledge in an appropriate and scholarly way. This aspect is developed in more detail in Chapter 4.

Theorization

Theorization, or theorizing, is a high-sounding term for what is quite a straightforward process. As noted at the beginning of this chapter, theories are simply models – ways of thinking about or categorizing knowledge about the world. By following the steps above (from 'observation' through to 'theorization'), you will have completed the essential process of theorizing and developed generalized categories that are connected by purpose and which illuminate one or more aspects of work based practice. The authors of this book strongly believe that learners should become more confident in engaging with theory discussion, and we encourage the notion of 'theory-in-use' developed by Donald Schön. Theory-in-use is that implicit in what we do as practitioners. Theory that we use to describe our actions to others can be described as 'espoused theory'. Theory-making makes strong use of comparison, connecting with existing theory, and seeing what is confirmed and what seems not to fit our own case. This is why the methodical and careful approach to coding and categorizing described above will pay off in terms of providing the basic ingredients for theory building.

Dilemmas for the reflective practitioner

Elliott (1991), writing in the context of action research for educational change, identified a number of dilemmas for reflective practitioners which we have generalized to all work based research settings. In each case, we have drawn on Elliott's analysis in suggesting ways the dilemma might be resolved.

Encouraging others to critique one's professional practice

Professional status carries with it notions of autonomy, high status, independence and personal expertise, all of which, in the minds of some, can be undermined by questioning and critique. Your success in encouraging others to question your own practice will depend on how successfully you can establish a climate of critical openness and respect for professional expertise that is not predicated on preciousness, vanity or aloofness. Setting clear boundaries to questioning is often helpful, for example disallowing or limiting references to other professionals. Always let colleagues know what you are doing and why, to help to create a supportive environment for insider research in the organization.

Gathering data

Some data may be difficult to gather. Information may be confidential, sensitive or only available to certain grades of employee. Insider-researchers often have to be patient, avoid taking pre-emptive or presumptuous action and, where possible, seek permission from a sympathetic authority.

Sharing data with professional peers both inside and outside the organization

Sharing data promotes a reflective conversation and is at the heart of transforming any professional culture. However, sharing data has the potential to bring latent conflict into the open where problem areas of practice become exposed which can give rise to 'finger pointing'. As an insider-researcher, you can agree to give those who provide data their say on what is shared, but you need to recognize that this accedes to traditional structures and spheres of authority which are often in tension with more democratic notions of reflective practice and action research. As an insider-researcher, you will often find yourself having to resolve real dilemmas of what to divulge and having to balance organizational interests with those of the research itself, and indeed of your continued access to the workplace.

Blurring the practitioner-researcher role

It is a particular characteristic of qualitative research that some blurring of roles may occur. As an employee, you will have access to data that are essentially in the private domain and restricted to the company or organization in which you work. As a researcher, you will be drawn further into the public domain, and it is the tension between the private and the public that can create dilemmas in selecting and sharing data. The more data is depersonalized and de-contextualized, the more it resolves the dilemma of the private and the public but becomes less valuable. Therefore, you must give considerable thought to what data can be made public and who you should seek to gain permission. No two cases are the same and such judgements have to be made and re-made for every single work based research project.

A reluctance to produce case studies of researchers' own reflective practices

There is an ongoing debate amongst researchers about the wider significance of reflective practice, often giving rise to concern about the extent to which findings can be generalized. This is a controversial debate which polarizes opinion, however a number of writers have noted the powerful potential for small-scale research, case studies and reflective practice to:

- tutor our judgement (Stenhouse, 1979)
- highlight internal contradictions in policy formulation and implementation (Finch, 1988)
- provide working recipes for an understanding of the abstract properties of social life (Rock, 1979)
- give a detailed understanding of the local context in which innovations are being attempted (Crossley and Vulliamy, 1984)
- tap the quiddity, the uniqueness of particular cultures, contexts and personalities (Hurst, 1987)
- be a powerful management tool that is highly sensitive to the perspectives of those directly affected by policies and procedures (Elliott, 1996)
- connect research with the everyday world through the use of fuzzy generalization (Bassey, 1998).

Each of these dilemmas, if left unresolved, has the potential to thwart even the most experienced work based researcher. In general, careful thought, planning, discussion with your supervisor and consultation with appropriate colleagues and managers in the workplace should point to ways of resolving most tensions you come across. However, you should guard against easy solutions that constrain professionalism and legitimate authority, privacy and territoriality. Helen Simons has powerfully argued the case for a distinctive methodology of insider-research/evaluation which rests 'upon the possibility of dismantling the value structure of privacy, territory and hierarchy, and substituting the values of openness, shared critical responsibility and rational autonomy' (Simons, 1985).

Discussion questions

1. Consider some benefits and disadvantages of coding research data. How might the disadvantages be overcome?
2. How might 'blogging' be used in an insider-research study as a tool for reflective practice?
3. Thinking about an organization you are familiar with, which of the dilemmas for the reflective practitioner seem most problematic, and how might they be overcome?

References

Argyris, C. and Schön, D. (1974) *Theory in Practice: Increasing Professional Effectiveness*. San Francisco, CA: Jossey-Bass.

Barton, T. (2008) 'Understanding practitioner ethnography', *Nurse Researcher* 15(2): 7–18.

Bassey, M. (1980) Fuzzy Generalisation: An Approach to Building Educational Theory. Paper presented to British Educational Research Association annual conference, 27 August, Queen's University Belfast.

Bennett, N., Crawford, M.and Riches, C. (eds) (1992) *Managing Change in Education*. London: Paul Chapman Publishing/Open University Press.

Boud, D. (2001) 'Using journal writing to enhance reflective practice', in L.M. English and M.A. Gillen (eds) *New Directions in Adult and Continuing Education* 90: 9–18.

Crossley, M. and Vulliamy, G. (1984) 'Case study research methods and comparative education', *Comparative Education* 20(2): 193–207.

Dewey, J. (1933) *How we Think: A Restatement of the Relation of Reflective Thinking to the Educative Process*, rev. edn. Boston, MA: D.C. Heath & Co.

Dewey, J. [1929] (1970) *The sources of a Science of Education*, reproduced in M. Skilbeck (ed.) *John Dewey*, London: Collier Macmillan.

Elliott, G. (1996) *Crisis and Change in Vocational Education and Training*. London: Jessica Kingsley.

Elliott, G. (1998) 'Teaching in post-compulsory education: profession, occupation or reflective practice?', *Teachers and Teaching* 4(1): 161–75, Reprinted in *Teachers and Trainers: Theories of Action*, Deakin University Faculty of Education Reader, (1999).

Elliott, J. (1991) 'A model of professionalism and its implications for teacher education', *British Educational Research Journal* 17(4): 309–18.

Finch, J. (1988) 'Ethnography and public policy', in A. Pollard, J. Purvis and G. Walford (eds) *Education, Training and the New Vocationalism*, pp. 185–200 Milton Keynes: Open University Press.

Freire, P. (1972) *Pedagogy of the Oppressed* (trans. Myra Bergman Rumos). Harmondsworth: Penguin.

Greenfield, T. (1975) 'A theory about organizations: a new perspective and its implications for schools', in M. Hughes (ed.) *Administering Education: International Challenges*, pp. 71–99 London: Athlone Press of the University of London.

Hurst, P. (1987) 'The methodology of qualitative research', *International Journal of Educational Development* 7(1): 69–72.

Locke, J. [1690] (1959) *An Essay Concerning Human Understanding*, 2 vols (ed. A. Fraser). New York: Dover.

Maslow, A. (1954) *Motivation and Personality*. New York: Harper and Row.

Matthews, R. and Pitts, J. (2001) *Crime, Disorder and Community Safety*. London: Routledge.

Miles, M. and Huberman, A. (1994) *Qualitative Data Analysis*, 2nd edn. Thousand Oaks, CA: Sage.

Mill, J. [1843] (2009) 'A system of logic: ratiocinative and inductive', www.gutenberg.org/ebooks/27942 [accessed 30 September 2009].

Pring, R. (1978) 'Teacher as researcher', in D. Lawton, P. Gordon, M. Ing, B. Gibby, R. Pring and T. Moore (eds) *Theory and Practice of Curriculum Studies*, 236–46. London: Routledge & Kegan Paul.

Queen's University Belfast (2007) Dissertation handbook, School of Education.

Rock, P. (1979) *The Making of Symbolic Interactionism*. London: Macmillan.

Schön, D.A. (1983) *The Reflective Practitioner: How Professionals Think in Action*. New York: Basic Books.

Schön, D.A. (1987) *Educating the Reflective Practitioner*. San Francisco, CA: Jossey-Bass.

Simons, H. (1985) 'Against the rules: procedural problems in school self-evaluation', *Curriculum Perspectives*, 5(2): 2–5.

Smith, P. (2001) 'Action learning and reflective practice in project environments that are related to leadership development', *Management Learning*, 32(1): 31–48.

Stenhouse, L. (1979) 'Case study in comparative education: particularity and generalization', *Comparative Education*, 15(1): 5–11.

Valkenburg, R. and Dorst, K. (1998) 'The reflective practice of *design* teams', *Design Studies*, 19(3): 249–71.

Wolcott, H. (1975) 'Criteria for an ethnographic approach to research in schools', *Human Organisation* 34(2): 112–24.

Woods, P. (1986) *Inside Schools: Ethnography in Educational Research*. London: Routledge & Kegan Paul.

Yelloly, M. and Henkel, M. (1995) *Learning and Teaching in Social Work: Towards Reflective Practice*. London: Jessica Kingsley.

10

Work based research in action

Key points

This chapter provides a window on work based research in action. The authors have collected a number of work based research case studies that illustrate different aspects of work based research. The idea of this chapter is to examine how work based learners have approached the task of carrying out insider research in an organization as part of a postgraduate or undergraduate course. The examples that we have collected illustrate the wide variety. There is no right or wrong method; all are different and one of the aims of this chapter is to show how they can generate new knowledge and insights.

Each of the chosen examples features an aspect of work based research that we have covered in this book. Using the subject index, you can cross-refer to the chapter(s) of the book that deals with each aspect. We are grateful to the learners on whose work we have drawn for the extracts, and they are acknowledged at the front of this book. Where literature sources are cited, the full reference is given at the foot of the extract.

Examples drawn from real work based projects

The research proposal

Work based researchers have in common a single need – to find an approach to answering research questions that meets the needs of the organization, the university and themselves. Organizational needs are often expressed in terms of perceived benefits to the organization, whereas work based researchers' needs often relate to their own personal and professional development, both in the organization and outside it. University needs most obviously relate to the requirements of the degree the learner is studying towards, and whilst these are usually un-stated in the research report itself, the university regulations always specify their pass/fail criteria. The first example identifies clear benefits for both the workforce and for the organization being studied, in terms of training needs and requirements.

Example 1

My project will focus on identifying the ICT competencies that are needed by the workforce, and anticipate future possible requirements to develop an understanding of the training needs of staff. In identifying their needs, it will enable effective planning to be undertaken to develop and train staff. The impact of this should realize service and staff service improvements, have a positive impact on staff morale and also assist the Authority in:

- planning for future ICT training requirements
- planning for and implementing e-learning
- aiming to achieve 'excellent' standards for e-service delivery
- facilitating the effectiveness of staff for alternative ways of working.

This project will link to the Authority's long-term aims and support the Vision Statement for a culture where learning and development is supported to help staff achieve their potential and to recruit and retain a talented pool of staff (internal document #1). It will also link to the Authority's Framework for Managing People (internal document #2) to ensure that the performance of each employee is monitored to identify whether they reach the required level of competence.

There are also links to themes and objectives in the ICT Strategy (internal document #3) for identifying the core business-related competencies required by staff to make best use of the available ICT.

In the context of Comprehensive Performance Assessment inspections (Audit Commission, 2006), the Transformational Government Agenda (internal document #4) and the Local Government Pay and Workforce Strategy (ODPM, 2005), it is essential for the Authority to focus on maximizing the capacity of the workforce to realize improvements in performance, use technology to effectively deliver public services and assist in achieving excellent ratings in corporate assessments for the quality of public services.

Undertaking this project will also meet my personal and professional requirement for developing my project management and research skills, assisting with my ongoing professional development and providing an opportunity for me to undertake a major project in the workplace that will impact on service planning and performance.

The aim of my project will be to increase the knowledge and understanding of the ICT competencies required by the workforce at [organization].

(Continued)

(Continued)

References
Audit Commission (2006) *Comprehensive Performance Assessment.* London: Audit Commission.
ODPM (2005) *The Local Government Pay and Workforce Strategy.* London: Office of the Deputy Prime Minister.

Another learner, looking at career development in a police force, conceptualizes the sometimes competing demands of different stakeholders on work based research in terms of the need to meet applied vs academic aims that lead to two different sets of research outputs. Note that in this example the academic aims relate particularly to the theoretical and methodological dimensions of the study, whereas the applied aims relate more closely to the benefits of the study for human resource management, and for the personal and career development of individual police staff. This different focus feeds into the different outputs, where the academic outputs consist of publication in different forms, whilst the applied outputs refer to professional and organizational strategic and operational contexts.

Example 2

Applied aims:
- provide a framework for career development discussions
- take a more flexible approach to career development
- increase self-awareness among police staff about their career values
- take a realistic approach.

Academic aims:
- validate the COI as a measure of the eight career anchors
- explore trends in the career values people hold today
- match anchors to jobs
- investigate the impact of career anchor congruence.

Applied outputs:
- a workshop for senior personnel held in 2008
- a presentation to the Corporate Strategy Group
- an MBA project on police staff careers
- interest from other forces
- national projects for the NPIA.

Academic outputs:
- seven UK conference papers
- two European conference papers
- an invitation to present at an international conference in 2010
- a publication plan.

A key question, of course, is to what extent the needs of different audiences can be reconciled and addressed by a single work based research project. One approach to handling this balance is to argue that the study will identify research questions and issues that can be explored by senior managers and others internal to the organization. Sometimes it is even possible to suggest a consultancy project to investigate particular aspects of an organization's operations. You would do well to reflect on the different needs that apply to your planned work based research, and to consider the extent to which these are competing or complementary. In most cases, attention to the language in which research aims, objectives and outputs are expressed will do much to increase the acceptability of research proposals in business or other applied contexts.

The starting point for selecting a topic for research is to think about why the topic is important to you, the student, to the organization, and to other stakeholders – in other words, to be clear about the rationale for your study. This example sets out a rationale in a clear and precise way.

Example 3

The review of [organization's] existing curriculum, concurring with the personal reflection undertaken during the compilation of my *accreditation of previous experiential learning*, served to highlight what I would identify as the central problem inherent in the provision of music education, which is the *career progression* of its graduates.

It is generally accepted by the practitioners who provide the courses rooted in this subject discipline that only a small proportion of graduates will achieve a meaningful career in their chosen field and (particularly in the case of those who are undertaking performance courses) it is acknowledged that very few jobs exist in the 'real world'.

It is also my personal observation that only a small minority of students will graduate with the required skills level to find immediate professional employment in the highly competitive field of contemporary music. For most, there is the possibility that their full-time employment in music will be transitory and fleeting or, alternatively, more accurately profiled as a portfolio career which takes place in conjunction with other non-music-related, income-generating activities.

This being the case, I question why there *appears* to be no reflexive mechanism in place to address and deliver a meaningful employment remit, or to develop a curriculum which is tailored to meeting real-world outcomes for those who choose this course of study.

My research project aims to design a product from the basis of a balanced critical report that will identify and justify the case for a combined subject-specific/personal development education strategy rooted in *real-world* professional experiences, and designed to address these issues.

(Continued)

(Continued)

My present role as a volunteer in an environment which prioritizes personal development through engagement with music will allow me sufficient autonomy to pilot the product in a related, but informal, educational setting.

Therefore, the research product will be a specific, tailored curriculum and its related implementation strategies, designed to improve and extend the existing remit of the [organization].

The project is also future-oriented as it will represent the basis of my professional practice as I develop a career in music-based education.

In this further example, the rationale for the learner's research proposal is explicitly tied into knowledge creation – both at the individual and organizational level. Potentially, this enables the student to draw upon the significant literature of 'learning organizations' and organizational theory, as well as work drawing upon psychological and/or sociological perspectives on individuals in social settings.

Example 4

The work based learning research will support the organization to learn and understand safety as it learns. Hence, this enquiry into organizational learning must concern itself not with a static entity called 'organization', but with an active process for organization work based learning which is, at root, a cognitive enterprise. Individual members will be engaged in attempting to know the organization and to know themselves in the context of the organization.

Many good work based studies generate useful theory derived from workplace practice. The theoretical foundations of the research or the lens through which the observations will be made are made explicit in the next example.

Example 5

Because I am a participant observer in the community of practice under study for long periods of time, a month on board the drillship intercalated by a month of rest, the ethnographic approach was selected as the more appropriate for this research. Although historically ethnography has been associated with anthropological studies, in the twentieth century, ethnography has featured increasingly in studies of education, organizations and communities (see, for example, Kanter, 1993). In fact, the context in which the community under study is interacting with the Safety Management System is extremely important in this project. Kanter (1993) highlights that people's attitudes and behaviours take shape out of experience they have in their work; in a nutshell, her definition is 'the job makes the person'.

The study falls under the qualitative research paradigm, with strong emphasis on the fieldwork that I have carried out as a participant observer (Fetterman, 1998; Kirk and Miller, 1986; O'Reilly, 2004).

This work based research was developed under the Interpretative Paradigm as opposed to the Normative Paradigm. Fetterman (1998) defines ethnography 'as the art and science of describing a group or culture' (p.1), while O'Reilly describes it as a 'methodology that acknowledges the complexity of human experience and the need to research it by close and sustained observation of human behaviour' (2004: 1), and these statements are extremely relevant to my research.

I used an *emic* perspective, which is defined by Fetterman (1998) as the insider's or native's perspective of reality. I find this concept of interest for my work based research, as I am a participant observer and therefore am aware of these perceptions, trying to value them in their context. This is in contrast to a priori assumptions about how systems work (O'Reilly, 2004), as I am taking a phenomenologically oriented point of view, which sees behaviours as determined by phenomena of experiences, rather than by external, objective and physical reality. In addition, ethnography enables me to observe and analyse human interactions with results not achievable with classical positivistic and quantitative approaches.

References

Fetterman, D.M. (1998) *Ethnography: Step by Step*. London: Sage.
Kanter, R.M. (1993) *Men and Women of the Corporation*. New York: Basic Books.
Kirk, J. and Miller, M.L. (1986) *Reliability and Validity in Qualitative Research*. London: Sage.
O'Reilly, K. (2004) *Ethnographic Methods*. London: Routledge.

It is worthwhile noticing in the above extract how the insider-researcher attempts to provide a rationale for the theoretical and methodological approach taken in the study. As we have noted throughout this book, transparency is an extremely important principle in work based research and nowhere more than in the explanation provided about theory and methods. Also note how the account positions the researcher in the research and – another example of good practice – how appropriate sources drawn from the relevant literature are cited in support of the researcher's position.

The role of the work based researcher

Coping with the shift in role from worker-participant to worker-researcher is a challenge faced by most work based learners researching their own organization. We hope not to dissuade anyone from undertaking work based research by presenting examples in this chapter of situations where role tensions have been experienced by students. Our objective is to prepare you for the challenge that insider research presents and to encourage you to reflect on strategies to minimize role conflict. Undoubtedly, we would argue, the benefits in terms of the richness and depth of data open to you will more than compensate.

The next extract demonstrates an unusual frankness on the part of the researcher regarding her transformation from teacher to researcher, and the subsequent feelings of humiliation and powerlessness. Her opening comments suggest that she was quite unprepared for the loss of status and authority consequent on abandoning her teacher role.

Example 6: The role of the researcher

Under the remit of divine orthodoxy, the social scientist is transformed into philosopher-king (or queen) who can always see through people's claims and know better than they do. (Silverman, 2000: 198)

I must confess that on beginning this research I was an unwitting follower of what Silverman (2000) refers to as the 'divine orthodoxy' of the researcher. I thought that I would be able to take individuals' comments and from within them discover the 'truth' of what they really felt, believed, thought. I thought that as a researcher I would feel in a position of power; it all sounded very glamorous, but in reality I found my new role humiliating. Rather than the confident researcher that I had hoped to be, I felt de-powered; it was a very degrading experience. From the security of knowing that I was a highly proficient teacher, I became a clumsy novice researcher. I had no role that provided me with any value at the school; on the contrary, rather than feeling indispensable, as I was in my last role as class teacher in a school with many discipline problems, I felt uncomfortably aware that I was no use to the school and was simply a nuisance. Rather than having my classroom, my domain, I was constantly concerned that I was 'sat in somebody else's chair' in the staffroom. I had nowhere to go. Even if I escaped to my car, I would be observed, and look a little pathetic into the bargain. My insecurity became acute as I attempted to elicit information whilst causing the minimum amount of disruption. Hammersley and Atkinson (1993) cited Johnson (1976), who describes the feeling perfectly:

Trying to be busy without hassling any one worker too much is like playing Chinese checkers, hopping to and fro, from here to there, with no place to hide. (Hammersley and Atkinson, 1993: 100)

References

Hammersley, H., and Atkinson, P. (1993) *Ethnography: Principles in Practice.* London: Routledge.

Silverman, D. (2000) *Doing Qualitative Research: A Practical Handbook.* London: Sage.

The challenge of maintaining the roles of participant and observer, worker and researcher can however be viewed positively, in terms of the personal journey involved, as in this next extract.

Example 7

I have also been wondering about the impact doing the research has had on me. As the research comes to an end, I find myself transitioning out of this organization and into a new role, one with an organization that wants me to focus on retaining and energizing their key talent. Although I did this work to understand more, in order that the organization could capitalize on the work I had done, perhaps I have inadvertently prospered. I wonder whether I have been in a parallel process with those who I have been trying to work with and for. As I have been trying to connect with them on their career journey and help engage them with their work, I have also been engaging more deeply with my work and have made a transition of my own.

Ensuring that the work based research project offers value for participants is an effective mechanism for engaging them and securing support for the project. More deeply, such an approach can demonstrate the care and concern for participants that, as we have often argued in this book, is a core value for the insider-researcher.

Example 8

During the first run of the programme, I was struck by how valuable it was for the participants to be able to talk with another person who was present and interested in them. I was also struck by their openness, honesty and willingness to challenge themselves when they hardly knew me at all. As a result, when it came to choosing my research project, I knew I wanted to investigate the impact of coaching on adults returning to an educational environment and experiencing coaching for the first time as part of a personal development programme.

Placing others at the centre of the research process raises important questions of influence, power and authority as well as knowledge exchange, democracy and care for others. The following table was devised by a learner carrying out a work based research project designed to explore reciprocal learning through creative community partnerships. She conceptualizes the study as a cooperative enquiry, and uses a rather splendid epithet – 'the gifts of difference' – to communicate to the reader the centrality of the method of collaborative enquiry for her study of learning partnerships. The collaborative methodology penetrates all aspects of the study, and impacts on context, findings, analysis, key concept and implementation.

Example 9

Research method

Cooperative enquiry: a collaborative form of qualitative action research, a cycle of idea, action and review which welcomes both divergence and convergence.

Community of inter-being: mindfulness. Sangha Richmond Community Building in Britain. Working with Scott Peck's model. National Coalition Building Institutes. Welcoming Diversity Programme.

Research questions for co-enquiry

Can there be a partnership of equality in any sense when two very different people come together, perhaps one seen as more powerful than the other, if the partnership is seen as a learning partnership? What would be the characteristics, the benefits and the prerequisites of such a partnership? Is it true that community partnerships between people of widely diverse backgrounds and experience – perhaps of apparent equality – can promote creativity, learning and validation for all?

Principal focus
Related concepts

QUESTIONS FOR A COMMUNITY OR SOCIETY AS A WHOLE

QUESTIONS FOR AN ORGANIZATION

QUESTIONS FOR A GROUP

QUESTIONS FOR ONESELF

LINKING	SOCIETY	REAL PEOPLE
BRIDGING	ORGANIZATION	OTHERS
BONDING	INDIVIDUAL	SELF

Learning from Creative Community Engaging in mindful learning → Whose responsibility is this learning? → Taking profound action individually → Building community of difference

Abbey Sutton Courtenay

Time and talents for Westminster

Building Community through Arts

Context: setting this study in context of social capital theory and the domain of social psychology
- 3 different types of social capital
- psychology of self
- psychology of order.

Findings: on what is important when bridging social differences, in answer to the research questions explored together. The major themes and issues raised by my co-enquirers, a purposive sample drawn from the participants in a range of partnerships.

Analysis: analysing the findings and exploring some possible interpretations especially of the pre-requisites of learning partnerships identified by my co-enquirers, to see what kinds of action we might need to take when building our social capital.

Key concept: is the key finding that to change our world we must first change our minds becoming aware of how we place others and ourselves? Is it a call for a shift in consciousness and for profound action rather than decisive?

Implementation: how might we use these findings to become aware of gifts of difference? Might we now have the beginnings of a self-facilitated guide to use alone or with others? What future enquiries and experiments might help us in raising our own awareness?

'Community occurs when the gifts of those on the margin are brought to the centre. Focusing on gifts rather than deficiencies changes everything.' (Peter Block, 2000 on the Social Architecture of Change)

'Real change comes ... when authentic commitment, passion and wholeheartedness are released. These are social phenomena and are created from the nature of how we come together and the quality of our relationship.'

'Our commitment to each other, our relationships, may be the determinant of our success more than the particular path we pick or next big thing we engage in ... Something shifts when we differentiate between decisive and profound action.'

'Profound action begins with an acknowledgement of how we, not they, contribute to the problem we are facing. Forgiveness ... is an antidote for all the ways we think other people need to change for the future to be different.'

'You might say we are creating a spiritual foundation which becomes the basis for real accomplishment. It is on this foundation that decisive action can change the world.'

Figure 10.1 'The gifts of difference': reciprocal learning through creative community partnerships – what we may gain and what it may take – a cooperative enquiry

Collaborative research often involves negotiation of aims and outcomes, and the approach taken will vary with the position of the insider-researcher in their organization. In this example, the benefits of an insider's knowledge about who to talk to, access to relevant resources and understanding of organizational context and priorities are contrasted with a negative research experience involving an external consultant.

Example 10

After scoping up some business model principles for how the organization works together, senior managers raised legitimate concerns about how people would react. Although there were clear calls from parts of the business at the working level, the high-level engagement needed to take a much softer approach. I therefore recast my work in the context of specific examples of good practice and opportunities for improving collaborative working.

I have developed a strong sense of the benefits of being an insider-researcher. I have a clear understanding of the context and issues recently reaffirmed by a critical incident in the organization. A review of IT demand planning undertaken by an external consultant had just been completed. The report contained some interesting observations and assumptions about our organizational complexity and its implications. However, it was heavily criticized by the Management Board because it did not stick to the original brief, made broad assumptions (many of which were inaccurate), was based heavily in theory, and was not written in clear and concise language to meet the needs of the audience. The report sank without a trace and was probably not value for money. This was a lesson in the disadvantages of being an independent researcher – the research was not fit for purpose and was not well received by the target audience. I have access to a range of materials, together with insider knowledge of the key people who will be able to help (including those I will interview). I am aware of, and therefore hopefully able to manage, the inherent bias I will have as a product of the organizational culture.

Reflective practice and the worker-researcher

Many learners draw on the research tradition of reflective practice in their work based research. The idea of the insider-researcher reflecting upon their own practice and that of others, formulating research questions and testing everyday assumptions is the core of the reflective practitioner tradition and can provide work based researchers with a useful theoretical lens through which research observations and analysis can be viewed, as the next three extracts demonstrate.

Example 11

I have become aware of my worker/researcher role and the importance of reflexivity. I have to accept, that no matter how I try, the world will always be viewed from my own perspective and that I must recognize that in my research. The development of my project has opened my eyes to other perspectives, which I believe would have otherwise remained dormant. For example, I had labelled a contact as being uncooperative in her attitude. However, when I looked at things from her organization's perspective and engaged her in wider conversation, I realized our goals were closer than I had thought. There was much common ground. I gently broached the issue of my project and our contact admitted she had just finished a work based Masters and offered to introduce me to all the contacts I would need. I ended up reversing my opinion of her entirely! Certainly the concept of *Weltanschauung* or 'worldview' has helped me recognize where my personal prisms or viewpoints lie and to broaden them.

Example 12

Another important work based dimension is the perceived gap between the view from the corporate centre and what is actually happening on the ground. I will need to be aware of this, both in identifying bias in my data and in my approach to interviews and discussions with colleagues across the organization. One CEO recently explained to me that, whilst some people from corporate centre were 'sensible', he was suspicious of the 'young suits'. It was not clear in which category he put me at the time!

Example 13

My dual role as worker/researcher excites me. Work based learning allows me to connect learning directly to what I do professionally. The old days of calculating the square root of a random number or the speed of two trains, if one leaves San Francisco at 1:00 pm and the other leaves New York at 2:00 pm, are long gone and I am happier for it. I know I am much better engaged in learning when I can connect it to real-life experience and have the learning be applicable to something of my choosing.

Reviewing knowledge and information

The next extract illustrates well how becoming immersed in the relevant literature relating to a research project can generate insights and help the researcher to formulate appropriate categories and codes. Particularly noteworthy is the learner's decision to utilize categories that were already in use in the organization's own competency model for CPD, since these overlapped with categories drawn from the literature and would enable the research outcomes to be presented in language familiar, and therefore potentially more acceptable, to those within the organization.

Example 14: Step 2.3 – Identify the thematic framework

During my initial literature review, I identified nine sources from which to establish developmental experience categories that would form the coding framework. There were numerous overlapping categories and I believed the categories covered the broad range of stories that would emerge through the interviews. I identified the common denominators by examining the underlying definitions. This enabled me to compress the 57 described categories into 21 categories. As an example of category compression, my list of 21 includes one titled 'Start up'. This was drawn from Start-up, Start from Scratch, Manage a Start-up and Starting from Scratch (Building Something from Nothing), described in four of the seven resources.

After receiving feedback on my research proposal, I returned to a literature review to find additional resources. I found that my developmental categories were in contrast to studies that used categories such as Self, Relational or Context (Janson, 2008); sense-making themes of Natural Process, Value Driven, Coping and Struggle, Symbolic/Parental Relationship, Self-Improvement and Role Model (Janson, 2008); or leadership development as a natural process, leadership development as a story of coping with difficulties, leadership development as a learning process and leadership development as finding a cause (Shamir et al., 2005). While these constructs could be valuable, I believed my 21 categories would resonate with the study participants and be more actionable for others who may apply the results of this study.

Similarly, I believed it would be helpful to identify categories to capture themes from the areas of learning. I reviewed, for example, McCall et al.'s 'lessons' including technical/professional skills, developing other people and persevering through adversity (McCall et al., 1988). This list of lessons overlapped considerably with our company's competency model and set of behaviours. So, instead of introducing a new language around these behaviours, I chose to use our company's competency model as that framework. This may enable me to apply learning from this research to recommend further exploration for any behaviour or competency additions or changes. (See Item 3, Appendix 4 for the Assurant Competency Model.)

I recognize that developing the framework from the literature review and using our company's competency model rather than letting the categories emerge from the study participants' stories could mitigate some new learning. I was committed to being cognizant about that potential limitation during coding and analysis.

(Continued)

(Continued)

References

Janson, A. (2008) 'Extracting leadership: knowledge from formative experiences', *Leadership* 4(1): 73–94.

McCall, M., Lombardo, M. and Morrison, A. (1988) *The Lessons of Experience*. New York: Lexington Books.

Shamir, B., Horesh, H.-Dayan, H. and Adler, D. (2005) 'Leading by biography: towards a life-story approach to the study of leadership', *Leadership* 1(1): 13–29.

Frequently, our research assumptions and preconceptions turn out to be an incomplete picture of the reality within the organization. This may be because we discover facets of the organization that we had not yet encountered, or because participants reveal information that is novel or confidential or, as in this case, the external environment changes and brings about new concerns. The alert researcher will seize such opportunities, for they present an invaluable opportunity to create new and meaningful insights into organizational culture and behaviour.

Example 15

On a less positive note, the focus group threw up the first negative thought associated with the coaching conversation; it was based on the reality of career advancement in the current economic climate. They were not clear that their desired career moves would be possible in the environment that was more cost-focused and in an organization where headcount was being reduced. They felt that if headcount was being cut, then [organization] would not need so many leaders. The sense that the researcher conveyed when we discussed it was that 'they were questioning whether the next career move would be there; yes, it is nice for someone to talk to them about what job might follow their current one, but would they have that opportunity if the economic pressures remain?' This is not an issue that had come to light at all in the questionnaire and was a very interesting new perspective.

The following five examples of methodological approaches are abridged examples of real projects and are included to give you some ideas about how to construct a methodology and the kinds of methodologies that you may consider using. In each of these extracts, and in different ways, learners discuss the choices open to them in terms of research design, and, to a varying degree, the rationale for their particular choices made. In the first example, the learner provides a heartfelt rationale for her constructivist approach to a doctoral level study of a secondary school; however, note that she explicitly 'rules in' using both qualitative and quantitative methods to acquire the data she requires.

A methodological approach

Example 16

My understanding of 'how we know things' has changed beyond measure during this research. Before beginning my research, I was of the positivist assumption that there were facts out there to be discovered: a few observations, interviews and questionnaires, and I would be able to present a clear picture of what made my study school tick. The reality was far messier and slightly terrifying. If there were facts out there just waiting to be unearthed, then how could two participants have completely different views on them? How could some members of staff use the descriptions of 'friendly', 'welcoming' and 'pleasant atmosphere' to depict the school, when others chose 'untidy', 'poor pupil behaviour' and 'frantic atmosphere'? Could this be the same school? And where did my views come into it?

Whereas at one time the researcher could have claimed authority in presenting the 'truth', such positivist traditions have now been challenged: 'The age of a putative value-free social science appears to be over' (Denzin, 1994: 501). I came to realize that, if anything, my voice held less value than the participants' because I had not lived the experience. Having progressed beyond the fantasy of my authoritative voice, then, my aim became largely ethno-methodological; I needed to discover and present the inhabitants' views of their social culture. Alongside this would sit my observations of the local infrastructure and neither would take precedence. It would involve both large- and small-scale data (for the overview and the minutiae) and would benefit from both qualitative and some quantitative methods.

References

Denzin, N.K. (1994) 'The art and politics of interpretation', in N.K. Denzin and Y.S. Lincoln (eds) *Handbook of Qualitative Research,* pp. 500–15. Thousand Oaks, CA: Sage.

Example 17 makes use of an 'evolving design' approach. The idea here is that at the outset of a work based research project, it can be difficult to appreciate what events, processes and interactions will be significant or interesting. Applying some flexibility to the research design is therefore helpful in such circumstances, enabling the researcher to develop research questions and ideas as the study progresses. This approach draws upon grounded theory and combines the benefits of systematic approaches to data collection, the flexibility to focus and re-focus analysis, and the ability to accurately capture the changing reality of social situations.

Example 17

The research strategy that will be used for this project will be a case study. Yin (2003) describes the case study as a research strategy that comprises an all-encompassing method – covering the logic of design, data collection techniques and specific approaches to data analysis – basically, a comprehensive research strategy. A consideration in choosing this research strategy was highlighted by Robson (1993) in that the work on the design of a case study can, and should, continue after the start of the study. When researching a real world/work based problem, this evolving design could be advantageous to me.

References
Robson, C. (1993) *Real World Research: A Resource for Social Scientists and Practitioner Researchers.* Oxford: Blackwell.

Yin, R.K. (2003) *Case Study Research: Design and Methods,* 3rd edn. Thousand Oaks, CA: Sage.

Example 18 is of Action Research and Appreciative Inquiry. The researcher has drawn from these two distinct research approaches to justify a whole approach that suits the kind of research that has been undertaken. Work based projects are often multi-methodology projects as has been explained in Chapter 7.

Example 18: Action Research synthesized with Appreciative Inquiry – a coaching professional wishing to research, explore, model and test the factors which are believed to contribute to the successful coaching of the leaders of organizational change, thereby evolving an effective, marketable coaching model

The methodological approach

I wish to arrive at a clear recommendation for the elements of a coaching model which will meet the needs of leaders in organizational change. For me, this will be achieved by evolving my coaching model and I believe that action research provides the learning cycles necessary for this necessarily emergent and responsive development process. Evaluation will include the commercial response to the resulting framework.

One of the reasons that action research is so appealing to me is that it will enable me to reflect and learn from any data collected in the context of my work, rather than be second-guessed by it. It will all be 'grist for the mill'.

It is an approach rather than a method (Bell, 1995), unlike action learning which appears similar in its dynamic, narrative-based approach to research, and involves conversation and dialogue. I would hope that my presentation of the outcomes of my research might also help 'tackle a problem or enhance the performance of … organizations … through changes to the rules and procedures within which they operate' (Denscombe, 2002), an outcome said to be inherent in action research.

My need, according to Lomax (2002), is to collect rigorous data which Judith Bell points out must provide evidence to support claims for action. Considering how I might collect the data from each question, I was delighted to find that the four phases of action research mapped easily on to the Appreciative Inquiry model (Cooperrider and Whitney, 2000) which influences my work, and so I have chosen to use the same headings below and to describe methods of collecting data, within the activities necessary for the project which are summarized there.

Phase I/Discovery – appreciating the best of what might exist, as well as the challenges it addresses: carry out a literature search.

1. What elements form an effective coaching model designed to support the learning of and from leaders of organizational change? What are the authoritative sources of such data?

Phase 2/Dream – envisioning a result and asking 'what is the world calling for?': summarize the results of the literature search and seek to elicit a response from buyers of coaching which demonstrates interest, if not demand, and, ideally, contributes to the research.

2. To what degree is there demand for such coaching as a strategic tool for organizational learning in change by experienced buyers of coaching services?

Phase 3/Design – co-constructing an ideal: host and record focus groups to present the model and invite discussion.

3. What examples of best practice emerge from accounts by participants, probably coaches but possibly triangulating coach/buyer/executive, involved in coaching the leaders of organizational change (to improve individual and organizational performance), including contracting, relationship management, supervision and communication of organizationally relevant themes?
4. What, if any, obstacles or barriers to entry have arisen, for instance, what type of issues have been resolved (or remained unresolved) for a process to operate (optimally) and how do these appear to have been contracted for by organizational clients, sponsors, supervisors, coaches and executive clients (and any other stakeholders)?

Phase 4/Destiny – establishing and sustaining the model: produce a presentation of final findings and present it to participants.

Return to Phase I/Discovery

1. What elements form an effective coaching model designed to support the learning of and from leaders of organizational change?

(Continued)

(Continued)

References

Bell, J. (1995) *Doing Your Research Project: A guide for first-time researchers in Education and Social Science*, 4th edn, p. 8. Buckingham: Open University Press.

Cooperrider, D. and Whitney, D. (2000) *Collaborating for Change: Appreciative Inquiry.* San Francisco, CA: Berrett-Koehler.

Denscombe, M. (2002) *Ground Rules for Good Research: A 10-Point Guide for Social Researchers*, p. 27. Berkshire: Open University Press.

Lomax, P. (2002) 'Action research', in M. Coleman and A.R.J. Briggs (eds) *Research Methods in Educational Leadership and Management*, p. 124. London: Sage.

Example 19 is a case study which incorporates a rationale for an interpretivist research design and an inductive approach to gathering qualitative data. Case studies can come in many forms and it is likely that if a small research project is based upon one organization, then a case study may be a viable research approach to use.

Example 19: Case study research design – a project evaluating an executive coaching programme involving the coaching of 15 senior managers of a Greek multi-national manufacturing company

Choice of research methodology and rationale

There is very little theoretical research that examines how or why executive coaching should work, when it will be most (or least) successful in changing executives' behaviours and '*under which conditions executive coaching will translate into greater organisational effectiveness*' (Feldman and Linkau (2005) p. 830, my italics). For this reason, I have chosen an interpretivist research design, starting with an inductive approach in order to gather qualitative data that will attempt to make meaning of people's experiences in order to better improve my own and others' professional practice, first and foremost. This I believe is the true value of work based research. I will explain my rationale.

I wonder if Feldman and Lankau's survey (2005) also highlights the difficulty of using quantitative methods and attempts to calculate the return on investment (ROI) to measure the true success of executive coaching. While evaluations of coaching programmes (like my current research) are not new, they are plagued with identifying coaching's real value in terms other than soft or fuzzy or what I would call attempts at 'hard' guesstimates offered by participants on ROI (McGovern, 2001). This leaves many companies preferring to use qualitative data to assess the value of coaching (Sherman and Freas, 2004). It also highlights the importance of practitioner work based studies in addition to systematic academic research in making further contributions to the field.

My research project, an evaluation of one coaching programme, is affected by the same difficulties and constraints I have described. For these reasons, I have chosen a qualitative in-depth exploration of people's experiences and the meaning they make of the coaching in order to offer some richer insights than numerical guesstimates and an opportunity to make some potential recommendations to the field of executive coaching, especially about the impact of coaching as an organizational change intervention.

I have chosen a research design which is interpretivist with an 'anti-foundationalist' ontology (Grix, 2004), where I see social reality as existing not independently of our experience, but as something that is 'socially and discursively constructed by human actors' (p. 61). I believe it is through people's experiences that I will achieve a richer understanding of coaching's effect on them and on the organization for investigating my research question. For this reason, I have also chosen an inductive approach, starting with understanding people's experiences and meaning, rather than a deductive hypothesis to test. I believe an inductive approach is more suited to work based learning for gathering a richer understanding and developing one's practice, rather than the testing of hypotheses which is more suited to formal academic research.

Case study research methodology and rationale

I have chosen an in-depth case study methodology to bring out the richness of a particular instance of executive coaching that incorporates the data collection methods of: semi-structured interviews; opportunities for anonymous written or spoken feedback through a third party; and information from participants in the 360° Feedback Profiles and my coaching notes.

One data collection method I should have liked to use was observation. The major advantage of observation as a research method is its directness. There are often huge discrepancies between what people say they do or will do and what they actually do. Its data can contrast revealing differences or usefully complement information from any other method (Robson, 2002: 310–11). Drawbacks concern cost and concerns about reliability and validity, and the risk of interviewers developing 'over-rapport'. Subjects can also modify their behaviour if they know they are being observed, trying to present themselves in a better light and thereby give misleading information (Clarke, 2003: 80–1). The reasons I did not use it were time restraints as well as distance. Over half of the participants were based outside Athens.

References

Clarke, A. (2003) *Evaluation Research: An Introduction to Principles, Methods and Practice*. London: Sage.

Feldman, D.C. and Lankau, M.J. (2005) 'Executive coaching and agenda for future research', *Journal of Management* 31(6): 829–48.

(Continued)

(Continued)

Grix, J. (2004) *The Foundations of Research* (Palgrave Study Guides). Basingstoke: Palgrave Macmillan.

McGovern, J. (2001) 'Maximizing the impact of executive coaching: behavioral change, organizational outcomes, and return on investment', *Manchester Review* 6: 1–9.

Robson, C. (2002) *Real World Research: A Resource for Social Scientists and Practitioner Researchers*, 2nd edn. Oxford: Blackwell.

Sherman, S. and Freas, A. (2004) 'The wild west of executive coaching', *Harvard Business Review* 82(1): 82–90.

Example 20 is of soft systems methodology and shows the stages of SSM applied to a diagnosis system in veterinary practices. Similar to action research, SSM incorporates a wide focus upon organizational practices and can be a most appropriate approach to methodology for work based projects.

Example 20: Soft System Methodology – introducing a diagnostic coding system for the PDSA (Peoples' Dispensary for Sick Animals)

On initial examination, it would be easy to assume that diagnostic coding was simply a process-driven system. Each time a diagnosis is made, a code is chosen from a list and data is then simply extracted as needed. It is, however, more complicated than first impressions suggest. How certain of the diagnosis must the clinician be to record it as a fact? How accurate do the stakeholders require this diagnosis to be? Do they all require the same level of certainty over the conditions coded? What will motivate those capturing the data to record the information accurately in a busy working environment? All these questions need to be addressed and are heavily influenced by human factors. SSM places a high degree of emphasis on these and takes into account the specific environments in which they are occurring.

The intrinsic nature of SSM is one of a collaborative approach and works best if many people are involved in the overall process, as opposed to a single person attempting to resolve the problem in isolation (Checkland and Scholes, 1990).

These stages could also be described as (Bowen and Shehata, 2001):

- 'finding out about the problem' (phases 1 and 2)
- 'systems thinking' (phases 3, 4 and 5)
- 'taking action' (phases 6 and 7).

An important concept of SSM is to realize that these stages do not represent a single process followed from start to finish. Often, stages of the process require repetition in order to reach accommodation and agreement on the final goal. This issue is addressed later by the 1988 representation of the methodology (Checkland and Scholes, 1990). When I look at these seven stages in the context of the PDSA's world, they become the following steps:

1. The PDSA recognizes the need for diagnostic coding and would like to introduce it as part of the routine of recording clinical data at its pet aid hospitals (PAHs).

2. A detailed analysis of the current situation as applicable to the PDSA.

    • Who has an interest in the data from coding?

        – Internal stakeholders
        – External stakeholders
        – Their levels of importance/priority
        – What do they want to do with the data?
        – What detail of coding and level of accuracy do they require?

    • Who delivers the data by coding?

        – Vets
        – Nurses
        – Any others?

3. Naming the system.

    • Root definitions
    • CATWOE

        – **C**lient: the identified stakeholders
        – **A**ction: vets, nurses and possibly other hospital staff
        – **T**ransformation: clinical histories into coded clinical histories
        – **W**eltanshauung: practical capture of diagnostic data throughout (PDSA PAHs)
        – **O**wner

            Director of Veterinary Services (DVS)
            Chief Veterinary Surgeon (CVS)
            The vet department.

        – **E**nvironment

            Funding
            Coding structures being developed by others
            Time frames.

4. Production of Concept Model(s) (CM).

    • Identify who is currently coding data and review what systems they are using.
    • Identify why their system of coding works in 'their world'.
    • Define what 'their world' is.

(Continued)

(Continued)

5. Comparison of CMs to 'the real world of PDSA' using one or more of the following techniques:

- CMs as base for ordered questions
- History with model predictions
- General comparison (most likely method)
- Model overlay.

6. Identify the required changes within the PDSA, ensuring they are both feasible and practical.

7. Development of an action plan for the implementation of the above changes.

Checkland's system has been developed further and in 1988 a 'new look' model was presented (Checkland and Scholes, 1990). Here, the methodology is refined into four phases in an attempt to remove the impression that SSM was a seven-step process to be followed from start to finish. There is a desire to resolve the problem – the PDSA has recognized the advantages to be gained from robust diagnostic coding and wishes to make it happen.

Facing up to this situation is a 'would-be improver'; this is the role I take in doing the project and as a user of SSM.

We now have the current situation and a would-be improver, both providing streams of structured enquiry which together lead to the implementation of change to the improve the situation. PAH staff will continue to record clinical histories while work is done on this project and from these will develop purposeful actions (the tasks) and areas of disagreement (the issues).

Theoretical models will be sourced and reviewed ('holons' as described by Koestler, 1967) and by comparing these to the real-world problem, they will illuminate the situation and act as a structure for debate about desired change. Existing coding systems will fulfil this role when compared to the real-life situation within the PDSA.

The desired outcome is then the emergence of realistic change that is practical to implement in the real world and so resolve or improve the problem. In the PDSA's case, this is the implementation of a system that meets the stakeholders' needs.

References

Bowen, S. and Shehata, M. (2001) *Soft Systems Methodology*. Calgary: University of Calgary.

Checkland, P. and Scholes, J. (1990) *Soft Systems Methodology in Action*. Chichester: John Wiley.

Koestler, A. (1967) *The Ghost in the Machine*. London: Hutchinson.

Conclusions and recommendations

Finally, we have chosen to reproduce two rather longer extracts which illustrate the very important matter of presenting conclusions and recommendations arising from work based research. Like all the other examples in this chapter, the extracts are drawn from live projects and are reproduced here to illustrate how other learners have approached this most important aspect of work based research – that is, its practical application in the workplace. We hope that the extracts will be a useful resource for your own personal reflection, and that they might also be used to stimulate group discussion in research methods workshops.

Example 21: Conclusions and recommendations

To arrive at recommendations, I returned to my research questions:

What variations, if any, are there in Food Section Managers' performance?

At a high level, the variances may not be deemed drastic, as the percentage of people within each band – Non-Achieve, Achieve and Exceed – could be viewed as an acceptable spread of proportions. It is at the point when the grading scheme (Chapter 6: 24–5) has been applied that the variances are most evident. Over a quarter (27 per cent, n = 10) are new to their role and only 5 per cent (n = 2) are performing to a level where advancement is possible within a six-month period.

It is also important to note that only a very small proportion of this group have the development tools in place to enable them to improve their performance. These are an up-to-date CPR and Development Plan. Without these tools, the individuals may not be aware of performance issues and would not have a strategy in place to overcome them.

Therefore, I conclude that there are indeed significant variations in Food Section Managers' individual performance that need addressing. Furthermore, this has been deemed as consistent with the commercial performance of the stores involved in the research. Corrective action should be taken by [organization] to rectify this and thereby improve business results.

What support/training is available to Food Section Managers to equip them with the necessary competencies to reach a sustainable optimal level of performance?

As discussed in Chapter 1, all new Section Managers attend a two-day business induction workshop. The content of this workshop is important, but does not aim to prepare new colleagues for the department where they will carry out their duties. It is made clear during this session that the individual will 'work shadow' an established Section Manager for a period of up to six months.

Therefore, it is true to say that all newly appointed or inexperienced SMs rely heavily on the support and coaching of more established colleagues. The issue here is that established colleagues feel unable to dedicate sufficient time to training their colleagues, and whether it is a reasonable expectation that they should be able to do so.

(Continued)

(Continued)

Also, when the findings of this research are considered – that is, the demands on established colleagues to deliver their individual objectives – is this a realistic expectation?

SMs have conveyed the reality of the situation in the 'real world', with opinions such as:

> I think the business lacks specific training to the job, or maybe it is expected to be all on the job learning through error. (Store G)

> [organization] was the only way of training yourself as a Food Manager but as I mentioned earlier, needed to be carried on outside of work time. Therefore, I feel that the development of Section Managers depended on how much of their spare time they could spend on the modules ... New managers are recruited and expected to 'get on with it'. They are fortunate if they have experienced colleagues (with time) to give them technical training. If not they are forced to muddle through. (Store E)

> All areas need regular refreshers. (Store K)

The group overwhelmingly agrees that, to acquire the necessary explicit knowledge, they require intensive and structured training. Extensive research clearly supports and encourages the need for ongoing training and development of employees. The expertise of employees has also proved to increase the willingness of individuals to share their knowledge, which in turn leads to increased individual commitment.

I conclude that at the time this research was undertaken, there was very little evidence of formal department-targeted training for SMs. I am aware, however, that the new Section Manager Career Path is due to be launched. I have not had access to this programme during this project.

What do Food Section Managers think would enable them to reach a sustainable optimal performance level?

The key finding was that all SMs agree that more training specific to Foods is essential. The training should cover all aspects of the role, with an emphasis on how to use the commercial resources effectively. The opinion of the vast majority of individuals is that the knowledge they have gained to date is either a result of their experiential learning or a result of completing Foods Unwrapped modules.

SMs have portrayed an interest in a training scheme whereby individual learning achievements are recognized. They believe that this would need to be structured, with an agreed time frame and individual programme plan that is fully supported – not only by the business but, more importantly, by store management teams. The group would like to have this training delivered by experts. This would be most beneficial if it were delivered by individuals who had both an in-depth knowledge of the food business and experience of delivering the Food Section Manager role itself.

Opinions vary as to what awards would be appropriate, with mixed views on accreditation-based schemes that involve third parties. The main concern is that training is essential to enable individuals to improve their work performance and drive their professional development.

Finally, the group agree that ongoing training, regular feedback and the provision of a support network would make a significant difference to their performance.

Do Food Section Managers receive sufficient support from line managers in terms of professional development?

This research suggested that SMs receive very little support from their line managers in terms of their individual professional development. The main focus appears to be on achieving commercial results.

The impact of constant change of line managers appeared to be the biggest barrier to this support. With a change of line managers comes a change of priorities, according to the group. The outcome of this was a decrease in motivation – as the cycle of 'proving themselves' commenced yet again. This, again, could be resolved if the individual had an agreed development pathway that could be proceeded with, irrespective of changes within the management structure within their store.

What effect, if any, has the cessation of the Foods Unwrapped Programme had on individual performance?

Although there was no evidence to suggest that the cessation of the programme has had a direct impact on individual performance, it is suggested by those individuals that did complete the modules that the majority agree that the programme did improve their work performance.

Recommendations

Taking all the findings of this research into account, I recommend that for [organization] to improve food business results, it is necessary to ensure that their food departments are managed by experts. [Organization] should appreciate the issues put forward by this research and acknowledge that this specific group aspires to becoming managerial experts in their field. The way to achieving this is to invest heavily in their professional development.

To the HR department, I recommend the following:

1. The Section Manager job profile should be revised. There should be separate documents for general merchandizing and Food Section Managers. This document should be a direct reflection of the objectives and the activities required to drive the relevant business unit forward.
2. To ensure continuous improvement, all SMs should have regular, ongoing and consistent performance reviews with their line managers.
3. Every individual must have an up-to-date development plan in place, with agreed timetabled, realistic and achievable targets set. This development

(Continued)

(Continued)

plan should be adopted and followed through, even when there is a change in line manager.

4. The pathways for career progression should be reviewed. These must be designed to be clear and consistent, with detailed benchmarks and frameworks that are transferable to all individuals. This 'one corporate way' should be adhered to by all management and HR teams.

To the Learning and Development Department, I recommend the following;

1. A project team should be put in place to take the finding of this research forward.
2. A training structure for SMs should be devised that is specific to the needs of food business.
3. To ensure that the training is robust and specific, the involvement of established, motivated and high-performing SMs is essential.
4. The training should be delivered by a team of experts that is dedicated to food trainer roles.
5. Learning should be ongoing and continuous. It should be both training and a refreshing opportunity. The experience of individuals should be deemed irrelevant.
6. Individuals should be recognized and rewarded for both their improved competence and work performance.

Finally, for a detailed discussion of the reflective insights on my personal learning, please refer to Appendix 3, Section 4.

Example 22

- Female dancers have shorter careers than male dancers.
- Qualitative data identify choice and control over the timing and circumstances of retirement as a key to influencing overall satisfaction with transition.

Recommendations

A small number of practical recommendations aimed primarily at the Ballet Company (BC) and the Dance Forum (DF) have been formulated, based on the evidence assembled.

1. To improve record keeping and evaluation of existing and emerging transition programmes

At present, the Ballet Company has no way of evaluating the outcomes of transition for their members and improving upon services offered to inform and aid dancers in this area. Evaluation is a vital step in the design of improvements, elimination of shortcomings and eventual expansion of transition programmes. Reaction to this study from dancers and management alike was enthusiastic and it is felt more regular and systematic study could provide benefits for both the organization and its members.

2. To raise the profile of the Dancers' Career Development within the Ballet Company

I don't remember being aware of the transition centre. Otherwise I think I would have felt I could find out what it was all about. (Ballet Campany Dancer)

The findings suggest that the Dance Forum is one of the key sources of practical, financial and emotional support for dancers in transition and is much valued by dancers who have used its services. However, formal contact between the BC and DF dancers is limited and many dancers are either unaware of the organization or badly informed about the resources they offer. The findings also suggest that dancers are waiting until the end of their careers to contact DF rather than using the organization's services to aid long-term planning.

It is suggested that yearly information sessions between DF representatives and BC dancers be made a priority. It is also suggested that the BC provides a simple informative guide about the DF (including services offered and contact details) to all dancers joining the company.

3. To improve and expand transition awareness and educational programmes, both in-house and in partnership with outside institutions

There needs to be a lot more focus and funding towards helping dancers prepare for careers after their life in ballet. There are not enough education or awareness programmes available for the dancers. (Ballet Company Dancer)

Although over 50 per cent of transition programmes undertaken by dancers were self-initiated from independent sources, the time demands of their career suggest on-site educational initiatives might be a more realistic means of promoting transition readiness and career development. However, the number of programmes available to dancers and participation levels are still fairly minimal. Dancer feedback suggests greater awareness and promotion of transition support should come from those managing the operation of the company. It is advised that more work be done to inform dancers of the opportunities available to them both in-house and in conjunction with outside institutions such as the university and the Ballet School. It is also suggested that the evaluation of existing programmes be undertaken with the aim of improving quality and accessibility and ultimately to inform the creation of new initiative.

4. To create a mentoring/job shadowing programme with the Opera House

A small number of dancers are already participating in programmes geared towards gaining experience or qualifications in alternative aspects of the

(Continued)

(Continued)

dance field, such as choreography or teaching. However, it is suggested that the opportunities for this sort of personal and professional development are increased. The Opera House has a huge range of expertise within its ranks and could provide a useful resource for dancers wishing to explore a variety of careers such as stage management, set, lighting or costume design, publicity, education or fund-raising. Time and financial constraints mean this sort of initiative would need to be well thought out and modest in scale. However, this approach would not only reap obvious benefits for the dancer, but for the institution which would gain the opportunity of developing and retaining talent in-house.

5. To develop and promote the Dancers' Career Developments networking database

I believe that support should continue beyond transition in the form of a network where people could share ideas and experiences. I feel any problems that I have had are more than likely being repeated elsewhere. It would also help with the emotional side of having been part of a large institution. (Ballet Company Dancer)

The enthusiasm with which this study was greeted by former dancers, including a willingness to share personal experiences and offer advice, suggests a more formal forum for networking/mentoring could be a useful transition resource. Although the Dance Forum has the capability to connect dancers, feedback suggests that dancers are not making use of this resource at present. It is suggested that this aspect of DF's services be further developed and promoted to raise awareness amongst current and former dancers.

6. To undertake further study into the relationship between motherhood and dance

Having kids I think really changes you and how you will transfer to normal life. If I was to have given up dancing not having had children, I think the transition would have been harder. (Ballet Company Dancer)

Although this study did not look specifically at the relationship between motherhood and dance, preliminary findings suggest motherhood provides new obstacles, challenges and perspectives for dancers. There is qualitative evidence to suggest that motherhood can be a catalyst to early retirement, the result of difficulties reintegrating, post-childbirth, and/or juggling the emotional and practical aspects of the career and childrearing. Many dancers also cite the role of motherhood in aiding their transitions out of dance and reframing identities. Certainly, it seems this is an important area, affecting both the careers and transitions of dancers, and is worthy of further study.

Using the extracts

The examples of work based research in this chapter are from live, work based research projects which have been submitted in partial fulfilment of the assessment requirements towards a postgraduate or undergraduate degree at a UK university. We hope that the extracts will raise interesting questions and issues for you to reflect upon in relation to your own work, and that they will be an additional and useful resource for group discussion on work based research methods.

References

Audit Commission (2006) *Comprehensive Performance Assessment.* London: Audit Commission.

Bell, J. (1995) *Doing Your Research Project, A guide for first-time researchers in education and social science,* 4th edn. Buckingham: Open University Press.

Bowen, S. and Shehata, M. (2001) *Soft Systems Methodology.* Calgary: University of Calgary.

Checkland, P. and Scholes, J. (1990) *Soft Systems Methodology in Action.* Chichester: John Wiley.

Clarke, A. (2003) *Evaluation Research: An Introduction to Principles, Methods and Practice.* London: Sage.

Cooperrider, D. and Whitney, D. (2000) *Collaborating for Change: Appreciative Inquiry.* San Francisco, CA: Berrett-Koehler.

Denscombe, M. (2002) *Ground Rules for Good Research: A 10 Point Guide for Social Researchers.* Berkshire: Open University Press.

Denzin, N.K. (1994) 'The art and politics of interpretation', in N.K. Denzin and Y.S. Lincoln (eds) *Handbook of Qualitative Research,* pp. 500–15. Thousand Oaks, CA: Sage.

Feldman, D.C. and Lankau, M.J. (2005) 'Executive coaching and agenda for future research', *Journal of Management* 31(6): 829–48.

Fetterman, D. (1998) *Ethnography: Step-by-Step.* London: Sage.

Grix, J. (2004) *The Foundations of Research* (Palgrave Study Guides). Basingstoke: Palgrave Macmillan.

Hammersley, H. and Atkinson, P. (1993) *Ethnography: Principles in Practice.* London: Routledge.

Janson, A. (2008) 'Extracting leadership: knowledge from formative experiences', *Leadership* 4 (1): 73–94.

Kanter, R. (1993) *Men and Women of the Corporation,* 2nd edn. New York: Basic Books.

Kirk, J. and Miller, M. (1986) *Reliability and Validity in Qualitative Research.* London: Sage.

Koestler, A. (1967) *The Ghost in the Machine.* London: Hutchinson.

Lomax, P. (2002) 'Action research', in M. Coleman and A.R.J. Briggs (eds) *Research Methods in Educational Leadership and Management.* London: Sage.

McCall, M., Lombardo, M. and Morrison, A. (1988) *The Lessons of Experience.* New York: Lexington Books.

McGovern, J. (2001) 'Maximizing the impact of executive coaching: behavioral change, organizational outcomes, and return on investment', *Manchester Review* 6: 1–9.

ODPM (2005) *The Local Government Pay and Workforce Strategy.* London: Office of the Deputy Prime Minister.

O'Reilly, K. (2004) *Ethnographic Methods.* London: Routledge.

Robson, C. (1993) *Real World Research: A Resource for Social Scientists and Practitioner Researchers.* Oxford: Blackwell.

Robson, C. (2002) *Real World Research: A Resource for Social Scientists and Practitioner Researchers*, 2nd edn. Oxford: Blackwell.

Shamir, B., Horesh, H.-Dayan, H. and Adler, D. (2005) 'Leading by biography: towards a life-story approach to the study of leadership', *Leadership* 1(1): 13–29.

Sherman, S. and Freas, A. (2004) 'The wild west of executive coaching', *Harvard Business Review* 82(1): 82–90.

Silverman, D. (2000) *Doing Qualitative Research: A Practical Handbook*. London: Sage.

Yin, R. (2003) *Case Study Research, Design and Methods* 3rd edn. Thousand Oaks, CA: Sage.

11

The development of a research proposal

Key points

This chapter is designed to take you through the key elements of writing a proposal for a work based research project[1], and it is structured in two parts.

Section 1 looks in detail at some characteristics of work based research, and directly addresses the fundamental issues of knowledge, theory and power, exploring the basic principles and conventions of knowledge claims when designing a project proposal for a work based research and development project. It acknowledges that your project is for the purpose of developing practice and is likely to make a difference in a work situation. The difference may be structural change, creative enhancements, or change in you, the practitioner, that in turn influences others. Change of some kind is almost always a key component of a work based project and therefore has to be accounted for in the proposal. We look specifically at all stakeholders in the research and how they might best be involved in both developing the research and putting the research into practice.

Section 2 is a practical user's guide to structuring your project, offering a well tried and tested framework that will meet the needs of most learners on undergraduate and postgraduate programmes requiring work based research. It explores the ways in which the notions of enquiry and research practice that have been previously developed can be presented as a coherent research project proposal, and recommends close cooperation with your advisor.*

*In this chapter, the term 'advisor' is used to describe the research supervisor or member of academic staff assigned to support you in your work based research project.

Section 1: What is work based research?

> Work based projects aim to develop personal and professional practice by research and development and to discover and develop knowledge embedded in that practice. Students are worker researchers and are thus enabled to make a contribution within their communities of practice, that is, in employment, for the community, in a family or voluntary organization and are therefore context bound. The reality of the project and the particularities that contribute to it create a situation where the student as worker researcher is closely involved in the internal specifics of the work. A more traditional university project would involve a leap of the imagination, a more removed stance. (Armsby and Costley, 2000: 35)

Many commentators have pointed to an important characteristic of work based research – its capacity to make explicit knowledge that is often taken for granted or tacit (for example, Eraut, 1992; Maclaren and Marshall, 1998; Maclure and Norris,1991). As a work based researcher, you have at your disposal an immensely valuable resource – your own experience of the workplace. However, in order to turn this experience into knowledge that can be accredited, it will be necessary to create knowledge through the 'transformation of experience' (Kolb, 1984). The key participants in this process are the university (academy) and the organization (workplace). As a work based researcher, you will span both as a participant in the work setting and as a learner carrying out a work based research project. Often, university learning is characterized as theory-based (theoretical) and workplace learning as practice-based (practical). Work based research actually helps to narrow the theory–practice gap, and many good work based studies generate useful theory derived from workplace practice.

Much valuable practitioner research is generated by the process of the practitioner reflecting upon their practice, and the term 'reflective practice' is often used to describe this method of carrying out work based research (see Chapter 9). Similarly, a widely used approach for work based research is the case study method, relying on the study of a particular case to generate evidence to answer research questions. Another commonly used approach to work based research is action research, in which practitioners carry out applied research with the explicit aim of making positive change and improvement, adding to the body of knowledge of understanding processes of development and change in the workplace. For the moment though, we can simply note that work based research is generally characterized as active, personal, experience-based, linking theory and practice, illuminative, situated and reflective.

Language and power relations in the workplace

In work based research, language and power are key issues since:

- the workplace is a site of multiple interests and communities of practice
- the interests of the key stakeholders – the researcher, the workplace and the university – may well not coincide.

Because of this, you should consider carefully what interests are operating in the workplace you are studying. As a workplace researcher, you will have a particular interest in setting up, carrying out and successfully completing a work based research project. However, an employer or manager may or may not support the project and, even if there is support, there may be assumptions about the research that you, the researcher, may not share. You will need to judge how feasible it will be to collaborate with others in the workplace, and you will need to balance any competing or contradictory influences on the aims, objectives, process and outputs of your study. There may be anticipated outcomes that are outside the scope of your project, and there may be unwelcome outcomes that challenge accepted values or assumptions. There are also sets of interests held by the accrediting body for your research, which will generally be a university. A university's regulatory framework governs all its students' work, no matter that the work will be primarily carried out beyond the university itself. The nature of the research report, its format, the timings associated with submission and the assessment regulations will all exert their influence upon your project.

Then, of course, there are your own preferences, values and perspectives which will necessarily bear on your study and which should be frankly acknowledged in your work.

Some commentators have highlighted the particular influence of a multiplicity of power relations and organizational internal hierarchies on work based researchers, and argued that these do not bear in the same way on the university-based researcher. So, as Siebert and Mills (2007: 313) suggest:

> One of the most serious challenges the work based researcher faces is ensuring reliability of their research by minimizing those hierarchies and power relations. This may mean devising tactics and strategies, in other words, displaying resistance, which is precisely what Foucault suggests is necessary, in the process of knowledge creation. The dense defences of managerial practice often conveyed in managerial rhetoric such as 'the right to manage', 'the bottom line' and 'getting the product out the door' can mean that reliability and objectivity are more difficult to achieve.

The topic of the study

How do I decide on a good research topic? This is a question posed by most learners when faced with the prospect of work based research. As a work based researcher, you are likely to have insider knowledge and practical experience which combine to suggest a number of possible research topics. We need to recognize the essential complexity of work based research, drawing as it does upon multi-disciplinary approaches, inter-professional working, professional and regulatory bodies, trades unions, employer/ employee perspectives and power relations and, of course, university regulatory and academic credit frameworks.

Our advice is to take a systematic approach, and to start by doing some creative, open-ended *thinking* about your research topic. If you are working collaboratively with one or two others, you can begin this phase by brainstorming possible work topics suitable for a research project.

Remember, though, the limitations of time, money and access: don't set yourself up to fail with a project that will be too expensive to carry out, that will take a year when you only have four months, or that will require access to an institution, cohort or data that may not be granted. Bearing in mind these practical limitations, though, be as imaginative as you can in thinking about your topic. Consider looking at work-related publications, internal documents and research journals to see what other practitioners and researchers have been doing. Newspapers, television and, of course, the Internet can be other useful sources of possible research topics. Remember, even if someone else has done a similar study, research can still have originality and therefore constitute a contribution to knowledge, for example if you base your study in a different setting, or in the same setting but engage with a different category of enquiry.

It is essential to consider carefully the typology (or category) of knowledge that you expect your research to reveal. For the most part, researchers do not simply dream up a research topic, nor do they enter into research simply hoping to find out something important or in which others will be interested. More usually, as a work based researcher, you will be attempting to uncover one of three broad categories of enquiry into work based policy and practice:

- illuminative – to understand and interpret
- developmental – to make improvements
- critical – to uncover power relationships.

These categories are not mutually exclusive and, like all models, you should adapt and modify to suit your own needs. Mezirow (1991) has suggested a classification of work based learning that closely coincides with these. categories:

- dialogic – the organization and the individual's place in it
- instrumental – skill development and improving productivity
- self-reflective – transformative, focusing on the individual's identity, relationships and the need for self-change.

Often the best approach is to identify what might be done better in the workplace in which you find yourself. Many practitioners are attracted to work based research because of its capacity to develop and make a difference to practice in a work setting. The difference may be structural change, creative enhancements, or change in you, the practitioner, that in turn influences others. Change of some kind is almost always a key component of a work based project and therefore has to be accounted for in the proposal. This might be a process, such as induction for new employees, or a quality-checking procedure for final products off the production line, or it might be something to do with the organizational culture such as how a company motivates its sales force. Alternatively, it might be more to do with your own attitudes, behaviours and performance.

Your choice of topic can be strongly influenced by your personality or by your personal experience of the workplace. For example, if you are working in a healthcare setting, your interests may lie in the way patients interact with the health professionals treating them, or your focus may be on the roles expected of managers, the way employees interact with each other and how changes are implemented. If you are a relatively experienced professional, then it is likely that your own practice will suggest a range of possible research topics. Discussions with work colleagues can often suggest suitable topics. In many cases, a team project is possible where you agree with one or more colleagues to carry out a shared research study, dividing tasks between the group or covering different aspects of a work-related issue or topic.

Alternatively, a supportive supervisor or manager may be an invaluable source of ideas for a project and can easily become a co-researcher in the work. Many excellent work based research projects are developed in this way, with the expectation that the study meets the needs of the work based researcher and the employer, and that both benefit from it in different ways. However, always bear in mind that different stakeholders have different interests and, as stated above, you will have to balance and resolve these to achieve your desired outcome of a high quality project that meets all the higher level assessment criteria.

The list of possible topics is almost endless, which of course is why many learners find this first part of the research process quite hard to pin down, but it is really important that you select an aspect of working life that interests you and preferably one you feel can be improved or enhanced. This should be related to your own interests and professional experience. It should also be an area/issue for which you have relevant research materials and references available to you in your university. As already noted, for most work based researchers, the employer also has an interest.

We can see that, in choosing a research topic, you will have to balance a number of interests:

- the benefits to the organization (community of practice)
- your obligations to the participants (care)
- your own career interests (personal benefit)
- the academic requirements of the university (accreditation).

Remember, when thinking about your work based research project, that every work setting is different. Organizations are infinitely variable. Large companies do things differently from small ones and no two large businesses operate identically. SMEs (small and medium size enterprises) are characterized by their diversity. The public and private sectors have quite different ways of operating and are highly variable, especially when it comes to governance and accountability.

You will especially need to consider the socio-cultural context in which your research is situated. Interpretivist researchers in the social sciences have rightly alerted us to the importance of *situatedness* in research. There are two aspects to this. As a work based researcher studying an organization, you must be aware of, and describe fully, whatever typology of knowledge you expect your research to reveal of the social and cultural environment in which the organization operates. This is important in order that the reader can understand and appropriately locate your work in the research literature. Not only this, but you must not assume that your findings can be applied to other organizations in different social and cultural settings. To their cost, many researchers have attempted to over-generalize their findings in an uncritical way to different countries and contexts which are dissimilar to those of their own study (see Elliott et al., 2010).

The rationale for the study

If your project is part of a taught course, one rationale for choosing a topic might be that it relates closely to one or more of the taught modules you have taken. If so, it is worth explaining carefully what aspects of your chosen topic particularly interest you, which elements of the taught module(s) relate and how the particular literature, approach or perspective that you have been introduced to in the taught part of your course will help to illuminate your chosen research topic. All this will help to convince the assessors that you have chosen your topic carefully and persuade them of the relevance of your project.

There may be some sound academic reason for selecting a particular topic. As new knowledge, theories or approaches are developed, they create new opportunities for work based research. For example, you might apply an approach to organizational analysis developed in one sector to a different sector or, if there are divergent views on a particular issue, you might explore whether these can be reconciled, using your organization as a case study. On the other hand, if some new policy or procedure is in place or being developed, this creates plenty of opportunities to test its impact on those who it will or does affect.

A good rationale for a work based research project is to test the findings of another work based study in a different setting. This is one way in which knowledge can be advanced through research, and brings in the idea of replicating research in specific contexts. Alternatively, especially if you are an experienced professional or practitioner in a particular field, your experience itself may provide a strong rationale for a potentially interesting and important topic. Take care, though, to move from experience to critical analysis; a simple recounting of experience based on anecdote or reminiscence is certainly not research, though it may lead to it!

You should write down all the reasons why you have chosen your topic. Refer to the guidelines for choosing a topic in the previous section, and note down each element that is relevant to your particular choice. Don't forget to include the personal rationale as well as reasons to do with skills, experience and future career. Don't be shy in making claims for your study; even at advanced undergraduate level, work based research projects have influenced the practice both of work based researchers and more widely across the organization.

Understanding methodology and methods

Remember that research methodology is not the same as research methods and techniques. Methodology is about how you, the researcher, see the world. How you see the world is another way of saying that you have one particular theoretical orientation rather than another. From this theoretical orientation, or position, are derived the research methods and techniques best suited to illuminate your enquiry, or to provide you with the answers you need to your research problem. Your work based research may well draw upon more than one theoretical position and this is quite acceptable – as long as you make clear that this is what you're doing. See, for example, Gerrish (2003), who reflects on her own decision-making in creating her ethnographic approach.

The two dominant research traditions (or paradigms) in social science are the positivist and the interpretivist. Positivist researchers maintain that to have knowledge about the social world, it is necessary to gather observable and measurable facts using methods drawn from the natural sciences. People are regarded as the objects of research, the researcher is independent of the research subjects, and values should remain external to the research. Research of this kind is typically characterized by quantitative numerical data that is subjected to statistical analysis to make predictions about future events.

By contrast, interpretative researchers maintain that to have knowledge about the social world, it is necessary to gather data about language, ideas, feelings and meanings which are frequently subjected to qualitative analysis to generate understandings about human behaviour and interaction. People are regarded as participants in the research, the researcher adopts a reflexive stance to acknowledge involvement in and impact upon the research process itself, and values are integral to research. Many interpretivist researchers, unsurprisingly, maintain that human behaviour and interaction can only be properly studied from an interpretivist perspective, since humans impose meanings, interpretations and values upon their own and others' behaviours and actions, and that we must understand these in order to make sense of the social world. Many positivists maintain that the work of interpretivist researchers is partial, biased, unreliable and cannot be generalized.

Although positivist and interpretivist research traditions are often presented as competing and distinct, nonetheless it is not unusual for work based researchers to draw upon both traditions. The general advice on this is to avoid painting your research into a single box, wherever possible. The fact is that insights have been, and will continue to be, generated from studies based in both traditions, and that many mixed method studies do draw on both positivist and interpretivist approaches.

There is a strong relationship between the research traditions described above and research methods. However, it is very important to make a distinction between paradigm and method. Essentially, it is the paradigm that provides the rationale for one particular method over another. Take the example of a study of six women managers in a government office with the objective of understanding their experience of the glass ceiling and career advancement. This study draws principally upon the interpretative paradigm and utilizes qualitative methods, primarily the in-depth interview and the focus group. The rationale for the choice of qualitative methods is that the research aims to give an account of the women's own work experiences and to relate this to their career development and aspirations, and it is principally through the rich description provided by the in-depth interview that their perspectives can be accessed. The focus group adds a further dimension because it is held to be likely that the women responding as a group will generate elements of consensus, divergence and priority in relation to the issues at hand.

Many commentators, for example Nikolou-Walker and Garnett (2004), and Armsby and Costley (2000), have concluded that work based research will generally be better aligned within an interpretative paradigm. For example:

> Work based learning is by design and necessity concerned with knowledge which is often unsystematic, socially constructed and action-focused by the worker researcher, in order to achieve specific outcomes of significance to others. These characteristics appear to fit more comfortably within an interpretative paradigm in which the researcher is an actor involved in the partial creation (through assigning meaning and significance) of what is studied. The nature of work based knowledge and the potential role of the university as co-creator and validator of such knowledge is at the heart of university work based learning. (Nikolou-Walker and Garnett, 2004: 300)

Your work based research project will be transformed from good to excellent if you take care to spell out your theoretical position – the approach to knowledge that you will take. The above section should help you to frame a discussion about knowledge and methodology in your project that will in turn provide you with an appropriate rationale for the research methods that you select and employ.

Section 2: Planning and writing your work based research project

According to Laurence Stenhouse, research is 'systematic and sustained enquiry made public' (Stenhouse, 1983: 185). It follows from this that, to carry out any piece of research, a well-planned and coherent research proposal is essential.

An influential art and culture critic reminds us that 'a way of seeing is also a way of not seeing' (Berger, 1967). What we like about this statement is that it reminds us that research is selective. As a work based researcher, you have the responsibility of selecting or scoping your research project. If you are an undergraduate, your research project will probably count for 30 CATS credits, or a quarter of your final year marks or, to look at it another way, about 120 learning hours. If you are following Masters programme, your research project will of course be more analytical, and might make up a slightly larger proportion of the course learning hours, but not greatly more. Either way, you won't want, or be able, to research everything. One of the hardest lessons to learn as a researcher is how to scope your study. Another hard lesson is when to stop, which is another aspect of the same problem.

The following guidelines[2] provide a simple framework to guide you in your discussions with your research advisor, and act as a checklist of the steps to take when planning your project – it complements the other guidelines available (for example, Bell, 2005; Blaxter, et al., 2006; Denscombe, 2003; Nikolou-Walker, 2008). Consultation with your advisor will be much improved if you systematically apply to the following tasks this tried and proved method of planning and structuring a good work based research project.

Project proposal

1 Selecting the topic of study

- Firstly, identify the broad topic or area of study – refer carefully to the guidelines in Section 1 of this chapter.
- Secondly, describe the nature of the more specific research issue or problem that you intend to address.
- Thirdly, develop a working title for the project for use at the head of your research proposal, in the first instance.

2 The rationale
A good research proposal makes clear *why* the topic is important. Specifically, you should carefully explain:

- why the topic is of general importance
- why it is of current importance in the context/country that you intend to study
- why it is important for you (for example, personal interest, skills, professional experience, future career and so on).

A carefully presented rationale will make it easier for you to explain the significance of your study which is most important if you want to make claims about the originality of your research and its contribution to the field of knowledge in which you are working.

3 Research aims and objectives

In this section, you should identify the broad aim or aims of your research. These will be initial working aims; they may change as your work progresses. Keep this concise and tightly focused because your project must be realistic in scope – and you may have little time and resources at your disposal.

Next, list five or six research objectives. These are more specific in nature. Remember, an objective common to many projects may be the critical review of the relevant literature. A second is often an overview of the context of your study. The third objective could then be to carry out a detailed case study. Other objectives could relate to implications for policy and practice, what outcomes or knowledge contribution might arise from the work, and implications to challenge or support existing theoretical literature, and for future research.

In light of the above, it may be appropriate to formulate a number of key research questions. Again, keep these concise, tightly focused and realistic.

The general aims, research objectives and specific research questions that you formulate will help you to narrow the broad field into a realistic project. This will also help you to demarcate exactly what literature is appropriate for you to review and use to shape your own critique/analysis.

4 The theoretical framework

In this section, briefly outline what theoretical literature you will use to guide the research and act as a starting point and conceptual framework. A full review of the literature often follows in chapter/section 2.

Your aims, objectives and research questions will have arisen in the light of your reading of the relevant literature, in combination with your own ideas and professional experience. State what this literature is and identify and define the main points of view, concepts and terminology you will use. While the perspective you adopt for your study and the concepts you apply may be derived from the work of other writers, it will become the basis of your own theoretical framework.

Remember, in concluding your study, your findings should be related back to the literature to support or to challenge existing knowledge.

5 Research methodology and methods used

Decide what research methodology you will use in your research. Work based research projects may be located in one or many disciplines or be trans-disciplinary. In order to meet the examiners' expectations, it is advisable to clarify at the outset whether the project is based in an academic discipline and, if so, upon which academic discipline or disciplines your study is drawing.

You must first decide what theoretical approach you will adopt, then move on to what methods or techniques for data collection and analysis you will use. You should describe these fully, along with a reasoned justification for your choice. Sometimes a separate chapter/section is used to describe and justify the methodology and methods. Always link the methods and techniques that you use back to your methodology – remember, methodology always drives methods, and you need to make this clear in your writing.

6 Research ethics

Discuss how you will deal with ethical issues related to your study. In particular, consider your own position in the research study, and your relationships with (duty of care towards) participants. Will you have access to confidential or sensitive data and, if so, how will this be authorized and handled? If your work setting includes children or vulnerable adults, what procedures will need to be followed, not only to protect subjects' privacy but to respect their feelings, emotions and their wider personal situation?

N.B. You can turn the above sections into a first draft of chapter/section 1 if you add an extra section here entitled 'Overview of the study'.

7 Sources of data

In this section, you should identify your main sources of data, materials and references.

At an early stage in planning your project, you must know at least where you will get the information you need. It is a good idea to list main sources. You may also be reminded by this to write to various official bodies/people for important material. This must be done at the outset if replies are to arrive in time to influence the shape and nature of the study.

8 Production schedule

Prepare a project work schedule. In this, you should map out a timetable for your work. Include all the months you will have available, then for each month write in the project tasks that you plan to do in that time. A Gantt Chart is a useful technique for planning and scheduling complex work based projects. Remember that writing up needs more than one draft and that you need to allow time for production.

9 Logistics, costs and so on

Logistics, anticipated costs and potential problems are a final set of issues to think about in planning your project.

10 A draft table of contents

On a separate page, try to indicate how you expect the written project to progress, the chapter/section titles, possible main sub-headings and so on. This will change throughout the study, but it can be helpful to have a working draft early on.

11 A working list of references
This should be begun early. From the start, learn the exact style and format for citing references at your university and use this style for your working bibliography.

Collaboration with your advisor

It is the responsibility of each learner to take the initiative in planning and producing a work based research project. Nevertheless, collaboration with your advisor is very important. The advisor will advise, guide and support, but the best quality of supervision is possible only if your advisor is kept well informed of your ideas. Remember also that university staff research commitments, consultancy work and holidays mean that, by the summer vacation period, you should be able to work relatively independently.

Submitting your project proposal

In view of the above guidelines, it is very sensible to initiate early collaboration with your advisor by first writing up a project proposal. For this task, the section headings used above should be followed. The proposal need not be too long, but it should incorporate the details noted for each section plus any other relevant information necessary to brief the advisor fully.

The document should be titled 'Work based project proposal'. This should be followed by the working title and your full name. Add the date of the draft for future reference and the level of the programme that you are enrolled in.

Good news

This proposal will then be the basis of further planning and discussion. It is an important document and one that will be useful draft material when you come to write up your project. Many of the sections of the proposal can be later expanded on to form separate chapters/sections. The proposed structure is also close to the basic framework expected for any work based research project. You can, of course, modify the structure if you believe that this is appropriate for your study.

Discussion questions

1. How important is personal experience in choosing a work based research project?
2. Identify some examples of tacit knowledge that might lend themselves to work based research.

3. What limitations might constrain your choice of project?
4. What sources of data can be drawn upon for work based research? How easy or difficult will each be to obtain?
5. Give examples of projects that are illuminative, developmental and critical.

Notes

1. In this chapter, the term 'project' is normally used to describe an extended work based research study produced to fulfil university assessment requirements at undergraduate or postgraduate level. A work based learning project may, in other contexts, be described as a 'study', 'thesis' or 'dissertation'.
2. The authors acknowledge Professor Michael Crossley, Graduate School of Education, University of Bristol, whose Research Guidelines are extensively drawn upon in Section 2 of this chapter.

References

Armsby, P. and Costley, C. (2000) *Work Based Learning and the University: New Perspectives and Practice*, pp. 35–42. SEDA no. 109, Birmingham: SEDA.

Bell, (2005) *Doing Your Research Project,* 4th edn. Maidenhead: Open University Press.

Berger, J. (1967) *A Way of Seeing*. Harmondsworth: Penguin.

Blaxter, L., Hughes, C. and Tight, M. (2006) *How to Research*, 3rd edn. Buckingham: Open University Press.

Denscombe, M. (2003) *The Good Research Guide for Small-scale Social Research Projects*, 2nd edn. Buckingham: Open University Press.

Elliott, G., Fourali, C. and Issler, S. (2010) *Education and Social Change*. London: Continuum.

Eraut, M. (1992) 'Developing the knowledge base: a process perspective on professional education', in R. Barnett (ed.) *Learning to Effect*, pp. 98–118 London: Taylor & Francis.

Gerrish, K. (2003) 'Self and others: the rigour and ethics of insider ethnography', in J. Latimer (ed.) *Advanced Qualitative Research for Nursing*, pp. 77–94 Oxford: Blackwell.

Kolb, D.A. (1984) *Experiential Learning: Experience as the Source of Learning and Development*. New Jersey: Prentice-Hall.

Maclaren, P. and Marshall, S. (1998) 'Who is the learner? An examination of the learner perspectives in work-based learning', *Journal of Vocational Education and Training* 50 (3): 327–36.

MacLure, M. and Norris, N. (1991) *Knowledge Issues and Implications for the Standards Programme at Professional Levels of Competence*, pp. 35–6 Norwich: Department of Employment, CARE.

Mezirow, J. (1991) *Transformative Dimensions of Adult Learning*. San Francisco, CA: Jossey-Bass.

Nikolou-Walker, E. (2008) *The Expanded University: Work Based Learning and the Economy*. Harlow: Pearson Education.

Nikolou-Walker, E. and Garnett, J. (2004) 'Work-based learning: a new imperative – developing reflective practice in professional life', *Reflective Practice* 5 (3): 297–312.

Siebert, S. and Mills, V. (2007) 'The quest for autonomy: a Foucauldian perspective on work-based research', *Research in Post-Compulsory Education* 12 (3): 309–17.

Stenhouse, L. (1983). *Authority, Education and Emancipation*. London: Heinemann.

12

Preparing and evaluating project outcomes and assessing the learning achieved

Key points

This chapter will address how you should determine the form, nature and context of the outcomes you specify will emerge from your work based project. These outcomes are essential objectives of a work based project and they must be feasible, actionable, measurable and credible. A clear specification for the outcomes makes their evaluation simpler as they can be tested against organizational and, where appropriate, academic criteria. In many cases, the two sets of criteria are similar in intent, but different in focus; the academic are used to assess the learning achieved and are usually assessed against practical outcomes concerning the reliability of a solution to an organizational problem.

Outcomes from work based projects

The outcomes of the project are critical in work based learning. Below is an example of the thinking of a work based learner.

Further realization has been about the dissemination of the material. I have been nervous all the way through about the fact that it has all been done in one part of the organization and therefore may not be representative enough to take out into other organizations. However, I have managed, without consciously trying, to mitigate this risk. By using an external peer to review the work, it helped me be confident that it feels relevant to other organizations. As a result, I have started a very informal presentation of the findings. By talking informally to people about my research project before it is ready, I have created a pull in the organization rather than having to push it into various forums. I hadn't consciously tried to do this, but it has made me realize that by identifying risks early, my subconscious has worked hard to find ways of mitigating them on my behalf. In future, I will do more thorough risk analysis of projects to make sure I give my subconscious the best chance.

An outcome from the project is not an afterthought; let's be clear about that. It is a manifestation of the research work that has been undertaken within the workplace project and is an essential part of it. Outcomes are embedded, grounded and nested in the research which explores the workplace or professional issue that comprises your research project. The outcomes are the natural progress of your project, as the conclusion of your project often marks your arrival at your learning goals. We talk more about how to present these outcomes to stakeholders in the next chapter, but here we want to consider the various forms outcomes may take and to what purpose they may be put.

Outcomes are considered at the beginning of your project, not tacked on at the end. Before writing your project, you need to articulate clearly what it is you want to achieve and establish how you will know when you have achieved it. Project outcomes are the changes that occur and the impact of your having conducted the project. Establishing outcomes at the outset of your plan will enable you to:

- define your goals for the research project
- focus the results of the research project
- evaluate the results and quantify the extent to which the project has achieved its goal
- be accountable to your organization, the community and funding bodies.

An outcome can be tangible, both physical and quantifiable, such as a prototype of a product or a work of art. Alternatively, it can be intangible, such as an increase in intellectual capital, as in property rights. In preparation for the research project and to help define useful outcomes for stakeholders, you might consider convening a stakeholder workshop. Its purpose is to list the relevant outcomes from the project from the point of view of stakeholders other than yourself. Indeed, as part of the development and negotiation of a meaningful learning agreement, the stakeholder meeting has great value as it ensures that expectations are clear for all parties at the inception of the project. Having developed these outcomes and established their relevance to the project and to the organization, they can be prioritized for each stakeholder and used to structure and then finalize the project. You gain a clearer focus on the project's usefulness and it is a way to validate your outcomes with all the stakeholders.

To help in the development and the definition of outcomes so that they are workable, we recommend a process termed the BBRDR model. This considers how the resultant outcomes match the 'who' or the 'what' in the following:

Benefits

What are the benefits the outcome will provide? This helps focus the research process. Moreover, it will form the production of the outcomes according to their evaluation criteria (see below).

Beneficiaries

Who are the people who benefit from the outcome? An understanding of who they are will enable you to comprehend the politics and power relationships of the project. It will also help you steer the project's other ethical research dimensions.

Roles

The outcomes may be produced by you or a team, but to be implemented by others they will usually need your help. A clear understanding of who does what with the outcomes within the community of practice for which they are designed makes them more effective and ensures that the evaluation of your work is fair and appropriate.

Dependencies

It is vital to be clear about what the outcomes depend on. If factors of an outcome for which you wish to claim credit are beyond your control, for instance the allocation of resources, then specify the extent in the research project. Instead of claiming that the outcome is the development of a new location for a manufacturing plant, it is more prudent to define the outcome as that of making recommendations which are acceptable to the company's board. This does not necessitate the recommendations being actioned by the board for your claim to be justified.

Risks

Dependency is just one of the risks to delivering the assigned outcomes. Job losses, closing down of the research project or a change in your own priorities can all impair your ability to deliver. These risks need to be assessed and contingencies developed to ensure that what you say will indeed be delivered.

Forms of outcomes

The outcomes need to motivate and activate others; they are the result of a research project inquiring into a pragmatic problem and are to be used to solve it. Outcomes may take one or multiple forms, for they reflect the problem being investigated and the nature and context of the solution. They represent potential ways of evaluation. They do not deal with the learning process of the project which in future we will term assessment of learning experiences (see below).

Books – these may be academic, professional or for general consumption. If an independent publisher agrees to publish your books – that is, you don't pay for its publication – this in itself is a recommendation of its worth.

Academic papers and trade publications – these are vetted as being of appropriate quality for a target audience. They carry the reputation of the journal or magazine and, as such, may form very acceptable evidence of outcomes of the project.

Reports – these would normally be commissioned by a member of the learning agreement and be intended to inform and have the potential to lead to change.

Recommendations – often accompanying a report, a set of recommendations specifies what should be done. It carries the authority of the author, based on the credibility of the research. If this is within the remit of the learning agreement, recommendations can also be published to wider audiences.

Training courses – taking and actioning the findings of a project might not be strategically in the control of the researcher. However, if one of the outcomes from the recommendations is to change something, to educate or to restrict, evidence that a training programme has been designed and delivered to achieve this is a strong indicator of the value ascribed to the research project by stakeholders to the learning agreement. They are lending it their reputation and often their resources.

Curriculum innovation development – the subsequent acceptance of a proposed curriculum indicates trust in the outcome and faith in the creators.

Prototypes – if the project is to design a tangible product, create a formula or write prototype software, provide evidence that the potential can be realized.

Framework and model – in coaching, for instance, the development of an approach or model to assist professional practice is an ideal outcome, as it directly benefits the profession.

Works of art – these are notoriously difficult to evaluate. To those whose professional opinions are valued, works of art may engender the same level of confidence as more conventional outcomes.

New polices, procedures and guidelines – proposing the adoption of recommendations from research to direct the future of the profession or an organization may form a worthwhile outcome.

Health and fitness programmes – anything with a wider, national or international audience that might need endorsement and then dissemination may prove a worthy outcome. Trying to stipulate actual, changed behaviour is not wise, for this is beyond the control of the devised programme and its authors.

Website construction – where interactive dissemination of findings and e-commerce opportunities are important to the research project, website design, construction and evaluation can prove important outcomes for a research project.

Criteria for the evaluation of outcomes

Outcomes are identified at the proposal stage of your project and should be made known to all the stakeholders. Most importantly, the stakeholder should have the criteria to evaluate these outcomes. These criteria need to be negotiated at the same time as the other elements of the learning agreement such as access, withdrawal from the research site and voluntary participation of research subjects. Not to agree these at the beginning of the project can lead to misunderstanding, disappointment and frustration. What each party took to be the consensus form of the outcome could end up different for each stakeholder. For example, if I expected as an outcome a recommendation for the re-engineering of my factory floor processes, with a detailed map, a timetable and estimated disruption times, I would be disappointed if I received a report discussing the effect of colour on workers' ability to concentrate at their machines! Although both would be valuable to my operation, only one would be what was expected.

The criteria for evaluation reflect the objectives to which the outcome relates and will vary according to the nature of the stakeholders' interest. For instance, if the work based project is to lead to an academic award, a set of learning outcomes might need to be evident in the outcome to satisfy the conditions of the award. Of course, the outcome will not represent the learning outcomes, for that is not its purpose; its part is the important role of offering evidence of learning criteria. Table 12.1 offers a number of project titles with outcomes and forms of evaluation.

Evaluation of the outcomes can take various forms, depending mainly on the needs of the interested parties, as indicated in Table 12.1. The following are just suggestions and need to be related to your project's specific needs in effecting change in your work community, professional group or on a wider policy issue.

Table 12.1   Example project titles with outcomes and forms of evaluation

Project	Typical forms of outcomes	Evaluation evidence
The development of a vocational course on marine seamanship	• A curriculum designed to gain approval of professional bodies • Endorsements from ship owners • Institution and (where appropriate) government approval for the course • Recruitment of students • Job places	• A letter stating that the curriculum is approved and exemption given against professional awards • Ship owners agree to the course and recommend students to it • The programme is run by the institution and receives funding from government, if appropriate • Student numbers match or exceed project targeted numbers • Students find job places whilst on course and subsequently obtain jobs
The development of software to improve the customer relationship management system of the organization	• A test programme • A support package	• The trial is signed off • User positive evaluations
An increased awareness of health, diet and exercise in one's lifestyle	• Increased media coverage • Dietary and exercise programmes • Books and lectures	• Media schedule with various appearances and viewer/listener penetration figures • Programme accept by professionals (doctors) as valuable • Books published by independent publishers • A series of open lectures
The introduction of a new strategic direction to an organization through action learning	• Action research adopted as an appropriate programme for change management • Revision of strategy with an implementation plan	• The running and evaluation of action research circles • Buy-in confirmation from staff and management
The development of burial and cremation policy	• Publication of recommendations • A research report on the acceptability of a new policy	• Recommendation adopted by profession and government • Research cited as an important contribution to the debate by

(Continued)

Table 12.1   *(Continued)*

Project	Typical forms of outcomes	Evaluation evidence
		professionals and academics
The introduction of Chinese medicine within higher education	• The development of an award-bearing course for a higher education institution • Recruitment to the course	• Recognition within the Chinese medical community of the worth of the programme • Matching of targeted demand with actual numbers
The development of an injection therapy module	• Provision of a rationale for the proposed approach • The development of detailed procedures	• Satisfying of all clinical requirements for the procedures to be adopted • Gaining of approval to trial the therapy
The development of an ethical framework for the profession of educational marketing	• The development of a compelling case for the adoption of a new ethical code • The development of a code that is feasible	• Establishing the core of the profession to accept the code • Having all stakeholders accept the content and form of the code
The development and implementation of an online English placement test: a case study	• Establishing the form of assessment required for an online test and valid proposed approach • Production of a programme that can fulfil testing specifications to a satisfactory standard form of the code	• Gaining acceptance from professionals on the approach to be adopted • Undertaking a testing programme and making research transparent for inspection and verification
The development of feedback in lay preaching	• Understanding the dynamic of feedback of quality within the context of lay preaching • Utilizing feedback in improving the quality of preaching	• Gaining community acceptance as to the form and measurement that will provide the feedback • Increasing the power, conviction and transformative power of preaching

Evaluations

Evaluating the work presented is all about finding out if it is of adequate quality, rigour and practical significance to satisfy and validate the achievement of the research project for the organizational and academic stakeholders. This should not take place when presenting the outcomes; at an early stage, the requirements should be converted into criteria against which the work presented can be objectively evaluated.

Before continuing, we should distinguish between our usage of the terms 'evaluation' and 'assessment'. Assessment refers to information and judgement about individual student learning, and we discuss it in the next section. Evaluation, on the other hand, is about gaining information and making judgements on the actual outcomes of that learning in terms of the effectiveness of the project's artefacts in matching the goals set out in the learning agreement. For instance, when we undertake a training course, we are often asked to complete an evaluation form of the course which includes:

• What was the quality of the classroom?
• Was it organized well?
• Were the lecturers' presentations up to standard?

These are questions of evaluation. If the object of the survey is to assess the learning that has taken place, the questionnaire would talk more in terms of:

• Has the learning objective been achieved?
• Was the course effective for the learners?
• What were the learning benefits?

Thus, the critical evaluation questions relate to evaluating what, why and for whom. To answer these, we will use the same process we used to construct the outcomes. By using the BBRDR model, we can compile an evaluation matrix of how the outcomes satisfy stakeholders to the project. To make the issue a little easier, let us assume there are three primary stakeholders, that is, signatories to the learning agreement. (Of course, there are likely to be more – the research participants, the workers and the community, but the three chosen will act as an example.)

Assessment of work based learning

As Murdoch (2004) has discussed, there has been considerable reluctance within the work based learning community to move towards a formal assessment system for work based learning – one that would stand up to close scrutiny. This is partly because of the perceived difficulties of achieving valid, reliable and comparable assessments, given the complex interactions of human, social, technical and practical processes in the workplace. To some extent, this has been overcome by seeking evidence that can be assessed by clear criteria. Taylor (2008) suggests that, as a mode of learning, work based learning is centred on reflection about work practices and about the process of learning, and is more process-oriented than classroom-based learning, with stronger elements of action and problem solving.

Table 12.2   What is expected of the learner

What learners should know and their learning advisors facilitate:

- what learning is (how learning implies change) – *learning theory*
- how to do it best (style, approach, fitness for purpose) – *learning theory*
- when they have learnt (description of and reflection about the learning) – *critical reflection*
- by what their learning is informed (its validity; how it stands up to scrutiny against outside evidence) – *critical reflection*
- what they need to learn (future learning) – *critical reflection*
- what they have learnt, know more about, become more able at doing (analysis and evaluation of the learning) – *capability.*

(Brodie and Irving, 2007: 14)

Brodie and Irving (2007) have developed an important and useful set of pedagogical principles in relation to work based learning that, they argue, work based learners themselves ought to know. These are shown in Table 12.2.

There are, of course, various ways in which these processes can be revealed in order that they may be assessed. We favour general learning criteria which judge on the basis of the demonstrated academic level of the research project's learning component. The mechanism for recognizing these revealed skills and experiences is professional judgement informed by level descriptors relating to the contextualized outcomes of learning. These descriptors are something between occupational standards and academic level descriptors. Moreover, these standards are applied to learning that you, the holder of these learnt experiences, determine. That is, they respond to what is intended to be shown and ask what the evidence is and how it builds into an architecture of learning to inform those unfamiliar with the actual learning, so they understand. Such an approach allows generic descriptors to be used; interpreted for each project, they also retain a stand on intra-project quality.

A practical example of these descriptors in UK higher education is provided in Table 12.3. These are currently used by the Institute for Work Based Learning at Middlesex University to judge the learning experience and achievement of professional Doctorate and Masters students. Similar descriptors at the appropriate level are used for the work based learning undergraduate level programmes.

Awarding credit based on individual, experiential learning within the work based project is recognized as fundamental to the awards (Doncaster, 2000) because they centralize you, the individual. That is, the award is individually focused and negotiated, thus concentrating on your own personal set of skills, knowledge and abilities, and your learning. Finding criteria by which to judge these unique characteristics is no simple task and the complex assessment process for this, which involves understanding claims from the claimants' perspective, has been outlined elsewhere (Armsby et al., 2006).

Table 12.3   Levels 4 and 5 assessment criteria for the MProf/DProf programmes at Middlesex University (effective 2009)

	Key term	Assessment criteria	
		Masters level	**Doctorate level**
A. Knowledge and understanding			
A1	Knowledge	Identification and appropriate use of sources of knowledge and evidence is wide-ranging, critical and often innovative.	Evidence that the candidate has depth and range of knowledge in a complex area and is currently working at the leading edge of practice underpinned by theoretical understanding.
A2	Research + development capability	Selection and justification of approaches to task/problem are self-directed and involve recognition, articulation and critical evaluation of a range of options from which a justified selection is made, based upon a reasoned methodology.	Demonstrates effective and critical selection, combination and use of research and development methods; can develop new approaches in new situations and contribute to the development of practice-based research methodology.
A3	Ethical understanding	Ethical understanding spans a range of contexts, where applicable prescribed codes and their rationale are critically understood and sensitively applied.	Demonstrates awareness of ethical dilemmas and conflicting values which may arise in professional practice and work situations; able to formulate solutions in dialogue with superiors, peers, clients, mentors and others.
B. Cognitive skills			
B1	Analysis + synthesis	Analysis and synthesis of information and ideas demonstrate critical awareness and result in the creation of knowledge of significance to others.	Demonstrates ability to analyse and synthesize complex and possibly conflicting ideas and information in order to redefine knowledge and develop new approaches.

(Continued)

Table 12.3   *(Continued)*

	Key term	Assessment criteria	
		Masters level	**Doctorate level**
B2	Self appraisal/ reflection on practice	Self appraisal/reflection on practice leads to significant insights which are likely to make a lasting impact upon personal and professional understanding.	Provides evidence of work with 'critical communities' through whom a new or modified paradigm is being established. Habitually reflects on own and others' practice so that self-appraisal and reflective inquiry are intertwined, thereby improving the candidate's own and others' actions.
B3	Planning/ management of learning	Action planning leading to effective and appropriate action is complex and is likely to impact upon the work of others.	Is autonomous in management of own learning; makes professional use of others in support of self-directed learning and is fully aware of political implications of the study.
B4	Evaluation	Is able to independently evaluate/argue a position concerning alternative approaches; can justify evaluations as constituting bases for improvement in practice.	Can independently evaluate/argue a complex position concerning alternative approaches; can accurately assess/report on own and others' work; can critique and justify evaluations as constituting bases for improvement in practice.
C. Practical skills			
C1	Awareness of operational context + application of learning	Application of learning involves indicating workable frameworks and/or models for practice which transcend specific contexts.	Can take into account complex, unpredictable, specialized work contexts requiring innovative approaches, which involve exploring current limits of knowledge and, in particular, interdisciplinary approaches and understanding.

Table 12.3

	Key term	Assessment criteria	
		Masters level	**Doctorate level**
			Is able to translate and disseminate theoretical knowledge into workable frameworks and/or models for practice.
C2	Use of resources	Effective use of resources is wide-ranging and is likely to impact upon the work of others.	Effective use of resources is wide-ranging, complex and is likely to impact upon the work of others.
C3	Communication/ presentation skills	Effective communication both in writing and orally is in an appropriate format to appeal to a particular target audience and is clear, concise and persuasive.	Can engage in full professional and academic communication with others in their field and place of work; can give papers/presentations to 'critical communities' for developmental purposes.
C4	Responsibility + leadership	Working and learning autonomously and with others spans a range of contexts, often in a leadership role, and is likely to challenge or develop the practices and/or beliefs of others.	Autonomy within bounds of professional practice with high level of responsibility for self and others. Ability to provide leadership as appropriate.

The criteria fall into three categories: knowledge and understanding, cognitive skills and practical skills. These represent three perspectives. Knowledge and understanding are facts, information, conceptual interpretations and so on that can be known; cognitive skills are what a person needs to have in order to effectively process that which is known; and, finally, practical skills enable the user to put into practice the knowledge that has been personally processed. Clearly, there is overlap in these abilities; thinking, being and acting must come together and synthesize in experiences. Claims unpick what is known, how it is known and evidence what has been achieved using that knowledge and personal skill. This explicit depiction of personal experience is empowering, as it recognizes the individual as a whole, consisting of thoughts, feelings and actions.

Any learning experiences can be assessed against these criteria and some will be more important than others for specific experiences. Work and experience imply action or practical application; hence practical skills are important in the assessment of work based learning and provide a convenient platform for recognizing achievement. However, it is the range of criteria and the unique expression of experiences synthesizing these criteria that provide a powerful tool for recognizing individuals' specific and personal knowledge, being, action and learning. The use of this form of explicit assessment criteria allows not only the functionality of your learning to be revealed, but also helps to describe the epistemology and ontology of your practice.

Concluding comments

In this chapter, we have shown that outcomes are central to the successful evaluation of a work based project. We have distinguished assessment from evaluation, stating that evaluation applies to outcomes, and assessment to the learning process that creates the outcomes. Each is important, but has higher priority depending upon which stakeholder to the learning agreement you happen to be.

Discussion questions

1. Why do we need to evaluate workplace learning explicitly?
2. Discuss a range of outcomes and consider the most appropriate form of evidence for each. Can one piece of evidence be used for different outcomes?
3. Discuss the difference between evaluation and assessment
4. Why is it critical to develop clear outcomes before the research is undertaken?
5. Can defining outcomes before the research influence the research process? Is this a problem for workplace research?

References

Armsby, P., Costley, C. and Garnett, J. (2006) 'The legitimisation of knowledge: a work based learning perspective of APEL', *International Journal of Lifelong Education* 25 (4): 369–83.

Brodie. P. and Irving, K. (2007) 'Assessment in work-based learning: investigating a pedagogical approach to enhance student learning', *Assessment and Evaluation in Higher Education* 32 (1): 11–19.

Doncaster, K. (2000) 'Recognising and accrediting learning and the development of reflective thinking', in D. Portwood and C. Costley (eds) *Work Based Learning and the University: New Perspectives and Practices*, SEDA Paper 109. Birmingham: SEDA.

Murdoch, I.J. (2004) 'Developments in the evaluation of work-based learning: a UK perspective', *Industry and Higher Education* 18 (2): 121–4.

Taylor, C. 2008. *The Assessment of Work-based Learning in Foundation Degrees.* Available at: http://escalate.ac.uk/1151 [accessed 10 March 2009].

13

Recommendations and presentations arising from the research

Key points

A critical area for work based practitioner research and development projects is making meaningful recommendations. These need to be explained both to an academic and a professional audience in order for them to be implemented. Academic audiences expect a through line within the project where recommendations are shown to arise directly from the project's findings, and they require adherence to specific academic assessment criteria. Professional audiences expect to be persuaded into implementing recommendations based on both the compelling outcomes of the research and the credibility of worker-researchers themselves. To have your recommendations taken seriously by colleagues, it is most beneficial if those making and implementing project recommendations have good standing in their networks of colleagues, understand the arguments and frame their advocacy to appeal to their audience.

Making recommendations justified by practitioner-led research is a central purpose of many work based research projects where the project's value is in its practical application. The two broad audiences for your project are the academic audience, who will formally assess the work according to the assessment criteria of the course programme specifications, and your work audience, to whom the project is likely to bring a worthwhile change or enhancement to practice. There will be a great deal of shared interest between these two audiences but, nevertheless, it is important that you have full understanding about how all the recipients of your research project are likely to receive your work.

You have planned to research an important and relevant element of your work as part of an educational course that will also be in some way significant for your organization or professional area. As this is the case, your project proposal will also plan the implementation of the project, giving at the planning stage the thought and consideration that are important for the practicalities of implementing the project. The outcomes of your work based research project are likely to contain recommendations for change or enhancement that may be small or large scale, at policy or practice level, and in a variety of forms. These recommendations arise from the research outcomes and are usually then shared with colleagues and others in the research, for example customers and other stakeholders. This is because your work based project is likely to be, or have the potential to be, used in your organization or other practice community.

From the perspective of your work situation, it is important to address the issue of who should implement the project's recommendations. For example, you are likely to be the main driver in their implementation, but it is also likely that your line manager will play an important role, at least in endorsing your work. There may also be an organizational committee, outside bodies such as partner organizations that become involved in disseminating your work, or perhaps government agencies with an interest at a policy level that should be informed about your recommendations. How these might be implemented should be detailed, and precisely what needs to be done should also be made clear so the change-makers, whoever they may be, know precisely what you recommend them to do. When and where the dissemination of your recommendations ideally takes place is also an important consideration, as the details of timing and place can have consequences on how ideas are received.

From the perspective of the academic community, conclusions leading to recommendations must be clearly drawn from the project's findings and should address the initial aims and objectives of the project. Recommendations should therefore always arise out of the research project and include important issues and findings to justify what is being proposed. Academic assessors are looking for rigorous research which follows a logical argument, from the initial aim to the final recommendations. The work will be assessed in relation to the assessment criteria so it is clearly important to study these carefully and address them in detail.

Some projects are based on an action research approach, where there are points in time during the research process when action is taken to make changes in the place where the research is situated. Other projects use a more evaluative approach, where the final outcome is likely to include recommendations for change arising from the evaluation. Similarly, case study approaches and other investigative approaches to research result in an analysis of the researched situation from which recommendations arise. Whatever approach is taken to your work based project, the recommendations should be an area – probably a whole section entitled 'Conclusions and recommendations' – given due consideration throughout the project.

Recommendations can be considered as both prescription and advocacy, drawn from the research and evolving into judgemental decisions then to be applied in specific situations. The recommendations can be made with or without provision for processes that specify activities taking place over varying amounts of time. The amount of detail in the recommendations will depend on the nature of the project and what it set out to achieve when it was set up and its objectives were stated. In any event, recommendations are likely to result in a clear, helpful and rigorous set of points that can be acted upon by others, where necessary, and offer vital and compelling alternatives in a work situation. They are the result of a thorough and considered piece of research informed by insider knowledge and should be candid, research-informed, specialized and coherent.

Setting out your recommendations

The results of your project may give rise to recommendations for change that need to be addressed by a range of stakeholders, for example colleagues in your organization, peers in other organizations, others in the same professional field, perhaps abroad, policy makers and so on. Although the core recommendations may be to colleagues and, not least, yourself, the innovations you propose are likely to be addressed to more than one audience. For example, if your recommendations involve changing the use of a room or building for specific purposes explained in your project, you need to make a case for the change to policy makers who will agree, or not, in principle. Next, you would recommend how the change would take place, how the use of the room would work in practice and who would be involved and so on. The secondary issues concerning actual processes often need to be shown as sustainable before the policy makers agree to make the change. So there are strategic reasons for making recommendations that not only provide the rationale for change, but also show that change is feasible. As well as feasibility, the rationale for change needs to be compelling, so the recommendations need to stimulate the reader into wanting to make the change by making clear sense and suggesting what positive impacts the recommendations could have.

Consider the best media to disseminate your work for the purpose – for example, bulletins, newsletters or formal presentations with an executive summary. Oral, written or both forms of dissemination can be used to make a set of recommendations to the academic and the professional audience. Alternatively, an outline that draws upon the project findings, cross-referenced with appendices setting out the work based actions in more detail, could be drawn up which could then be used for differing audiences in the work situation.

There are two examples of recommendations arising from work based Masters projects in Chapter 10 that demonstrate the range of stakeholders in the projects to whom recommendations for change are addressed. The rationale for making the changes is shown to be informed by the research.

Considering the practice situation in depth

There is no set way of introducing your recommendations into your particular situated practice. There are bodies of knowledge, referenced in the sections below, which consider how changes in practice may be influenced by a range of both internal and external factors. These texts are worthy of consideration because they can help you think deeply and strategically about how your recommendations might be received and implemented. Practitioners who consider their situation in depth are more likely to understand how to undertake broad and wide-ranging influences on particular practices.

Practice is frequently theoretical. That is, it refers to theory that informs it, of which practitioners or others may or may not be aware (Carr, 2005; Kemmis, 2005). There is no doubt that many practitioners operate successfully without a great deal of recourse to theory but are intuitive about the worth of actions they decide to take. Making a case for change always involves practical reasoning (Aristotle, 1995; Gadamer, 1977; Gauthier, 1963), using knowledge in the face of uncertainty, guided by a practical knowledge-constitutive interest in acting wisely and prudently in given circumstances (Carr and Kemmis, 1986; Habermas, 1974). It is likely that the most successful people take actions based on their experience, their intuitive knowledge of their practice and their ability to interpret theory. It is this combination that is likely to produce practices that make a real, positive impact on work situations. Theory can arise in many forms, often directly out of practice, and the two can be thought of as being mutually constitutive.

A further consideration is the need to avoid making assumptions about your research project's validity as a free-standing piece of evidence with a theoretical 'truth' of its own. To provide data from your project as hard facts and to state that these alone should bring about a change in practice can go against the human dimension of the community that is to effect it. There is a 'positivist' scientific tradition whereby, to be truly scientific, facts and values are separated. This is sometimes regarded as meaning that precise values are not included in reporting research outcomes. A contrasting academic stance adopted in the interpretation of data is that this position is solely a technicist view, and can threaten to empty practice of its moral dimension. This is not a price professional practitioners should be prepared to pay in exchange for the alleged 'certainties' of the restricted range of 'evidence' that 'counts' in positivist approaches. Changes in real-time situations are never so straightforward.

Theorists and practitioners who have written extensively on the influences on practice are cited in this chapter to provide further reading to assist your thinking about strategies for implementing your research.

Your insider credibility within your organization or professional community

How your recommendations are received in your work situation may depend on your current position within your organization or professional community, your reputation and how people have received both you and your work in the past. You require others to recognize the validity of your research – your credibility – which will be based upon other professional and personal issues of managing your identity as a worker undertaking research within your own organization or community of practice.

The presentation of the research results and recommendations is likely to contain more than the technical results of the research, that is, the 'evidence'. You are presenting the rationale for your recommendations as well as the measurable outcomes or outputs. A valuable contribution to the research that you are able to offer as an insider-researcher is the individual perspective of a professional practitioner. Your practice involves meaning and intention and the data you collect will be interpreted according to your own experiences and knowledge as a practising professional. In the conduct of your work, your intentions, values and commitments are therefore crucial (Kemmis, 2006).

The arguments that support your project's recommendations can be derived from the empirical evidence that has emanated from your research project (Costley, 2007) and from the dialectal logic derived from your practice (Costley and Doncaster, 2000). In order to persuade your audience about your proposed changes, the recommendations need to move them to action by convincing them that the recommendations are worthwhile (Beckett and Hager, 2002). The worker-researcher, whose insider status in the work situation ensures familiarity with both the research and those for whom it is destined, needs the recommendations for change to be first accepted and then implemented, and this requires more than excellent research and argument. How they are received also depends on your own credibility as a worker.

Your credibility within your work situation is likely to influence decisions regarding acceptance or rejection of the recommendations and their implementation by the audiences at whom the research has been aimed. It may rest on a number of factors such as how well you are known, which in turn may depend on how long you have worked within a particular community. Other factors are your reputation, your position and perceived importance, and your character (discussed further below). Much of the knowledge and understanding that you bring to interpreting data and how you perceive your project arises from your own identity and subjectivity (Benhabib, 1992). The relationships you form as a practitioner and the subject of your work, along with those who represent the objects of your work (other colleagues, clients and students), provide opportunities for a reflexive practice where working relationships change and relate to the needs and ideas of others (Cunliffe, 2004). It may be that it is the extent to which you have engaged in such reflexivity that embeds and confirms your insider status as someone who shares and acts with others.

You will have certain learned capacities and competences gained from experience, from training and previous education. Added to this and, indeed, merged with it, your identity and emotional responses unfold within the human and social action of your work situation and inevitably against the background of your own, individual biography. Much theoretical work has been derived through scholarly work in relation to individuals' biographies and the relation it has to their work and lives (Hodkinson et al., 2004, 2008). Your practices are frequently preserved, maintained and developed through the way your professional role has developed and the particular functions or roles you have undertaken.

Working practices nearly always involve and express values, and are often value-laden, like the value of care for those with whom you work, and come into the remit of your working life (Noddings, 2002). Social norms guide us through many of the moral and ethical concerns we encounter there and other, more nuanced, morals, ethics and virtues are still evident to those with whom you work.

It is almost always important to have had your work endorsed from the outset by someone who is perceived by others to have such credibility, and this is no less the case when presenting the outcomes of the project work to implement the outcomes. Further, the form of the actual recommendations will also sway others who do not have access to the underlying evidence or argument that supports the recommendations. An understandable and compelling interpretation of the research findings, whilst drawing on the data, depends on your ability to persuade, often orally or in presentational form (Wolcott, 2001). You will need to take this into account and engage with individuals and networks that can support you.

As an insider-researcher, you know how initiatives are likely to be received within your organization or professional field. For instance, you will know which people would be open to your ideas and be willing to listen, or to facilitate wider dissemination of the work, how systems work and the best timing for presentations or sending out information about your project. Whatever the context for your research, it is likely that you are the best person to drive the implementation of your work based project. Added to your insider knowledge, you now also have precise and rigorous data which you have interpreted with your expert knowledge of the work situation. In essence, the whole project from inception to implementation is likely to be orchestrated by you. However, as we will discuss below, you are operating in a situation where there are 'extra-individual' features that can affect your actions.

The influence of your organization or professional community

Practice is always historically formed and the product of structured, local (in this situation, among these people) and more global history (Foucault, 1970). It is frequently preserved, maintained, developed and regulated in institutions and organizations, and in the cooperative work of professions. In the traditions of communities of practice, your work situation has historical and social meaning and significance beyond the particular measurable effect of particular acts of particular practitioners at particular times. It is wise to recognize the extent of these embedded and more macro influences upon the propositions you recommend.

Your organization or professional community is invariably located in a particular cultural tradition of particular societies and groups (Toulmin, 1972). Practices are always constructed in cultural and linguistic times and places with social and material–economic dimensions. These involve structured systems of relationships between people, and people and things (see, for example, systems theory and activity theory) which may include relations of economic exchange (see Bourdieu's 'economic capital', 1986). Practices frequently involve systemically structured material interactions, for example role-related functions and economic transactions such as payment for services. You may need to interact with several communities that are thus variously located and with whom you may need to engage differently. This demands sensitivity on your part about how your communications will be received by others.

Your work is always culturally and discursively formed and structured, being realized in languages and discourses. For example, Bourdieu (1986) uses the term 'cultural capital' to mean the knowledge, experience and or connections gained through the course of life that can lend advantage to someone from a privileged background, especially through education. In addition, work is frequently subjected to discursive regulation through law, policy and standards (see Lyotard, 1984, on performativity). Further, it is represented by symbolic forms that codify it, making connections to what Foucault (1980) explains as power/knowledge, where only those with certain knowledge and understanding are in a position to act. Inter-subjectivity would involve relating and discussing with others, which is necessarily grounded in the reasoning of language (Habermas, 2003), making it important that your reasoning is communicated clearly and convincingly. This requires an understanding of yourself and others as social, political and cultural beings.

There are nearly always possibilities for inviting the opening of communicative space and the creation of a more public and open discourse in which practitioners, clients and others explore issues and themes of common concern or interest (Habermas, 1987; Kemmis, 2000). This invites what Habermas has termed 'communicative action' – that is, collaborative action oriented towards mutual understanding, inter-subjective agreement and consensus on what to do. These forms of social integration of people such as practitioners, clients and others, for example in care via nursing, in education via teaching and in sustenance of people and land via farming, demonstrate the possibilities for discussion, debate and consensus and the importance of consulting all stakeholders about relevant issues (Giddens, 1984).

Presenting the research project and the art of persuasion

Some universities require an oral presentation and *viva voce* to assess research projects undertaken as part of a degree programme. Work based courses usually look for an ability to select and order your materials for the presentation and to be clear about the whole purpose and outcome of the project. They normally require you to convey the essence of the project clearly and coherently to deepen the assessor's understanding, and they require you to respond to questions displaying a depth of understanding that also confirms the authenticity of the project within its research context.

Practical presentation skills are an important factor here. To some extent, the ability to present well can be learned. It is worthwhile undertaking training in this area to ensure you are presenting to the best of your ability and using the most appropriate forms of presentation. You can also access the many texts and websites with good advice, for example Vitae's *Preparing for a Presentation* (2008).

A key factor in actualizing many work based projects is the oral representation of ideas and of any proposed changes or innovations to work communities. As well as presenting the results of your research project to an academic audience, you should be prepared to present it to a professional audience. The basis of such a presentation may be your recommendations. In work based learning, this focus on presenting work to others is important, as the subject of research is a working environment where practical issues are investigated. The results of these investigations may have a significant practical impact. The rest of this section deals with oral presentation within the sphere of your work with a view to actualizing the proposed recommendations.

Some of the qualities associated with constructing a compelling argument can be found in Aristotle's *Rhetoric,* an ancient Greek treatise on how practical judgements can be communicated in public. Aristotle (1995) writes that they who have practical wisdom (*phronēsis*) must also have moral excellence because the good character of the rhetorician 'may almost be called the most effective means of persuasion [s]he possesses' (1995: 14). The orator should be perceived to have good sense, excellence in moral character and goodwill. From this, we can conclude that it is not just the findings of the research project that are important in persuading colleagues to implement them; it is also a matter of who is endorsing the recommendations towards action, and how this is done.

The character of those making recommendations needs to complement the recommendation process; their views need to be credible, reliable and unbiased. Indeed, they must be seen to engage and carry the audience for whom the recommendations are intended. This may have special importance for work based researchers, whose relationship with their audience is more personal (Gibbs and Costley, 2006) than that of those making recommendations based on, for example, the deliberations of a committee.

In a contemporary work setting, a worker's credibility may depend partly on their position within an organization or community of practice, and also on whether they are perceived by others as being someone who regards the welfare of others or the company as a priority. It may depend on emotional intelligence and qualities of leadership. Putting a work based project into action often depends on who is driving it and, maybe because of the proposer's position and personal reputation, whether there is an element of compulsion.

Aristotle recognizes that to evoke emotions in the audience is an important component of the presentation of an argument, and for this he develops the use of the enthymeme,[1] which draws in the audience with its simple structure, and can be employed in the form of an example. Given that the audience is unlikely to be as expert as the researcher, it seems plausible that adopting the enthymeme which is based upon 'one or other of four things: probabilities, examples, evidences, signs' (Aristotle 1995: 13–14) offers advantages of style and content.

The use of appropriate enthymemes and emotional contexts is intended to prove the truth of statements and can disrupt our interpretation of our conditioned and accepted everyday practice to help us be moved to make a change. The presenter demonstrates understanding of a situation and the actions needed for communal benefit. Thus, the ability to present research results goes beyond persuasion to include the development of judgement and a sound practical understanding and social awareness. The recommendations must move the audience to act and so must be persuasive, clear and reasonable. This engagement with the audience's emotion is difficult to achieve and sustain, but it can be accomplished in structuring recommendations by the use of the enthymeme, which assumes not only the rationality but the emotionality of the audience.

Three elements of persuasive communication to best present an argument are thus deemed to be: the credibility of the speaker, the disposition of the audience and the content of the message. A fuller discussion of the relevance of Aristotle's work on rhetoric to work based learning is given in Gibbs and Costley (2008).

Dissemination and diffusion of your recommendations in the professional sphere

More contemporary work on presenting and disseminating ideas in practice situations can be found amongst the literature on organization theory, especially in organizational change. Recent thinking in this field focuses on the diffusion of ideas both across and within organizations through the production, sharing and transfer of knowledge. It is now recognized that informal, uncodified, 'tacit' knowledge has high value in work situations and there a few formal processes for sharing such knowledge.

Greenhalgh et al. (2004) carried out a review of the literature on the spread and sustainability of innovations in health service delivery and organization, and consider six key questions for discussion:

- Innovations: what features (attributes) of innovations influence the rate and extent of adoption?
- Adopters and adoption: what is the nature of the adoption process – and why do some people adopt innovations more readily than others?
- Communication and influence: what is the nature of the diffusion process and in particular how does social influence promote the adoption of innovations?
- The inner context: what elements of the inner (organizational) context influence the adoption and assimilation of innovations in organizations?
- The outer context: what elements of the outer (environmental) context, including aspects of inter-organizational communication, influence the adoption and assimilation of innovations in organizations?
- Implementation and sustainability: what are the features of effective strategies for implementing innovations and ensuring that they are sustained until they reach genuine obsolescence?

Each of the questions can have specific consequences when disseminating and diffusing ideas in organizations and there are also many cross-cutting issues that can impact on successful implementation. The Teaching Quality Enhancement Fund (TQEF, undated) makes a useful checklist available that suggests approaches to effective dissemination.

Whatever strategies you choose to put in place to successfully embed the recommendations of your project in your organization, they will be made easier and more effective if you think the strategies through at the planning stage of the project. It has to be part of your thinking and in turn these strategies could make a difference to the topic of your project and the way you undertake the project (your methodology). It is without a doubt a valuable exercise to read some of the literature available in this area.

There should not be any insurmountable problems in appealing to both an academic audience and a professional audience; people often write on one topic and produce results that are then arranged for differing audiences. There may need to be some amendments to the final project. For example, the recommendations section of your work may need to be extended for the professional audience, whilst the methodology section of your project is likely to be reduced, and it may be that you decide to write an executive summary for the professional audience.

From Aristotle, it seems that we might conclude that those who are most able to direct and move others with their arguments do so through derived recommendations for action. If this is a work based learning project undertaken for a university course that states that it intends to relate the academic nature of the project to a practical outcome, then the academic outcome will support your consideration of how the recommendations need to be implemented in your particular context. The main reason people undertake such projects is to make an impact in their organization or professional field and receive academic recognition. The strength of your recommendations can secure the former, which should also help to achieve the latter.

Note

1 An enthymeme is based on probable opinions that aim at persuasion. The following humorous quotation is an example: 'There is no law against composing music when one has no ideas whatsoever. The music of Wagner, therefore, is perfectly legal' (Mark Twain).

Breaking it down, the three parts are:

- There is no law against composing music when one has no ideas whatsoever (premise).
- The music of Wagner, therefore, is perfectly legal (conclusion).
- Wagner has no ideas (implicit premise).

References

Aristotle (1995) *The Complete Works of Aristotle* (ed.) J. Barnes. Princeton, NJ: Princeton University Press.

Beckett, B. and Hager, P. (2002) *Life, Work and Learning*. London: Routledge.

Benhabib, S. (1992) *Situating the Self: Gender, Community and Postmodernism in Contemporary Ethics*. Cambridge: Polity Press.

Bourdieu, P. (1986) 'The forms of capital', in J. Richardson (ed.) *Handbook of Theory and Research for the Sociology of Education*, pp. 241–58, New York: Greenwood Press.

Carr, W. (2005) 'The role of theory in the professional development of an educational theorist,' *Pedagogy, Culture and Society* 13 (3): 333–46.

Carr, W. and Kemmis, S. (1986) *Becoming Critical: Education, Knowledge and Action Research*. London: Falmer.

Costley, C. (2007) 'Integrating research and workforce development activities', in *Incorporating the Learning People do for, in and through Work into Higher Education Programmes of Study*, pp. 88–95. UVAC/LCCI Commercial Education Trust.

Costley, C. and Doncaster, K. (2000) 'Citation and related argumentation strategies in reflective essays by work based learners', in S. Mitchell and R. Andrews (eds) *Learning to Argue in Higher Education*, pp. 107–18, S. New York: Heineman/Boyton Cook.

Cunliffe, A.L. (2004) 'On becoming a critically reflexive practitioner', *Journal of Management Education* 28 (4): 407–26.

Fisher, J. (1987) ' Kemmis's idea of a dialectic in educational research and theory', *Educational Philosophy and Theory* 19 (1): 29–40.

Foucault, M. (1970) *The Order of Things: An Archaeology of the Human Sciences.* London: Tavistock.

Foucault, M. (1980) *Power/Knowledge: Selected Interviews and Other Writings 1972–1977* (ed.) C. Gordon. London: Harvester.

Gadamer, H.-G. (1977) 'Theory, science, technology: the task of a science of man', *Social Research* 44: 529–61.

Gauthier, D.P. (1963) *Practical Reasoning: The Structure and Foundations of Moral Arguments and their Exemplification in Discourse.* London: Oxford University Press.

Gibbs, P. and Costley, C. (2006) 'An ethics of community and care for practitioner researchers', *International Journal of Research and Method in Education* 29 (2): 239–49.

Gibbs, P. and Costley, C. (2008) The Application of Practical Wisdom in the Artifacts of Research: Making Recommendations. Paper presented at AERA conference. Available at: www.mdx.ac.uk/wbl/research/publications.asp

Giddens, A. (1984) *The Constitution of Society.* Cambridge: Polity Press.

Greenhalgh, T., Robert, G., Bate, P., Kyriakidou, O., Macfarlane, F. and Peacock, R. (2004) How to Spread Good Ideas: A Systematic Review of the Literature on Diffusion, Dissemination and Sustainability of Innovations in Health Service Delivery and Organization. Report for the National Co-ordinating Centre for NHS Service Delivery and Organisation R&D London: NCCDO.

Habermas, J. (1974) *Theory and Practice* (trans. J. Viertel). London: Heinemann.

Habermas, J. (1987) *The Theory of Communicative Action* (Vol. 2 of *Lifeworld and System: A Critique of Functionalist Reason*) (trans. T. McCarthy). Boston, MA: Beacon.

Habermas, J. (2003) *Truth and Justification* (ed. and trans. B. Fultner). Cambridge, MA: MIT Press.

Hodkinson, P., Biesta, G. and James, D. (2008) 'Understanding learning culturally: overcoming the dualism between social and individual views of learning', *Vocations and Learning* (1): 27–47.

Hodkinson, P., Hodkinson H., Evans, K. and Kersh, N. with Fuller, A., Unwin, L. and Senker, P. (2004) 'The significance of individual biography in workplace learning', *Studies in the Education of Adults* 36 (1): 6–26.

Kemmis, S. (2000) 'System and lifeworld and the conditions of learning in late modernity', *Curriculum Studies* 6 (3): 269–305.

Kemmis, S. (2005) 'Knowing practice: searching for saliences', *Pedagogy, Culture and Society* 13 (3): 391–426.

Kemmis, S. (2006) 'What is Professional Practice? Recognizing and respecting diversity in understanding of practice', Available at: www.csu.edu.au/research/ripple/docs/Kemmis%20Prof%20Practice%20Chapter%20060419_14.pdf [accessed 30 October 2008).

Lyotard, J.-F. (1984) *The Postmodern Condition: A Report on Knowledge* (trans. G. Bennington and B. Massumi). Manchester: Manchester University Press.

Noddings, N. (2002) *Starting at Home: Caring and Social Policy.* Berkeley, CA: University of California Press.

Toulmin, S. (1972) *Human Understanding, Vol. I: The Collective Use and Evolution of Concepts.* Princeton, NJ: Princeton University Press.

TQEF (undated) NCT Project Briefing No. 2: Approaches to Effective Dissemination. Available at: www.engsc.ac.uk/downloads/resources/brief02.pdf

Vitae (2008) *Preparing for a Presentation.* Available at: www.vitae.ac.uk/1640/Preparing-for-a-presentation.html [accessed 5 January 2008].

Wolcott, H.F. (2001) *Writing up Qualitative Research.* London: Sage.

Index

Exciting Early Years and Primary Texts from SAGE

978-1-84787-518-1 978-1-84787-393-4

978-1-84787-190-9 978-1-84787-524-2 978-1-84860-127-7

978-1-84787-593-8 978-1-84860-119-2 978-1-84860-224-3 978-1-84860-197-0

Find out more about these titles and our wide range of books for education students and practitioners at **www.sagepub.co.uk/education**